Popular Bohemia

Popular Bohemia

Modernism and Urban Culture in Nineteenth-Century Paris

Mary Gluck

HARVARD UNIVERSITY PRESS

Cambridge, Massachusetts

London, England

2005

Copyright © 2005 by the President and Fellows of Harvard College
All rights reserved
Printed in the United States of America

Cataloging-in-Publication Data available from the Library of Congress
Library of Congress catalog card number: 2004054379
ISBN: 0-674-01530-4 (alk. paper)

For Lajos

Preface

This book was conceived over a dozen years ago as a brief overview of recent scholarship on modernism, undertaken for a general series on modern European intellectual history. At the time, I had no way of knowing that the project would extend well into the new century nor that it would lead me to radically revise my assumptions about modernism, as well as my practice as an intellectual historian. Modernism as an autonomous realm of cultural activity, and intellectual history as the exclusive study of canonical texts became increasingly problematic as I worked on the book. I eventually abandoned both assumptions in favor of a more flexible conception of culture that valorized not only high culture but also popular and everyday forms of expressivity.

The quandaries and uncertainties that were an integral part of writing this book were not unique to my case. My engagement with the historical problem of modernism in the early 1990s came at a time of intense critical debates, which saw the fracturing of professional discourses and inherited narratives about modernism. Intellectual historians, literary critics, social philosophers developed widely divergent ideas about the meaning of modernism and about the relationship between aesthetics and modernity, which to some extent have not healed to this day. The proliferation of their ideas on the subject produced a cacophony of voices that seemed at times to preclude meaningful intellectual dialogue. It is this state of affairs that prompted Roger Shattuck to proclaim the death of modernism as a serious critical enterprise. "Modernism," he wrote in a witty article in the *New Republic* ("The Poverty of Modernism"; March 14, 1983; 30), "is not a meaningful category of literary and art history. It's a featherbed for critics and professors, an endlessly renewable pretext for scholars to hold conferences, devise special numbers, and gloss each other's work into powder."

Shattuck's pessimism about the fate of modernism proved to be mistaken, and his obituary somewhat premature. Modernism not only survived within the academy, but underwent a remarkable renaissance in the course of the 1990s. The founding of the journal *Modernism/Modernity* in 1994 and the establishment of the Modernist Studies Association in 1999 are only the most important indications of the newfound vitality and broadening impact of the field of modernist studies. This book is an attempt to rethink the conditions and possibilities of this new critical preoccupation with modernism from the specific perspective of the cultural and intellectual historian.

In the writing and research of this book, I have incurred a number of obligations that I am happy to acknowledge. Brown University has provided time off from teaching duties, research funds for travel, and funds for the duplication of images for the book. The Mellon Dissertation Seminar in Literature and History that I ran during the summer of 1996 and 1997 was an invaluable opportunity for rethinking the premises of intellectual history within an interdisciplinary setting. I am grateful to Alvin Kernin for his support and commitment to the project. A year at the National Humanities Center in North Carolina was probably the crucial experience in the genesis of this book. It provided the necessary leisure and the congenial intellectual environment in which to fully conceptualize the arguments of this book.

Among colleagues, I would especially like to thank Walter Adamson and Andreas Huyssen, who read early versions of chapters of this book. Walter Adamson, Paul Breines, and John Toews wrote letters of support on my behalf for which I am most grateful. In the History Department at Brown, Abbott Gleason has not only read parts of this manuscript but has been an unfailing source of support and encouragement.

Lindsay Waters at Harvard University Press has been an ideal editor, who has been an encouraging presence throughout the preparation of this manuscript and whose steadfast commitment to intellectual values has been exemplary. The two anonymous readers for Harvard University Press have contributed in major ways to improving the manuscript. I am grateful for their careful reading and their astute suggestions, which I have followed closely.

Bohemia is essentially a collective enterprise that rejects the myth of individual creation. This book came into existence in the context of an intensive intellectual partnership that has assumed many of the aspects and functions of bohemia. Lajos Császi has been a source of inspiration, audience, and critic throughout the writing this book. It is dedicated to him with love and gratitude.

Contents

Popular Bohemia

The Historical Bohemian and the Discourse of Modernism

What is the function of the artist in a commercial civilization? Can modernity produce a heroic culture comparable to the classics? When is art truly "modern" rather than merely "contemporary"?[1] Such broadly synthetic questions appear somewhat anachronistic to our ears, accustomed to the narrower categories of twentieth-century modernist theory and criticism. They were, however, of deep relevance to Parisian artists, men of letters, journalists, and critics throughout the nineteenth century. Indeed, these were the characteristic frames through which they attempted to understand and come to terms with the unprecedented relationship between modern art and modern experience that had developed in the course of the early nineteenth century. Their debates, controversies, and meditations about the interrelated problems of modernism and modernity form the subject of this book.

One of the noteworthy features of the discussions that will concern me is the fact that they took place outside established artistic circles or academic culture. They cannot be found in formal aesthetic treatises, in university lecture series, or in prestigious literary journals. Victor Cousin's highly regarded textbook about the nobility of the artistic function, *Du vrai, du beau et du bien* (The True, the Beautiful, and the Good), may have summarized official views on the subject of art, but it had no real impact on contemporary artistic debates.[2] It was in the mass circulation newspapers just coming into their own after 1830, in chatty prefaces attached to popular novels, in hastily written salons about art exhibitions, in colloquial essays about everyday life, and in collections of caricatures and humor magazines that the tangled questions of artistic modernity and the artist's life were first formulated and fought out.[3]

Most of the protagonists of these debates and polemics have fallen into oblivion, though a few have survived the vicissitudes of time, and a handful have even become classics. No one now remembers the name of Petrus Borel, but his fellow romanticist Théophile Gautier is still invoked as the formulator of the theory of *l'art pour l'art*. Jules Janin remains almost entirely unknown, but his contemporaries Honoré de Balzac and Charles Baudelaire are often cited in discussions of urban flânerie. Emile Goudeau has more or less disappeared from accounts of fin-de-siècle artistic life, but his counterpart Joris Huysmans is invariably celebrated as the founding father of decadence. Victor Segalen is only now being discovered by theorists of postcolonialism, but his fellow exoticist Paul Gauguin has long been an icon of modernist Primitivism. One of my goals in this book is to bring back into focus these lost voices and figures of nineteenth-century criticism and to reintegrate them with their better-known contemporaries, who have themselves been often understood out of context. Recognizing their inner continuities, their intertextual references, their often parodic dialogues with each other allows us to uncover a hidden world of aesthetic discourse that has been swept aside by more familiar models of modernism formulated in the early twentieth century.

The task of rescuing marginalized currents from what E. P. Thompson has aptly called "the enormous condescension of posterity" is, however, only part of the objective of this study.[4] My more general interest in the fragmentary and ephemeral debates about art and the artist that took place in nineteenth-century Paris is inseparable from contemporary concerns. It is, in fact, part and parcel of that broad current of theoretical preoccupations and cultural sensibilities that, under the title of postmodernism, has refocused scholarly attention from the realm of high art and canonical culture to popular, commercial, and nontraditional forms of expressivity. In the spirit of these trends, I will argue that modernism or avant-gardism,[5] seen as a radically new cultural practice and artistic identity that emerged sometime around 1830, cannot be understood exclusively in terms of an interiorized realm of high culture, nor can it be seen as a direct reaction to an external world of social and political crisis. On the contrary, the origins of modernism will be presented here as an inseparable part of the humble and neglected regions of popular culture and everyday experience that found increasingly commercial articulation by the middle of the nineteenth century.

This contention is not particularly original nor very astonishing in light of the theoretical and methodological innovations of the past two and a half decades. Although Fredric Jameson has recently pronounced post-modernity finally over and a cultural reaction against its critical achievements in full swing,[6] academic and disciplinary practices have, nevertheless, been unalterably transformed by its insights. Reflecting on these changes in connection with New Historicism, Catherine Gallagher and Stephen Greenblatt have concluded that the "cultural turn" in literature has radicalized and democratized the field and vastly expanded "the range of objects available to be read and interpreted."[7]

Culturalist insights have penetrated into the assumptions of practicing historians and critics of modernism on many levels. To mention only two examples, Thomas Crow had already suggested in the early 1980s in a brilliant rereading of Adorno's theories that modernist art is incomprehensible without taking into account its popular "Other." "From its beginning," he wrote in what was meant to be a programmatic article, "the artistic avant-garde has discovered, renewed, or reinvented itself by identifying with marginal, 'non-artistic' forms of expressivity and display."[8] An even more dramatic acknowledgment of the interconnectedness of modernism and mass culture was provided by the exhibit "High and Low: Modern Art and Popular Culture," at the Museum of Modern Art in 1990. As the curators of the exhibit, Kirk Varnedoe and Adam Gopnik, affirmed, "the story of the interplay between modern art and popular culture is one of the most important aspects of the history of art in our epoch." Indeed, they continued, this story was inseparable from the process of aesthetic renewal whereby artists revitalized their idiom by "re-imagining the possibilities in forms of popular culture."[9]

Paradoxically, the frequent acknowledgment and even celebration of the interconnections between avant-garde art and popular culture has not transformed the structures and assumptions of established historical narratives of modernism. Andreas Huyssen characterized these narratives as part of a generalized "discourse of the Great Divide," which constitutes the identity of modernism precisely through its opposition to, and radical incompatibility with, the products of a commercialized mass culture. It is true, Huyssen admitted, that "modernism's insistence on the autonomy of the art work, its obsessive hostility to mass culture, its radical separation from the culture of everyday life, and its programmatic distance from political, economic, and social concerns was always challenged as soon as it arose," but this challenge was never successful. "Thus, the opposition between modernism and mass culture," he concluded, "has remained amazingly resilient over the decades."[10]

How can we explain the persistence of the ideology of aesthetic autonomy in spite of postmodernist perspectives and empirical findings in the field? Is there a different way of conceptualizing modernism that could offer a richer, more inclusive, more democratic alternative to discourses of the Great Divide? What would be the theoretical precondition and the empirical basis for such a revision? Before engaging these questions, a brief detour to existing narratives of modernism will be necessary to expose the deep strains of cultural and ideological consensus, not to speak of commonsense experience, that continue to support and nourish such narratives.

The philosophic foundations of notions of aesthetic autonomy are usually seen to lie in the late eighteenth century, with the Kantian theory of disinterestedness, articulated in the *Critique of Judgment* in 1790; or, alternately, in the 1930s and '40s, with Theodor Adorno's critical theory, developed in opposition to "the totalitarian pressures of fascist mass spectacle, socialist realism, and the ever more degraded mass culture of the West."[11] While these theories continue to define the field philosophically, it is noteworthy that on the empirical level most metanarratives about modernism have developed independently from professional aesthetic philosophy. Practicing literary critics, sociologists, and cultural and intellectual historians have articulated their own versions of aesthetic autonomy, whose differences seem, at first sight, to override any commonalities they may have. For purposes of illustration, I will briefly focus on three different types of formulations that have provided widely divergent explanations about the origins, functions, and implications of aesthetic autonomy in the modern world.

The first and perhaps the most familiar example has conceptualized modernism as a counterculture or an "adversary culture," whose task is to affirm values, perceptions, or intuitions that have been excluded from social and political modernity. Modernism as an adversary culture presupposes a fundamental contradiction at the heart of modernity that can only be resolved through a process of cultural differentiation. In Matei Calinescu's words: "Modernity in the broadest sense, as it has absorbed itself historically, is reflected in the irreconcilable opposition between the sets of values corresponding to (1) the objectified, socially measurable time of capitalist civilization . . . and (2) the personal, subjective, imaginative *durée,* the private time created by the unfolding of the 'self.' "[12] The conflict between a rationalized outer world and a fluid inner subjectivity was not the only antinomy invoked in discussions of aesthetic autonomy. For the philosopher Charles Taylor, autonomous or "epiphanic" art was also seen as the indispensable locus of spiritual, religious, and metaphysical values marginalized by secular modernity. "There is a kind of piety which still surrounds art and the artist in our times," he illustrated, "which comes from the sense that what they reveal has great moral and spiritual significance; that in it lies the key to a certain depth, or fullness, or seriousness, or intensity of life, or to a certain wholeness."[13]

Such conceptions of aesthetic autonomy have found a powerful counterpart in the work of the sociologist Pierre Bourdieu, who substituted for the notion of the adversary culture the more hard-nosed concept of the literary field. The creation of the literary field, Bourdieu maintained, was directly linked to the pressures of a commercial and capitalist cultural marketplace, where the nonutilitarian values of aesthetic production needed to be protected and legitimated. The ultimate implications of the phenomenon, however, were parallel to the more general visions of aesthetic autonomy contained in the notion of the counterculture. The literary field, too, was constituted, according to Bourdieu, "as a world apart, subject to its own laws."[14] It was, he admitted, nothing less than a "symbolic revolution" that emancipated the artist from the crudest pressures of modern capitalism, giving him unprecedented "independence vis-à-vis economic and political powers." The modern artist, in Bourdieu's depiction, was a "social personage without precedent," who had become a "full-time professional, dedicated to his work, indifferent to the exigencies of politics as to the injunctions of morality, and recognizing no jurisdiction other than the specific norms of art."[15]

There is, finally, a third, explicitly historical, conceptualization of the meaning of aesthetic autonomy, which found its most important expression in Carl Schorske's remarkable studies of Viennese and European aestheticism, *Fin-de-Siècle Vienna* and *Thinking with History*. Schorske's work, which set the agenda for a whole generation of intellectual historians of modernism, saw aesthetic autonomy as a retreat from the historical world into the interiorized realms of the psyche and of art.[16] Modernism, in this version of the theory of aesthetic autonomy, was not simply an alternative culture embodying values left out of social modernity; nor was it merely a professional space where the artist's autonomy in the capitalist marketplace could be protected. It was conceived, rather, as a tragic renunciation of the historical imagination itself, which had remained throughout the nineteenth century "a privileged mode of meaning-making for the educated classes."[17] Growing out of an experience of crisis, disruption, and political failure, modernism was seen by Schorske as "not so much *out* of the past, indeed scarcely *against* the past, but detached from it in a new, autonomous cultural space."[18] As illustration of the point, Schorske invoked the image of the nineteenth-century city, which still contained vestiges of a public culture of modernity. City planners "appropriated the style of bygone times to lend symbolic weight and pedigree to modern building types from railway stations and banks to houses of parliament and city halls. The culture of the past provided the decent drapery to clothe the nakedness of modern utility."[19]

One of the important consequences of Schorske's essentially tragic vision of an ahistorical modernism that had abandoned tradition as a way of making sense of the world was the privatization of culture and the emergence of the interiorized or psychological self. Among Schorske's students, it was Debora Silverman who worked out most thoroughly the consequences of aesthetic privatization in the arts. Her important study, *Art Nouveau in Fin-de-Siècle France: Politics, Psychology, and Style,* is devoted to the task of tracing how French art nouveau changed from a public culture of "technological monumentality" to an organicist, decorative culture, in which "modernity, privacy, and interiority were deeply linked."[20]

Is there a common conceptual ground underlying these widely diverging formulations about the historical meaning of modernism? How can we explain the fact that different disciplinary traditions, theoretical assumptions, even ideological preconceptions, nevertheless yield almost identical conclusions about the place of art in modern life? The paradox cannot be explained in terms of an internal analysis of these works, for it lies in an unacknowledged consensus that is itself part of what Habermas has called the philosophic discourse of modernity. According to this discourse, modernity is coextensive with the development of autonomous reason that is capable of validating its own laws independent of tradition.[21] This unprecedented historical condition is further associated with a series of social-structural revolutions such as capitalism, parliamentary democracy, and bourgeois individualism that have in turn created the conditions of social differentiation and cultural autonomy in modern life. The discourse of the Great Divide thus turns out to be not so much an aesthetic theory about the constitution of modernist art, as a philosophic hypothesis about the nature of modernity.

At this point, it is possible to return to the questions with which I began this broad overview of aesthetic autonomy and to raise once again the problem of an alternative vision of modernism, capable of incorporating within it popular and everyday forms of culture. The detour through the discourses of the Great Divide has made it apparent that such an inquiry cannot avoid the general philosophic problems of modernity, whose formulae have become deeply entangled with aesthetic definitions of the modern. Our starting point thus needs to be, not how to generate new conceptions of modernism that are no longer defined by notions of autonomy; but rather how to open up new perspectives on modernity that are no longer anchored within the philosophic traditions of rationalism.

As it turns out, such alternative versions of the modern have always existed side by side with the more familiar social scientific models, even though they have never been granted equal status or legitimacy with their more successful counterparts. First thematized in the middle of the nineteenth century by artists like Baudelaire, this alternate version of the modern has been associated with the elusive and dynamic experiences of urban life and consumer culture. The idea of *modernité,* as Baudelaire tentatively called it, was to find more sustained articulation in the works of theorists such as Georg Simmel, Henri Bergson, and Walter Benjamin, who transformed the concept into an aesthetic and phenomenological category of great subtlety, capable of giving expression to the novel realms of consciousness, subjective experience, and aesthetic creativity opened up by modern life itself. *Modernité,* wrote David Frisby, was essentially about "the modes of experiencing that which is 'new' in 'modern society.' "[22] The valorization of this alternate version of the modern became central to some postmodernist theorists, who rightly saw in it a counterpart of their own cultural projects. As Scott Lash and Jonathan Friedman put it, they were interested not in the modernity of "Rousseau's Geneva of natural rights and *volonté générale,* but instead of Baudelaire's Paris of the fleeting, the transient. This modernity signals not the destruction of the particular by the universality of the Cartesian *cogito* but the reassertion of the sensual baroque allegory . . . It is a modernity which most contemporary social theory—be it structuralist, poststructuralist, critical theory, positivist or rational choice—rather emphatically rejects."[23]

The theoretical horizon opened up by the concept of *modernité* obviously has far-reaching implications for our understanding of the aesthetic practices of the avant-garde. Modernists, viewed from these new cultural spaces, no longer appear as the intransigent antagonists or tolerated outcasts of modernity, but rather, as its authorized interpreters and public voices, who possess the unique power to give visual and textual representation to the unprecedented experience of modern life. The very idea of what Calinescu has called the "two modernities"—one conceived as the realm of practical life and the other that of aesthetic creativity—loses relevance in this context.[24] The notion of a singular *modernité* makes possible what Marshall Berman tellingly referred to as a "modernism in the street" or a "low modernism" fully open to the multifarious influences of everyday life as experienced in the city.[25]

Historians of bohemia have implicitly acknowledged this version of modernism when they placed the figure of the modern artist squarely within the empirical and symbolic spaces of the urban scene. Walter Benjamin, too, has explored, through the exemplary figure of Baudelaire, the intimate links between the artist of modernity and the disorderly urban milieu of the *bohème*. As Benjamin made apparent, Baudelaire was not simply a physical inhabitant of the *bohème* of mid-nineteenth-century Paris, but a full spiritual citizen as well, sharing and incorporating in his work the ambiguous style of the political conspirator, the commercial values of the mass circulation newspaper, and the sensational outlook of the popular novel. "Baudelaire knew what the true situation of the man of letters was:" Benjamin summarized: "he goes to the marketplace as a flâneur, supposedly to take a look at it, but in reality to find a buyer."[26]

Benjamin's brilliant but fragmentary depictions of Baudelaire's relationship to the *bohème* only suggested, but did not map out, the points of conjuncture between the aesthetic practice of modernism and the cultural phenomenon of bohemianism. The effort to locate this elusive realm needs to begin with a more extensive, more systematic picture of the development of bohemia itself. Two comprehensive histories of bohemia, that of Jerrold Seigel and of Elizabeth Wilson, have formed the invaluable context and starting point for my own search for the symbolic spaces where modernism meets bohemia.

Bohemia, as both Seigel and Wilson have reiterated, is notoriously difficult to grasp as a concrete social or cultural reality. "Our clichéd idea of the rebel artist," wrote Wilson, "turns out to be a Frankenstein's monster of a figure, patched up from competing and incompatible characteristics."[27]

Seigel, too, confirmed that, "bohemia cannot be charted, graphed, and counted because it was never a wholly objective condition."[28] Despite such difficulties, both historians have offered working definitions of bohemia that fixed at least provisionally its shifting and unstable boundaries. For Seigel, these boundaries were closely affiliated with those of middle-class life, constituting a liminal space where the conflicts and contradictions of modern individualism could be acted out and negotiated.[29] For Wilson, on the other hand, bohemia was a more explicitly political, even utopian, space, from where the "repressive authority of bourgeois society" could be challenged.[30] Different as these perspectives are, they have at least one thing in common: the concern with the social and political implications of bohemia in its relationship with bourgeois life.

In my own engagement with bohemia, the preoccupation with borders and demarcations has been equally pressing, though, given my specific interest in modernism, I have tended to draw these lines somewhat differently from either Seigel or Wilson. Rather than considering bohemia as a symbolic space outside or on the fringes of bourgeois culture, I have looked at it primarily as a discursive configuration where the preconditions of avant-garde art and identity were forged. This reformulation of bohemia assumes a "native point of view," where the artists' own concerns and interpretations are privileged over a more general or objectivist vision. Bohemia, viewed from the point of view of avant-garde artists, provides many of the familiar images of provocation and nonconformity associated with "*épater le bourgeois.*" But new aspects of bohemia also become visible that are perhaps even more important and intriguing. Indeed, the aspect of bohemia that will primarily preoccupy me will be not so much its adversarial or symbiotic relationship with bourgeois culture; as its parodic and dialogic associations with popular culture. It is this complicated and much-neglected connection, I will argue, that provides insight into the popular sources of avant-garde identities and aesthetic creations throughout the nineteenth and early twentieth centuries.

The explicitly cultural-aesthetic focus that I am proposing here clearly does not exclude or contradict the more socially or politically oriented approaches of Seigel and Wilson. It simply refocuses attention to different aspects of the same phenomenon. Nevertheless, it is a more or less unfamiliar point of view that ends up problematizing the ways that the boundaries between bohemia and modernism have tended to be drawn by general historians of bohemia. It is a common assumption, reiterated by Seigel and

Wilson as well, that bohemia was not synonymous with modernism and that the two phenomena needed to be distinguished from each other. As Seigel put it, "The avant-garde and Bohemia were not the same, and should not be confused. The separation between genuine art and Bohemia, insisted on by Baudelaire, Flaubert, the Goncourt brothers, and even Rimbaud, would have been reaffirmed by many later modernists."[31] Elizabeth Wilson, too, expressed caution about conflating the ideas of modernism and bohemia. "Modernism and the avant-garde," she pointed out, "were closely connected to Bohemia, although not coextensive with it."[32]

The conceptual distinction between modernism and bohemia has good empirical grounds, since, as is well known, not all bohemians were avant-garde artists. Obviously, bohemia was much broader than modernism, containing within its borders disaffected youth on the verge of serious careers, marginalized types with problematic livelihoods, and outright criminal elements that often intersected with professional revolutionaries, conspirators, and anarchists. In 1842 Honoré Daumier gave visual expression to this heterogeneous social space, providing unparalleled insight into the sociological composition of bohemia. Daumier's *Bohémiens de Paris* (Bohemians of Paris), wrote a reviewer, contains "the debris of all professions, stations and classes: the man of letters side by side with the dog catcher, the retired lawyer next to the political refugee, the imperial official with the clothes merchant. It is the inventory of all hazardous activities, the history of all appetites waiting in Paris for a windfall. It is the bottom of society, exposed with a hand that is both vigorous and spirited."[33] (Figures 1–4)

The need to emphasize a clear distinction between bohemia and modernism has cultural and ideological aspects as well. For Seigel, the boundary between the two realms serves to protect modernism from the disorderly, subversive, and disreputable elements of bohemia. For Wilson, on the other hand, the same demarcation has just the opposite function, to help safeguard and distinguish the utopian political possibilities of bohemia from the formalizing and aestheticizing impulses of modernism.

My own reading of bohemia tends to de-emphasize these divisions, without fully erasing or eradicating them. The question that interests me more is not the distinction between the social and cultural-aesthetic aspects of bohemia, but rather the contradictions within its cultural-aesthetic manifestations. In order to make clear what I mean by these contradictions, it is useful to remember that the idea of bohemia has always been more

Figure 1. Honoré Daumier, *Le Marchand d'habits* (The clothes peddler). One of a series of twenty-eight images by Daumier entitled "Les Bohémiens de Paris," representing examples of bohemian types from the early 1840s. Published in *Charivari*, September 1840–April 1842. Courtesy of the Boston Public Library, Print Department.

Figure 2. Honoré Daumier, *L'Acteur des funambules* (The actor at the Funambules).
One of a series of twenty-eight images by Daumier entitled "Les Bohémiens
de Paris," representing examples of bohemian types from the early 1840s.
Published in *Charivari*, September 1840–April 1842. Courtesy of the
Boston Public Library, Print Department.

Figure 3. Honoré Daumier, *Le Réfugié politique* (The political refugee). One of a series of twenty-eight images by Daumier entitled "Les Bohémiens de Paris," representing examples of bohemian types from the early 1840s. Published in *Charivari*, September 1840–April 1842. Courtesy of the Boston Public Library, Print Department.

Figure 4. Honoré Daumier, *Le Préfet de l'Empire* (The imperial prefect). One of a
series of twenty-eight images by Daumier entitled "Le Bohémiens de Paris"
representing examples of bohemian types from the early 1840s. Published
in *Charivari*, September 1840–April 1842. Courtesy of the Boston Public
Library, Print Department.

complex than its social image as a marginalized condition at the edge of bourgeois life and metropolitan existence. Indeed, as most historians of bohemia have acknowledged, the real interest of bohemia for posterity resides in the fact that it was also a myth about the artist's life invented by artists and mediated, perpetuated, and reinvented by popular culture. Elizabeth Wilson summarized this symbolic aspect of bohemia well: "Bohemia, as a recognized concept—a way of life encompassing certain forms of behavior and a particular set of attitudes toward the practice of art—came into existence only when writers began to describe it and painters to depict it. From the start this was a myth created in literature and art, often when artists fixed their own transient circumstances as permanent or archetypal examples of how the artist ought to live."[34]

Rarely thematized, however, is the fact that the myth of bohemia was itself fractured and characterized by two antithetical, though interrelated, narrative conventions. I have labeled the first, more familiar, version of the bohemian myth "sentimental bohemia," since it was associated with realistic tales about the lives and tribulations of artists and tended to appeal to middle-class literary sensibilities. The second, less familiar, version, I have called "ironic bohemia," since it was concerned with the parodic gestures and ironic public performances of experimental artists and aimed to differentiate the artist of modernity from his middle-class counterparts. The aesthetic innovations of avant-garde culture and identity were to be associated almost exclusively with this latter version of bohemia, rather than with the former, and will form the focus of this study.

Since the differentiation between a sentimental and ironic bohemia is central to my argument, it is important to look a little more closely at what I mean by these categories. This is all the more necessary, since the contours of ironic bohemia have tended to disappear from our cultural horizons, having been absorbed and transformed into the more accessible images of sentimental bohemia. In the nineteenth century, however, the two versions of bohemia were still visible to astute observers. The critic Sainte-Beuve, for example, differentiated in 1866 between the ironic bohemia of the 1830s, which he associated with Théophile Gautier and his Romanticist friends; and the sentimental bohemia of the 1850s, which he saw embodied in Henry Murger and his more plebian cohort. "The world of Murger," he elaborated, "is more natural and haphazard. The rue de Canettes . . . lives from day to day, it does not have the vision of a past horizon, the exalted enthusiasm for the old, non-classical, Gothic masters, nor the contempt for mediocrity, the horror for everything that is vulgar and commonplace, the feverish ardor for renewal."[35] Sainte-Beuve's suggestive, though idiosyncratic schematization needs further elaboration if we are to appreciate the importance of his distinction.

Murger's amusing and sentimental vignettes about artists' lives in the Latin Quarter were published serially in the popular literary journal *Le Corsaire-Satan* between 1845 and 1849, but it was only after they were transformed into a popular musical in 1849 that they reached a wider audience. Performed in November 1849 at the Théâtre des Variétés under the title of *La Vie de Bohème,* the play became an instant success and bohemianism the subject of discussions in salons, on the boulevard, and in contemporary newspapers. Tourists soon flocked to the Latin Quarter and to the Café Momus in search of "real bohemians" and the supposed glamour of the artist's life. Imitations of Murger's tales followed in due course, and it is perhaps through its most successful adaptation, Puccini's *La Bohème,* that Murger's characters have remained alive for posterity. Murger had clearly succeeded in producing more than a best-selling play; he had given birth to one of the most enduring stereotypes of nineteenth-century culture.

This stereotype was created out of conflicting elements that were profoundly in tune with his middle-class public, who longed for realism and lighthearted wit after the failed idealism of revolution and social upheaval. He assured them in the published version of his stories in 1851 that his volume was not a romance but "only a series of social studies, the heroes of which belong to a class badly-judged till now, whose greatest crime is a lack of order, and who can even plead in excuse that this very lack of order is a necessity of the life they lead."[36] Murger's bohemian stories had two central themes that were of equal fascination to contemporary audiences: the artist's life as an alternative to bourgeois norms of respectability and conformism; and the artist's calling as a counterpart to modern commercial and professional identities. (Figure 5)

The artist's life as presented by Murger stood for enjoyment and spontaneity in opposition to puritanical self-restraint and a rigid work ethic. It exemplified a novel code of personal conduct that was frankly playful, sensual, and intimately linked to a public world of urban sociability. "Bohemia," Murger reminded his readers, "does not exist and is not possible anywhere but in Paris."[37] Murger's bohemians lived their lives on the boulevards, and in the parks, cafes, restaurants, and dance-halls of the city and nonchalantly ignored the social conventions and etiquette of respectable society. "The Bohemians know everything and go everywhere," claimed Murger, "according as their boots are polished or down at the heels. You meet them one day with their elbows on the mantelpiece of a fashionable salon, and the next day sitting at table under the arbor of a low dance hall. They could not take ten steps anywhere on the boulevard without meeting a friend, or thirty steps anywhere without meeting a creditor."[38]

Murger's stories presented not only an appealing myth about the artist's life, however, but also a well-conceived ideology of the artistic career. The bohemian artist, he reminded his readers, could no longer afford to remain naïve or ignorant about practical life. In contrast with his Romanticist predecessors, whom Murger dismissed as a "race of obstinate dreamers for

Figure 5. Honoré Daumier, *Le Bois est cher et les arts no vont pas* (Firewood is dear and paintings are not selling); 1833. Depiction of the hardships of the artist's life in the early 1830s. Courtesy of the Boston Public Library, Print Department.

whom art has remained a faith and not a profession," the bohemian artist had gained a foothold in the literary and artistic marketplace. Indeed, for Murger the true bohemians were artistic professionals whose products were recognizable in the market and able to command a price comparable to that of other commodities. "Every man," Murger concluded, "who enters an artistic career without any other means of livelihood than art itself, will be forced to walk the paths of bohemia . . . we repeat as an axiom: bohemia is a stage in artistic life; it is the preface to the Academy, the Hôtel Dieu, or the Morgue."[39] Murger's reconfiguration of the bohemian artist into the successful professional had a surprising conclusion. For in the process, he was also declared to be the rightful heir of such classics as Homer, Michelangelo, Molière, Shakespeare, and Jean-Jacques Rousseau. The successful bohemian, it turns out, was not only a full-fledged participant in the literary market, but also the representative of canonical high culture and the future academician.

These contradictory strains within Murger's sentimental bohemia explain the different possible interpretations that have crystallized about the meaning and implications of bohemia. For historians like Wilson, bohemia's nonconformism and explicit challenge to moral conventions, social authority, and political hierarchy have made it a radical symbol of emancipation from middle-class life. Bohemia was, she claimed, "the 'Other' of bourgeois society, that is to say it expressed everything that the bourgeois order buried and suppressed. In that sense it was an image of utopia."[40]

A more conservative reading of bohemia, however, is equally possible. For Murger's stories not only affirmed, but also neutralized, the radical potential of the bohemian life. Bohemia, in the parting words of one of its heroes, could only be a transitional phase in an artist's life.

> We have had our moment of youth, carelessness and paradox, he summarized for the audience the meaning of what had transpired in the play. All of this is appealing and the subject of a good novel; but this comedy of amorous follies, this frittering away of idle days with the prodigality of people who think they will live forever, all this has to end . . . Poetry does not exist only in a disorderly existence; in improvised pleasures; in love affairs that last the life-time of a candle; or in a more or less eccentric rebellion against prejudices that will always dominate the world . . . It is not necessary to wear a summer overcoat in the middle of winter to have talent; one can be a real poet or artist while keeping one's feet warm and eating three meals a day.[41]

Bohemia, reduced to a form of apprenticeship in the artist's life, had wide appeal precisely because it was perceived to be both subversive, but also safe. For this reason, Seigel was justified in asserting a symbiotic relationship between bohemia and the bourgeois world. "Bohemian and bourgeois were—and are—part of a single field," he wrote: "they imply, require and attract each other."[42]

These admittedly complex images of sentimental bohemia have been so successful in defining the myth of the modern artist's life, that they have almost completely filtered out alternate versions of the bohemia myth. Yet, Murger's bohemia was preceded by an earlier and more ironic formulation of the modern artist's life that was to have greater impact on the actual strategies and practices of modernist and avant-garde artists. Turning to Théophile Gautier's cultural images of bohemia involves a transition from a realistic and sentimental universe of social representation to a theatrical world of masquerades and disguises. Gautier's parodic short stories, first published in 1833 under the title *Les Jeunes France,* did not yet use the word "bohemian" in reference to its young artists, but they can be regarded as the prototypes of Murger's later stories, which were in many respects indebted to Gautier.

The essential differences between these two versions of bohemia can easily be gauged from Gautier's ironic Preface to the short stories. In place of Murger's somewhat didactic and overly emphatic explication of the role of the bohemian artist in modern society, Gautier performed the role through an ironic alter-ego, who addressed the reader in a colloquial and self-deprecatory manner. Gautier's bohemian persona was an essentially unheroic and comic figure, whose informal form of address subverted all traditional expectations about the exalted mission of the artist. "I resemble those relentless chatter-boxes," he confessed, "who grab you by the button-hole of your suit, monsieur, or by the tip of your white gloves, madame, and trap you in the corner of the salon in order to hold forth on all the observations gathered in a fifteen-minute pause in the conversation. On my honor, I have no other objectives. I don't have great things to do, nor do you, I think."[43]

The apparent transparency and accessibility of this garrulous self is quite illusory. It represented only one among a number of parodic masks or poses that Gautier successively assumed in the course of his ironic monologue. At times he presented himself in the guise of the Parisian flâneur, whose extravagant celebration of the urban scene mirrored and parodied the popular flâneurs of urban fiction. Almost without transition, he reappeared as the jaded aesthete, who declared his hatred for nature and his preference for art over reality. At still other times, he posed as the ordinary bourgeois, whose black uniform made him impossible to distinguish from other people on the street. Indeed, the essential point of Gautier's remarkable Preface was to act out the paradoxical nature of modern artistic identity that could only come into being through parody and masquerade. To become an artist in the modern world, Gautier implied, meant by definition to assume an elaborate array of colorful and theatrical disguises. Acting on this premise, Gautier concluded his monologue with his new image as *Jeune France:* he adopted a pseudonym, grew his hair long, grew a mustache, and acquired a colorful historical wardrobe, modeled on the heroes of the popular theater.

Gautier's self-conscious masquerade had a number of seemingly contradictory implications. It signaled the modern artist's retreat from direct social and political action and a determination to model himself on characters taken from the realm of popular art and urban legend. At the same time, however, this was hardly an escapist gesture, since it also implied a mock-heroic magnification of the artist's persona and sphere of influence. He was not marginal to his society in any sense, but a public figure engaged in a theatrical performance that presumed a captivated audience. As Gautier confessed, "I want to be the quintessential incarnation of all varieties of Don Juan, just as Bonaparte was that of all the conquerors."[44] Gautier's bohemian, in contrast to Murger's, was not interested in becoming a success in the literary marketplace. On the contrary, he channeled his creativity into constructing his own life and identity, rather than creating works of art. "To the devil with verse, to the devil with prose!" the protagonist of the Preface exclaimed. "I am a 'viveur' now, I am no longer the hypochondriac, who pokes his fire between his two cats, building useless castles in Spain apropos everything and nothing."[45]

Gautier's parodic enactment of artistic identity forms an interesting contrast to the more familiar bohemian types that Murger helped popularize. Both were stylized figures that came into existence in the realm of popular culture and both dramatized the nature and dilemma of the artist's life in modern society. Yet, the two figures represented fundamentally antithetical values, strategies, and affinities in their relationship to modern culture. While Murger's heroes were essentially individualized selves, conceived in terms of the sentimental conventions of middle class literature, Gautier's version of the artist was a formulaic figure, constructed according to the typologies of the popular theater. Murger's bohemia may have superficially challenged notions of bourgeois propriety and convention, but on a deeper level it was in essential harmony with the aesthetic values and epistemological categories of middle-class life. Gautier's bohemia, by contrast, was fundamentally incompatible with middle-class conceptions of life and identity. Its parodic performances, elaborate disguises, and carnivalesque gestures destabilized all notions of social authority, foundational truths, or essentialist identities. It pointed to new cultural spaces outside of bourgeois modernity that were closely linked to urban popular culture. Unlike sentimental bohemia, which was ultimately defined by its relationship with bourgeois culture, ironic bohemia was constructed out of an ongoing parodic dialogue with popular mass culture. My title, *Popular Bohemia,* refers to this defining relationship. It argues that ironic bohemia needs to be seen as also a popular bohemia, which rescued the culture of everyday modernity and transformed it into enduring aesthetic forms that have come to define modernist culture.

In his superb study of nineteenth-century modernism, Richard Terdiman has already characterized such strategies as counter-discourses used to oppose, subvert, and destabilize the homogenizing tendencies of dominant culture. Modernists, he pointed out, "sought to project an alternative, liberating *newness* against the absorbing capacity of those established discourses."[46] Extending Terdiman's insights to the manifestations of ironic or popular bohemia, I have been particularly interested in the uses of parody in generating images of the "new" in the context of a commercial popular culture. Parodic recontextualization, I will argue, was used by modernist artists not only in a negative sense, to oppose the dominant discourses of the hated bourgeoisie; but also in a positive sense, to absorb and transform the creative potentials of modern life.[47]

As a consequence, the discourses of ironic or popular bohemia that I will be exploring in this book are best characterized, not as a dualistic, but as a triangular, relationship in which the artist plays the central, mediating role. Perhaps no one captured more powerfully the type of this figure than the lithographer Honoré Daumier, who invariably pictured the type of the modern artist as a painter in his studio, standing in front of his easel, with a nude model in classic draperies in the background and a black-clad visitor in the foreground. Significantly, the focus of the image was directed neither on the model nor on the half-finished work of art on the easel, but on the artist himself, deeply engrossed in conversation with the visitor, who might be a buyer, a critic, or simply a friend. (Figure 6)

The attempt to recreate the conversation between Daumier's artist and his allusive visitor, as well as to reconnect the links between aesthetic image, artist, and commercial culture, will be the task of the following

Figure 6. Honoré Daumier, *Entrez donc, monsieur . . . ne vous gênez pas . . .* (Enter, sir . . . make yourself comfortable . . .); 1847. Conversation between painter and his client. Courtesy of the Boston Public Library, Print Department.

pages. Conceived as a historical archeology of popular bohemia, its subject is, by definition, discontinuous, since many of the forms of popular culture on which it is based have fallen into oblivion or disrepute. The recovery of these lost versions of popular culture will suggest the underlying continuity between what have often seemed fragmented or autonomous expressions of popular bohemia. In the course of the nineteenth and early twentieth centuries, popular bohemia was to reconstitute itself several times according to the shifting patterns of popular culture and everyday modernity. In the 1830s, the bohemian artist used the theatrical costumes and gestures of the melodrama in order to give expression to his special conception of modernity. By the 1850s and '60s, he assumed the black frock coat and impersonal demeanor of the urban flâneur to signal his modernity. In the 1870s and '80s, the cultural type of the bohemian changed again, to be re-enacted as the androgynous figure of the decadent, who used the dramatic gestures of the hysteric to give expression to the public role of the artist in modern society. Finally, during the decades before World War I, the bohemian came to be associated with the figure of the Primitive, whose function was to radically recreate not only the cultural type of the modern artist, but also the aesthetic conventions of modernist art.

2

The Romantic Bohemian and the Performance of Melodrama

The decline of public culture and the privatization of individual life are among the deepest anxieties about modernity that have found recurring expression by social and cultural critics. According to Juergen Habermas and Richard Sennett—perhaps the most influential recent articulators of this general idea—a discursive culture of rational citizenship and a theatrical world of urban sociability, still available in the eighteenth century, had disappeared from Europe by the middle of the nineteenth century. In its place was left a new commercial civilization of privatized individuals who had become alienated from each other and had become passive spectators of a commodified urban world.[1]

This dominant vision of the bourgeois public sphere has been challenged in recent years by what could be called a revisionist tradition, focusing on the inner contradictions and unacknowledged ideological agendas implicit within classic theories of the public sphere.[2] Indeed, even Richard Sennett recognized that the concept of privatization did not apply seamlessly to the realm of modern cultural representation. Here, he acknowledged, the ancient metaphor of society as a *theatrum mundi* continued to hold sway:

> Human life as a puppet show staged by the gods was Plato's vision in the *Laws;* society as a theater was the motto of Petronius' *Satyricon.* In Christian times, the theater of the world was often thought to have an audience of one, a God who looked on in anguish from the heavens at the strutting and the masquerades of His children below. By the eighteenth century, when people spoke of the world as a theater, they began to imagine a new audience for their posturing—each other, the divine anguish giving

way to the sense of an audience willing to enjoy, if somewhat cynically, the playacting and pretenses of everyday life. And in more recent times, this identification of the theater and society has been continued in Balzac's *Comédie humaine,* in Baudelaire, Mann, and, curiously, Freud.[3]

The concept of theater was to be central in the formation of bohemian culture as well, whose characteristic gestures were deeply embedded in the conventions of early nineteenth-century popular theater. It is, thus, entirely appropriate that the founding act of bohemia should be associated with a theatrical scandal whose transgression of social and cultural norms shocked all of Paris. The "Battle of *Hernani,*" as the event came to be called, is worth recounting in some detail, since it represents the first time the bohemian appeared as a public figure of general relevance in French cultural life.[4] The battle took place on the opening night of Victor Hugo's *Hernani,* scheduled to be performed at the Comédie Française on February 28, 1830.[5] The controversial play was eagerly awaited by Parisian audiences, who saw the event as a showdown between Romanticism and classicism and as an apotheosis of the battle between the moderns and the ancients that had been raging for at least two decades.[6] Seats were sold out for opening night weeks ahead, and Hugo was bombarded for complimentary tickets by such luminaries as Benjamin Constant, Adolphe Thiers, and Prosper Mérimée, who had been unable to obtain tickets at the box office. Fearing that *Hernani* might become the occasion for political turbulence, the pro-government paper, *La Quotidienne,* warned: "However great importance the performance of *Hernani* may have for the republic of letters, the French monarchy cannot be concerned about it."[7]

What, in fact, occurred during the opening night of *Hernani* was a different kind of scandal from what the audience anticipated. The real outrage of the evening hinged, not on the innovations of Hugo's play, but on his youthful followers, who gathered to support the Romantic dramatist against his classicist foes. According to Hugo's account of the event, his own actions helped transform the performance of *Hernani* from an aesthetic controversy of predictable outcome into a cultural scandal of major proportions. This innovation had to do with the author's decision to forego the well-established custom of hiring professional clappers to ensure the success of his play and to rely on his own unpaid supporters among the students and artists of the Latin Quarter. When reproached for the foolhardiness of this venture, Hugo responded that a new art form needed a new audience that would resemble the play and that this new audience was to be found among "the young people, poets, painters, sculptors, musicians, print makers etc," who would come to support the play of their own free will.[8]

Hugo's calculation that he could rely on the loyal support of the hundreds of students, artists, and intellectuals who idolized Romanticism was not mistaken. The defense of *Hernani* was organized by his young admirers with all the skill and precision of a military campaign. Key followers, like Gérard de Nerval, Théophile Gautier, and Petrus Borel generated lists of recruits among their acquaintances in the Latin Quarter and made sure that they showed up on opening night. Inside the theater, the young Romanticists scattered in small groups in the pit and the galleries and performed as coordinated cheering squadrons for the play. They countered every hiss from the audience with louder applause and acclamations. By all accounts, the commotion in the audience rivaled in interest and dramatic passion the actual play being performed on stage. A reviewer of the play commented the following day: "The spectators were on the same plane as the actors on the stage and they performed as epileptics."[9] Thanks in large part to the effectiveness of the youthful hecklers, the success of *Hernani* was assured by the fourth act. Before the actual conclusion of the drama, Hugo was approached by the representative of a publishing house, offering to publish the play for the sum of 6,000 francs. The deal was concluded between the fourth and fifth acts and was signed at a nearby tobacco vendor's, with Hugo receiving 6,000 francs in cash on the spot.[10]

During the next four months following the scandalous first night (there was to be a run of forty-five performances), the young Romanticists continued their organized defense of *Hernani*, which had overnight become a sacred cause. Writing eight years after the performance, Gautier remembered *Hernani* as a mock-heroic battlefield on which "the champions of romanticism and the athletes of classicism clashed and fought with all the unparalleled fury and passionate ardor that only literary antagonism can provoke; each verse was taken and retaken in assault. One evening, it was the Romanticists who lost a speech, the next, they recaptured it and the classicists, beaten, brought to another line a formidable artillery of hisses, bird calls, screeches, and the combat was re-engaged with even more spirit."[11]

From the perspective of forty years, Gautier was to provide an even more revealing evaluation of the "Battle of *Hernani*." The opening night of *Hernani*, Gautier recalled, was "the greatest event of the century, since it represented the inauguration of free, youthful, and new thought on the debris of old routine."[12] It was the battle "of youth against decrepitude, of long hair against baldness, of enthusiasm against routine, of the future against the past."[13] The visual contrast between the youthful defenders of Romanticism and its superannuated opponents provided a living panorama of the state of contemporary culture. More important still, it illuminated the real significance of the "Battle of *Hernani*." The mock-heroic battle was ultimately not about the triumph of Romanticism over classicism, a foregone conclusion by 1830, but about the emergence of radical artists as a recognizable, collective presence in the public life of Paris. It is far from a coincidence that the term "artist" began to be used during this period as a general term to encompass all kinds of creative endeavors, rather than just painting or drawing.[14] In contrast with the older generation of Romanticists, the artists of the 1830s were identified for the first time not by what they did, but by how they lived and what they looked like. They performed their identities through outrageous gestures, eccentric clothes, and subversive lifestyles that came to be associated with a distinctive phenomenon: the artist's life.

Extravagant clothing and appearance played, in fact, a central symbolic and ideological role in the confrontation between the young Romanticists and their opponents at the "Battle of *Hernani*."[15] Their striking costumes distinguished Hugo's followers not only from the classicists, but also, significantly, from the older generation of Romanticists who dressed according to formal bourgeois conventions. Victor Hugo's bemused description of the appearance of his young supporters on the opening night of *Hernani* provides telling proof of how clothing redrew cultural boundaries, not only between Romanticists and classicists, but also, implicitly, between Romanticists and bohemians. "From one o'clock onward," Hugo recounts,

> the numerous pedestrians of the rue Richelieu saw a growing band of wild and bizarre characters, bearded, long-haired, dressed in every fashion except the reigning one, in pea jackets, Spanish cloaks, waist coats à la Robespierre, in Henri III bonnets, carrying on their heads and backs articles of clothing from every century and clime, and this in the midst of Paris and in broad daylight. The bourgeois were stopped short in their path, stupefied and indignant. M. Théophile Gautier was a particular insult to their eyes, in a scarlet satin waistcoat and thick long hair cascading down his back.[16]

Gautier, too, makes special mention of the important role that costume played in the activities of the young Romanticists. They were convinced, he writes, that the evening that was to inaugurate "free, youthful, and new thought" needed to be celebrated "with an appropriate toilette, some costume, splendid and bizarre, that would honor the master, the school and the play."[17] The champions of the future took pride in not looking like notaries and modeled themselves on characters from Renaissance paintings, romantic dramas, and Gothic novels. Even those who could not afford the expense of satin, velvet, and military braid, necessary to duplicate their visions of Rubens or Velázquez, still managed to look colorful and Romantic in make shift costumes. Of all the imaginative outfits of the evening, Gautier's red satin waistcoat, meticulously tailored for the occasion, seemed to be most successful in capturing the spirit of provocation and eccentricity that was the essence of the event. It became the symbol not only of the "Battle of *Hernani*," but of Gautier's entire career. As he ruefully remarked in his reminiscences, "if the name of Théophile Gautier is pronounced in front of a Philistine, even if he had never read a line of verse or prose of mine, he will know of me by the red waistcoat that I wore on the opening night of *Hernani* . . . This is the image that I leave for posterity. My poems, my books, my articles, my trips to foreign lands will be forgotten; but people will remember my red waistcoat."[18]

In order to understand the serious symbolic implications of these seemingly frivolous gestures, it is necessary to extend our analysis beyond the "Battle of *Hernani*," to the broader landscape of Parisian artistic and intellectual culture.[19] The fashion for beards, long hair, and historical costumes did not begin with the "Battle of *Hernani*," but went back to the late 1820s, when artists and intellectuals began for the first time to dress up in clothes that affronted the conventional dress code of the bourgeoisie.[20] Young men were to be seen everywhere, sporting Venetian outfits from the sixteenth century, Polish military uniforms from Brandenburg, Hungarian hussars' mantles, and oriental robes of all kinds, which were worn as markers of artistic identity and personal distinction.[21] The young artists in historical costumes carefully distinguished themselves from the fashionable dandies or "lions" of the time, who dressed according to the latest fashion imported from England.[22] After 1830, the taste for exotic costumes among young people became so pervasive that visitors to Paris invariably commented on it as a central feature of the city's cultural landscape. Frances Trollope, writing of Paris in 1835, repeatedly returns to the spectacle of the *jeunes gens de Paris* (young people of Paris) who were visible everywhere and whose gestures were seen by everyone as "something great, terrible, volcanic, and sublime."[23] The theatricality of these costumes prompted another visitor in 1835 to comment: "One would have thought that certain of the newer plays had sent out their character into the street."[24] (Figure 7)

So deep-seated was the association between eccentric historical costumes and the modern artistic life that it was still echoed in popular definitions of social types that became prevalent in the 1840s. In obvious reference to the fashion of the previous decade, we find the following definition of the "Man of Letters" in the multivolume encyclopedia of urban social types, published in 1842 under the title of *Les Français peints par eux-mêmes (The French Painted by Themselves)*: "The man of letters wants to transform himself and to appear like the resuscitated inhabitant of another century . . . One can thus encounter the hairstyle of Saint-Louis in the omnibus, the beard of Henri III on the railway, and the hat of the Duke de Guise in

Figure 7. Honoré Daumier, *Mon cher, je vous félicite . . .* (My dear fellow, I congratulate you . . .); 1838. Bohemian artists, depicted with long hair, eccentric clothing and exaggerated manners. Courtesy of the Boston Public Library, Print Department.

the restaurant.[25] (Figure 8) The same fantastic tastes that prevailed in the clothing of the modern man of letters could be found in the furnishings with which he surrounded himself:

> The literary celebrity has attempted the grotesque rehabilitation of the furniture of the Middle Ages . . . and soon every man of letters had his domed chest, his worm-eaten table with clawed feet, his shelves supported by gargoyles. Ancient platters, ancient frames, ancient chairs, ancient porcelains, ancient tapestries were the delight of the innovators of the age, and the fanatical partisans of progress surrounded themselves with daggers, halberds, clamors and armored plates, transformed into the inoffensiveness of decorations.[26]

Why did the young Romanticists choose to enact their opposition to bourgeois modernity through the literal embodiment of medieval, and more generally, exotic characters? What were the cultural implications of their carnivalesque performances? The dominant approach to this question has generally taken a political and ideological turn. It has been argued that young artists who idolized the medieval world were motivated by historical nostalgia; by a regressive desire to return to an original golden age that had been lost to modernity but still haunted it.[27]

Plausible as this explanation is on the surface, it becomes problematic on closer examination. In the first place, the young bohemians were neither conservative nor religious in outlook, and therefore lacked the kind of ideological or philosophic investment in the Middle Ages that characterized reactionaries such as Edmund Burke or Joseph de Maistre. Indeed, their essentially irreverent and transgressive temperament put them on a collision course with conservatives of all casts, who saw in the Middle Ages a normative ideal for modern societies. In the second place, the young Romanticists had no direct experience of, or interest in, an empirically definable medieval history, literature, or culture. As Gautier's early stories and later drama criticism made amply clear, their vision of the Middle Ages came, not from history books or archives, but from Gothic novels, fashionable romances, romantic dramas and melodramas, whose colorful images saturated the world of popular culture.[28] In the context of the time, one has to conclude that their stylized medievalism represented not so much a conservative repudiation of the modern world, as a polemical gesture of support for the popular forms of modern urban culture. Through these gestures, bohemians signaled that they were opposed, not so much

Figure 8. Illustration from Elias Regnault, "L'Homme de lettres" (The man of letters), showing artist in historical costume and medieval setting. From *Les Franççais peints par eux-mêmes: Encyclopêdie morale du dix-neuvième siècle,* vol. 3 (Paris: 1. Curmer, 1841), 220. Courtesy of Brown University Library.

to modernity in general, but to a particular bourgeois manifestation of modern culture that was emerging and being codified in the 1830s.

The testimonials of the bohemians themselves reinforce this interpretation. Arsène Houssay, for instance, a member of Gautier's early circle, explained that their outlandish costumes signaled their "common revolt against all prejudice, I might say against all laws."[29] Characteristic of their group, wrote Maxime du Camp some years later, was "a general repudiation of acceptable habits and common customs," especially those of the "abhorrent bourgeois."[30] His scarlet waistcoat, claimed Gautier, represented a "symbolic protest against the grayness of modern life."[31]

The young Romanticists of the late 1820s and early 1830s were by no means the first group to associate outrageous costume and eccentric lifestyles with radical ideological and aesthetic agendas. They were preceded by a long-forgotten sect of young artists in post-Revolutionary Paris, variously referred to at the time as *Observateurs de l'homme, Illuminés des arts, Primitifs, Penseurs, Méditateurs de l'antique,* or *Barbus.*[32] In the 1830s, the memory of the *Barbus* was still alive among Parisian radical artists, due in large part to the efforts of two sympathetic chroniclers of their exploits, Charles Nodier and Etienne-Jean Delecluze.[33] Significantly, both of these writers linked the contemporary cultural scene with the earlier movement of artistic rebels.

According to George Levitine, one of the few modern historians to take note of the *Barbus,* the majority of the group had been affiliated with David's studio, from which they seceded around 1797, in apparent protest against the painter's growing neoclassicism. The young artists advocated a radically new kind of primitivist art, defined by ethical and cultural ideals they associated with three revered sources: the Bible, Homer, and Ossian. Theirs was essentially a utopian vision that linked longings for a purified social order with demands for a more dignified and activist role for the artist in society. The *Barbus,* according to Levitine, were asking the modern artist "to step out of his studio in order to change the course of established culture."[34]

The novelty of their position came from the fact that they made their claims, not through manifestoes or aesthetic treatises, but through nonconformist dress and behavior. The *Barbus* became notorious in the Paris of the period. They wore their hair long and sported beards and striking costumes, consisting of sheet-like cloaks, white pantaloons, red waistcoats, turbans, and other assorted clothing that simulated primitive Grecian,

Scandinavian, and orientalist garbs. (It is, in fact, more than likely that Gautier's celebrated red waistcoat was modeled on the garb of the *Barbus* and served as a secret code to his contemporaries.) Nonconformism and eccentricity in physical appearance were used by these early bohemians not simply to shock the public, or even to distinguish themselves from ordinary people, but to provide visual images of their innermost ideals. For the *Barbus,* as for their later descendants, costume was laden with meaning and symbolism; it was used to make cultural references and to act out collective identities. Their clothes and external demeanor were, as Delecluze acknowledged, a philosophic and ideological statement at the same time, indicating their search for spiritual homes in a place other than the present. "Long beards sported by isolated men in a population without beards," he concluded, "are sure proof of a desire on their part to restore, to regenerate, some old custom or ancient tastes that had been worn out by time."[35]

It is impossible not to recognize in these activities the prototype not only of bohemianism, but of a more general phenomenon that came to be described in the twentieth century as youth movements. The sociologist Dick Hebdige has entitled such movements "spectacular subcultures," since they create collective and personal identity through public spectacle and performance. According to Hebdige, the defining feature of all "spectacular subcultures" is the ability to invest objects, gestures, and everyday practices with significant meanings through the invention of "style." The function of "style" is obviously to differentiate members of a group from the larger society. In the process, however, those who define themselves in this way also bring into doubt the implicit values and norms of the majority. As Hebdige emphasized, subcultures disrupt and destabilize the "authorized codes through which the social world is organized and experienced" and pose "symbolic challenges to a symbolic order." Subcultures, however, need to be understood in even broader terms than this. Ultimately, their importance lies in the fact that they are inseparably linked to the unacknowledged contradictions of mainstream society itself. Members of subcultures, in other words, act out more than their own dissatisfactions and alienation. They are also mirrors of latent ideological, economic, and cultural tensions that exist within the larger culture as a whole. Theirs is, in Hebdige's words, "a coded response to changes affecting the entire community."[36]

Such theoretical insights are of particular value in interpreting the social and cultural implications of bohemia in the 1830s. They help explain why the passing eccentricities of a handful of young artists barely out of adolescence could suddenly become the object of serious interest to contemporaries inhabiting mainstream culture. Indeed, they point to the enduring resonance of the bohemian phenomenon in general, which has always carried meanings beyond the colorful lifestyle of rebellious artists. Jerrold Seigel has acknowledged this when he perceptively associated bohemia with the liminal spaces where the inner contradictions of bourgeois society could be acted out and resolved.[37] The question is, "What were the historically specific forms of this conflict and why did they emerge at the particular time that they did?"

In order to answer these questions, it will be necessary to return to the popular cultural scene of the 1830s, where the problem of bohemia was first enacted as the conflicted experience of modernity itself. Gautier, who presented the "Battle of *Hernani*" as a microcosm of French society, was referring to this general collective experience when he declared in his reminiscences: "It was sufficient to cast one's gaze on this public to be convinced that this was no ordinary occurrence; what was at stake here were two systems, two parties, two armies, it is no exaggeration to say, two civilizations, who hated each other cordially."[38] Gautier did not specify the identity of these two civilizations that clashed in the Comédie Française in 1830. Clearly it was a matter of implicit knowledge that he could assume his audience to possess without further explanation. For later observers, however, it needs to be reconstituted from scattered, ephemeral evidence that has often lost its direct relationship to future developments.

At the core of Gautier's polarized vision of French culture was a profound experience of cultural crisis and disruption associated with the rise of commercial art and literature in the early 1830s. The problem can, perhaps, be best accessed through Sainte-Beuve's influential article, "La littérature industrielle" (The Industrial Literature), which he first published in 1839 in the *Revue des deux mondes*. The essay gave expression to the growing antagonism between a thriving urban commercial culture, associated with the mass circulation newspaper, the popular theater, and the sensationalist novel; and an increasingly moralistic and conformist official culture, reflecting the tastes and interests of respectable middle-class audiences. The "industrial literature" became the code name for a whole range of popular phenomena that threatened to undermine the stability and coherence of a bourgeois establishment.

The roots of these developments clearly reached back into the late eighteenth and early nineteenth centuries. Their short-range causes, however, were associated by Sainte-Beuve with the Revolution of 1830. According to him, it was the revolution that had disrupted the integral development of literature and helped unleash a period of anarchy and commercialism in culture. The problem of commercialism was by no means new, Sainte-Beuve admitted. To a certain degree, all ages had produced an "industrial literature," insofar as individuals have always written to make a living and to sell their literary products on the market. For Sainte-Beuve, the novelty of the current situation lay in the fact that the public sentinels of collective values, who had stood guard over literature during the Restoration, had abandoned the field of literature for politics. Their "brusque retreat created a vacuum" in literature, which had become a no-man's-land, without vigilant tribunes to exercise a restraining authority.[39] The tendency, Sainte-Beuve acknowledged fatalistically, was inseparable from the "invasion of literary democracy." Just as the forces of democracy could not be reversed, so the "industrial literature" could not be erased. Its growth, however, could be slowed down and restricted to its proper channels, he concluded, so that the polluted waters of the new commercial culture might be kept from entirely flooding the world of discriminating taste. He ended his article with the declaration of a moral crusade against the "industrial literature," in the name of aesthetic excellence and moral standards. "To conclude: two literatures coexist side by side, and will increasingly coexist in unequal proportions, intertwined like good and evil in the world and inextricable till the day of judgment: let us try to advance and ripen judgment by firmly aiding the good and limiting the other."[40]

The polarized cultural scene depicted by Sainte-Beuve defined the artistic and professional horizons of the young bohemians who flocked in support of *Hernani* in the 1830s. Their performance was in fact an integral part of the culture war that Sainte-Beuve proclaimed against commercial art in 1839. As their gestures and costumes vividly illustrated, they were on the side of popular commercial culture and opposed to Sainte-Beuve's moralistic and elitist vision of art. Yet, the nature of their position was paradoxical and cannot be subsumed within the starkly simplified dichotomies of Sainte-Beuve's moral polemic. Indeed, Sainte-Beuve's own position was more complex than meets the eye and needs some explication. He was not, as might appear at first sight, a cultural conservative arguing against modern literature in the name of classical standards and traditions. The controversy over the "industrial literature" was not, in other words, a replay of the battle between the ancients and the moderns that had been waged off and on since the seventeenth century. The opposing sides in Sainte-Beuve's cosmic moral struggle were different expressions of a distinctly modern literary culture, with common roots within Romanticism.

It is useful to recall that as recently as the late 1820s, the meaning of a "modern" literature was unambiguously associated with Romanticism. Victor Hugo's manifesto of 1827, the "Preface to *Cromwell*," gave a working definition of the concept of literary modernity that was uncontested by most educated observers. According to his magisterial account of the historical trajectory of the "modern genius" ("le génie moderne"), the essence of the "modern" was encapsulated in the concept of the grotesque, which, according to him, had been gaining increasing expression in literature since late antiquity.

> In the thought of the moderns, he asserted, . . . the grotesque has an immense importance. It is everywhere; on the one hand, it gives rise to the deformed and the horrible; on the other, to the comic and the buffoon . . . If [the grotesque] passes from the ideal world to the real world, it produces inexhaustible parodies of humanity. The creations of its fantasy include types from the Theater della Arte like Harlequins, Crispins, Scaramouches, which are grimacing silhouettes of man.[41]

It is highly significant, however, that Hugo did not equate the modern with the grotesque. He insisted that the modern genius was born of a fruitful marriage between the grotesque and the sublime and had already found its poetic flowering in the works of Shakespeare. By reframing the explosive energies of the grotesque with the ordering principle of the sublime, Hugo was in a sense divesting it of its radical potential and lifting it into a reformulated pantheon of art in which Shakespeare occupied the pride of place.

Within less than five years, this Romantic definition of modernity became outdated. Its cautious attempt to create a compromise between the grotesque and the sublime was shattered, in no small part, by the commercial tendencies that Sainte-Beuve denounced in 1839. The decade of the 1830s saw a dramatic transformation of cultural production and consumption.[42] In literature, the emphasis shifted from poetry to prose narratives, as the publishing industry transformed itself into a more explicitly commercial enterprise. The imperative to introduce cheaper and more accessible literary fare that appealed to larger and more diverse audiences brought about structural as well as substantive changes in literary production. Books became less a luxury and more a consumer item within the means of a growing literate audience. *Cabinets de lecture* or circulating libraries further aided in making this new popular literature widely available for a small fee. "There is scarcely a woman living in the provinces," Stendhal observed in 1832, "who does not read five or six volumes a month, many of them read fifteen or twenty."[43]

In 1836, an even more revolutionary innovation appeared on the cultural scene that was to have profound consequences for writers and artists. The invention of the inexpensive daily newspaper by Émile de Girardin created the first truly popular literary market in modern Europe. Girardin understood that if he reduced the price of his newspaper to half its original cost, he could sell more and make up the difference of profit in increased volume. But in order to guarantee mass circulation, he introduced a lighter, more popular literary fare, including gossip columns, fashion articles, and above all, the serial novel or the *roman feuilleton*. His newspaper, *La Presse,* was an immense hit, setting the pattern for all popular papers in the future. As business-minded editors like Girardin were to discover in the 1830s and '40s, the success of a newspaper could be made or broken by the serial novel it happened to be publishing. When Eugène Sue's *Les mystères de Paris* or one of Alexandre Dumas's novels was being run, subscriptions to the daily would double and then again decrease once the run of the novel was finished. Daily newspapers competed for the privilege of publishing novels of such popular writers and often paid extravagant sums of money for them. For the first time, vast fortunes could be made in the commercialized literary market, at least by the small minority who succeeded in producing popular best sellers.[44]

These new conditions of aesthetic production and consumption generated not only deeply conflicted reactions, but diametrically opposing conceptions of literary modernity, whose internecine battles were to echo throughout the decade. One of the earliest and most explicit confrontations between the opposing sides came in 1833 in the context of a highly publicized debate between the journalists Désiré Nisard and Jules Janin. The arguments put forth by the two sides are worth exploring, not only because Sainte-Beuve took most of his categories from them, but more importantly, because Gautier himself was to refashion their elements for his own radical construction of the bohemian artist.

Désiré Nisard was the defender of the concept of an elevated and moral literature in opposition to the characteristics of the emerging commercial culture. His designation of the new literature as "light literature" ("littérature facile") was analogous to Sainte-Beuve's concept of "industrial literature" and, in fact, the two men's ideas are almost interchangeable on the subject. Both critics shared a profound anxiety about the danger that threatened modern culture from the forces of commerce and democracy. As they both pointed out, in the newly competitive environment dominated by money and prestige, authors became self-promoting entrepreneurs, and literature a product of cynical calculation rather than of profound study and reflection. The result was, Nisard concluded, a "light literature," which required "neither study, nor application, nor choice, nor care, nor critique, nor skill, nor, finally anything that is difficult."[45]

Far more interesting than these familiar denunciations of commercial popular culture, however, was these critics' characterization of the phenomenon in terms of a seeming paradox. Both Sainte-Beuve and Nisard noted that the real problem with the new culture lay in the fact that it managed to be simultaneously sensational and formulaic. In other words, it made its appeal in terms of raw emotions, unchecked fantasies, irrational passions; but it used standardized forms, repetitive formulae, conventional frames, for the presentation of this inflammable material. As Sainte-Beuve tellingly put it, in works like the melodrama, the gothic novel, or the "forty-franc-newspaper," "the world of industry penetrates the world of dreams, transforming fantasy in its own image, but at the same time becoming fantastic itself."[46] The ultimate danger of this new kind of literature was that it brought about the materialization of life and the denial of its transcendental significance. It created a world, wrote Nisard, where "it is the body that speaks to the body, and not the soul to the soul; where man has the appetites of the animal and not the animal the refinement of man."[47] Sainte-Beuve repeated the same idea when he contended that under the changed conditions of modern life, art became "active, agitated, ambitious, daring everything, and treating the most refined passions of civilization with the bluntness of the state of nature."[48]

What was to be of lasting significance in Nisard's and Sainte-Beuve's evaluation of the new popular culture was their insistence on the revolutionary implications of the phenomenon for society at large. The emergence of a sensational and commercially oriented literature that deliberately disregarded moral decorum, aesthetic traditions, and social conventions signaled a social and moral dissolution, as well as a cultural revolution. It implied the liberation of culture from the control of elites and experts and the emergence of a kind of literary and artistic autonomy that had no historical precedent. Culture had become emancipated from genteel control in the same way as the modern citizen had, and with the same problematic implications for bourgeois observers. As Sainte-Beuve put it, industrial literature "has succeeded in silencing the critics and in occupying a place almost without challenge, as if it were alone in the universe."[49]

The central irony of these denunciations, an irony that the young bohemians were to fully exploit, was their uncanny resemblance to established theories of *l'art pour l'art*. The theory of *l'art pour l'art*, first introduced to France by Benjamin Constant, had been popularized through Victor Cousin's influential lecture series, *Du vrai, du beau et du bien* (The True, the Beautiful and the Good), which he first gave in 1818 after his 1817 trip to Germany. As a direct result of Cousin's efforts, *l'art pour l'art* became an integral part of academic eclecticism and the official aesthetic philosophy of the bourgeoisie.[50] Confusingly for later historians of modernism, both bourgeois and popular formulations of contemporary art came to be referred to as *"l'art pour l'art,"* even though their conceptions of aesthetic autonomy were diametrically opposed to each other. For bourgeois advocates, the concept of autonomy implied the dissociation of art from the everyday realm of utility and contingency. For popular supporters, aesthetic autonomy implied freedom from academic rules and moral and religious constraints.

One of the earliest and most eloquent spokesmen for this popular version of aesthetic autonomy was the journalist Jules Janin, who had been personally singled out in Nisard's attack against popular literature. In contrast to Sainte-Beuve's and Nisard's brilliant polemic against commercial culture, Janin's counterargument appears at first sight to be both less familiar and less compelling. Assuming the role of a champion of cultural democracy, Janin appealed to common sense and everyday experience, rather than to universal moral or ideological criteria, in his defense of the new culture. He juxtaposed the liveliness and experimental energy of popular literature with the tediousness and sterility of established culture and warned that all those who would deny their tie to the new tendencies were condemned to irrelevance. They would become like those academicians who study Sanskrit, Hebrew, Greek, the sciences, and other "difficult and superfluous things," that produce "useless knowledge, with profit neither to the spirit nor to the heart."[51]

Behind Janin's populism was a more profound set of considerations that confronted the two central criticisms against popular commercial culture—its sensationalism and its formulaic nature—with an alternative set of interpretations. Sensationalism, for Janin, was not the potentially destructive unleashing of individual passion and egotism that Nisard and Sainte-Beuve feared, but, on the contrary, a spirit of improvisation and informality Janin considered in tune with the spirit of the age. It made possible a "literature of everyday life" ("une littérature pour tous les jours") that "attains everything easily, laughingly, without pretension; with little learning and systematization, like a charming and adorable young girl who only wants to please you."[52] Indeed, the recurring image of the new literature in Janin's polemic was that of the carefree grisette or courtesan, who defies the rules of decorum and convention and, in a sense, becomes the incarnation of personal freedom in an age of repression, constraint, and conformism. The new, feminized literary culture, which Janine called, with deliberate ambiguity, "la fille de joie littéraire" (the phrase had a double meaning and could refer to either a lighthearted young woman or a prostitute) was not only not reprehensible, but in a sense, identified with the forces of spiritual and individual opposition to the repressive forces of the modern state and society. Its true position in the modern world was implied by Janin through the fate of Prévost's literary heroine, Manon Lescaut, who was condemned to deportation by the "terrible police prefect."[53]

Janin was equally positive about the formulaic, conventionalized aspects of the new literature. While Sainte-Beuve and Nisard had condemned these as destructive of moral and aesthetic standards, Janin represented them as a potentially integrating force that brought different segments of a fractured social order together in common enjoyment and escape. The new literature, he claimed, "is a relaxation of youth and the distraction, if not the consolation, of old age." It circulates in reading rooms, salons, attics, and porters' lodges of the city, creating common ground between "the great lady and the grisette, uniting the worlds of the humble and the privileged."[54] The new literature, Janin concluded, fulfilled the cherished dream of artists who had hoped to touch the entire population in its everyday life.

Janin's impressive achievement in this debate was to redefine the very terms in which the problem of commercial culture had been cast by Nisard and later Sainte-Beuve. Instead of associating popular mass culture with a disreputable cast of hack writers and opportunistic journalists, he identified it with the most creative and popular figures of the day: with Charles Nodier, Victor Hugo, Alexandre Dumas, Frédéric Soulier, Eugène Sue,

Balzac, Alfred de Vigny, indeed, with Sainte-Beuve himself, who in 1834 had not yet turned against the new tendencies. Popular culture, Janine implied, was not a pathological and reprehensible product of commercial civilization, to be quarantined like a moral contagion. On the contrary, it was the incarnation of the modern age's most vital and creative tendencies. It was not a "light literature" at all, as Nisard had contemptuously dubbed it, but in Janin's terms the "young literature" that contained the seeds of future creativity.

The confrontation between Nisard and Janin went to the heart of contemporary literary conflicts. The debate raised for the first time essential questions about the nature of cultural modernity in a postromantic age. On the one side was a bourgeois conception of the modern, which valorized moral control and social deference; on the other was a frankly popular vision, which celebrated the emancipatory potential of commerce and everyday life. It is within the force field of these opposing camps that the first generation of bohemians was to consciously shape their public identities as artists. They had a natural affinity with Janin's position. Their common enemy, too, was bourgeois philistinism, masquerading in the mantle of classical aesthetics and transcendental moral standards. Yet, their reenactment of the Nisard-Janin conflict had a uniquely parodic edge that radicalized and in many respects transformed its original meaning.

Gautier, who was to become one of the standard-bearers of the Parisian literary avant-garde of the 1830s, played a pivotal role in thematizing and giving new meaning to these cultural debates. His celebrated Preface to *Mademoiselle de Maupin* became the focal point of his repudiation of the claims of moral art and bourgeois culture. Frequently celebrated by critics as one of the earliest pronouncements of the theory of *l'art pour l'art*, the Preface has rarely been seen for what it actually was: a parodic replay of the famous Nisard-Janin debate, which had taken place only three years before the publication of the novel in 1836.[55] Gautier echoed almost without modification Janin's characteristic images and rhetorical strategies on behalf of popular culture. Gautier, too, personified popular literature as an appealing grisette who is juxtaposed with moral literature, represented as an unglamorous, if respectable, grandmother. He also identified popular culture with the forces of youth and made the same appeal to pragmatism and common sense in not condemning their lighthearted affirmation of everyday life.

Gautier's narrative differed from Janin's, however, in one fundamental, but crucial respect: it transformed the antagonists of the Nisard-Janin debate into allegorical figures who articulated their respective positions, not on the pages of newspapers, but on the stage of the popular theater. Thus, Nisard was cast in the conventional role of the henpecked husband frequently found in the comédie-Vaudeville, who used his numerous female relatives as foils for his own calculated denunciation of vice and sexual license on the contemporary stage. On the other side, the composite figures of Janine-Gautier were depicted as heroes of the melodrama, acting out their cultural agendas in the exotic guise of a Turkish Sultan, surrounded by his harem of muses, or of a Roman patrician, participating in an exotic and barbarous banquet.[56]

The deliberate recontextualization of the cultural battles of the 1830s from the realm of polemical journalism to that of the popular theater had a number of complex functions and consequences. On the most obvious level, it demystified the controversy and transformed it into a mock epic. The contestants were not political champions of great causes, but fictional characters associated with the two most common forms of popular theater at the time: the comédie-Vaudeville and the melodrama. In Gautier's ironic recasting of the debate, the stakes had been changed as well as lowered; it was no longer about high and low culture, or about morality and immorality, but about two parallel versions of commercial culture. In other words, Gautier denied the spokesmen of middle-class conventions the implicit claim that they were the standard-bearers of universal values and the heirs of classical culture. The conflict between bourgeois and popular art was brought down to a level playing field and shown to be what it actually was, a rivalry between two versions of the modern. And in this rivalry, the aesthetic and existential superiority of the melodrama over the comédie-Vaudeville was shown to be self-evident. The moralizing hero of the comédie-Vaudeville was not only a ridiculous figure, who used the clichés of conventional culture to affirm his scarcely disguised economic interests; but most importantly, he was an impotent artist, incapable of creating original literature. By contrast, the melodramatic hero, who acted as the foil for the true artist, was a colorful, passionate, and bountiful persona, capable of affirming the varied appetites of the liberated self. The sexualized imagery that Gautier invoked to characterize the newfound creativity of the modern artist was extravagant and intentionally provocative. The representative of bourgeois art was presented as a spiteful and impotent eunuch forced to watch the sexual pleasure of the sultan surrounded by his harem of muses.

Gautier's famous declaration for *l'art pour l'art,* or "the uselessness of literature" was merely a subtheme of this larger confrontation with the moral critics of popular culture. He countered Nisard's original charge that popular commercial culture had emancipated itself from the critical constraints of morality and convention by the proposition that it needed to escape these constraints even more completely if it was to be truly creative.

> For myself, Gautier declared, I am among those to whom the superfluous is necessary—and I prefer things and people in the inverse ratio to the services that they perform for me . . . I should most joyfully renounce my rights as a Frenchman and as a citizen to see an authentic picture of Raphael, or a beautiful woman naked: Princess Borghese, for example, when she posed for Canova, or Julia Grisi, when she enters the bath. I should very readily agree, myself, to the return of that cannibal, Charles X, if he brought me back a hamper of Tokai or Johannesburg from his castle in Bohemia.[57]

Far from defending the purity of the work of art against the contagion of a popular culture, as has often been argued, Gautier was simply rearticulating a parodic version of Sainte-Beuve's accusation against commercial culture and affirming a counter-ethic of passionate experience, of psychological excess, of erotic, aesthetic, and culinary gratification. Recontextualized within the cultural matrix of the 1830s, Gautier's celebrated theory of *l'art pour l'art* turns out to be a defense, not of aesthetic high culture, but of popular commercial culture.[58]

The Preface to *Mademoiselle de Maupin,* however, transcended the problem of *l'art pour l'art,* with which it came to be associated. For Gautier and his contemporaries, the issue at the heart of this text was not simply the affirmation of artistic autonomy, but also the redefinition of modern culture itself, which was fatally divided between middle-class and popular values. The most general questions raised by the Preface were, who had the right to define the meaning of cultural modernity and what would constitute its central values? Would the art of the future reflect a middle-class ethos of moralism and conformity or populist instincts of hedonism and expressivity? The conflict could have no final or definitive solution, for, as Sainte-Beuve already realized in 1839, the two literatures embodied the codes of two versions of modernity, destined "to coexist side by side . . . till the day of judgment."[59] Their relative status in the cultural hierarchy of modern society would not be equal, however, and their unequal relationship was already apparent by the mid-1830s, when Gautier was writing

the Preface to *Mademoiselle de Maupin*. It was bourgeois modernity, symbolized by the conventions of the comédie-Vaudeville, that was to displace
the populist melodrama as the legitimate voice and authentic incarnation
of modern culture. Yet, the comédie-Vaudeville did not entirely succeed in
appropriating the mantle of modernity for itself. The expressive formulae
of the melodrama continued to exist in modern society, but in a radically
new form. They were to be preserved and transcribed into a uniquely
modern aesthetic idiom, associated with the artist of modernity. It is to this
broader cultural metamorphosis that I now turn, which witnessed the
transformation of the bohemian self from an essentially carnivalesque urban
performer into an aestheticized allegorical hero by the late 1830s.

The melodrama as a source of heroic identification and as an aesthetic
model for the artist of modernity may appear both paradoxical and coun-
terintuitive at first sight. Yet, within the context of the period, this was far
less surprising than it seems. In order to appreciate the inner logic of this
development, a brief detour to the world of popular theatrical genres will
be necessary. In post-Revolutionary France, the melodrama had a far more
positive and central status as an art form than it has been credited with
subsequently.[60] Moreover, its original meanings and connotations were still
available to young Romanticists in the 1830s. Gautier not only wrote ex-
tensively about the great figures of the melodrama, but also openly admitted to an inner affinity with the tradition. "O Guilbert de Pixérecourt!
O Caigniez! O Victor Ducange!" he exclaimed. "Misunderstood Shake-
speares, Goethes of the Boulevard du Temple, with what pious care, with
what filial respect . . . we have studied your gigantic conceptions, forgotten
by the previous generation!"[61] In linking the revered icons of Romanticism
with the popular boulevard playwrights, Gautier was implicitly suggesting
two important, and potentially subversive, ideas. In the first place, he was
signaling the common cultural and ideological origins of the melodrama
and Romanticism, something rarely acknowledged by celebrated Romanticists like Victor Hugo. And in the second place, he was going back to the
buried, populist origins of Romanticism by thematizing its melodramatic
roots.

These roots were still partially visible in Victor Hugo's 1827 Preface to
Cromwell, which explicitly identified modernity with the grotesque; that is,
with a vision of excess, turbulence, and chaos. "It is a curious object of
study," Hugo noted, "to follow the evolution and the march of the grotesque in the modern era. At first it is an invasion, an eruption, an over-

flowing; it is a torrent that has broken its dam." Hugo's aesthetic meditation on the grotesque is revealing in that it implicitly relates the dynamic, explosive, uncontrollable quality of modern life with political experience. For, according to Hugo, the grotesque found its most characteristic expression in the "catastrophe of empires" and "the conflict of public events that had penetrated to the level of ordinary individual consciousness in modern society."[62] The reference to the French Revolution is unacknowledged, yet unmistakable. Indeed, it forms the repressed subtext of Hugo's manifesto; it gestures to the more robust and less refined theorists of the melodrama, which, earlier in the century, had explicitly linked the culture of modernity with the radical project of revolution.

This claim was perhaps most fully spelled out in an anonymous treatise of 1817, the *Traité du mélodrame,* which systematically explored the connection between revolutionary politics, inner experience, and modern culture, as exemplified by the melodrama. "It is sufficient to note in the interest of the chronology of art," wrote the anonymous author, "that the first plays that were an emanation of this divine substance [the melodrama], attained their success during the revolution. Great political convulsions have this characteristic that they inject into the spirit a kind of inner anguish which devours it and even when the storm passes, the anguish remains."[63]

The melodrama was, however, more than a simple reflection or an aesthetic mirror of the political turbulence associated with the events of the revolution. It was also a therapeutic response to it, providing comfort and intensity of experience to the suffering individuals who lived through the terrible convulsions of the age. "Where would we be," our theorist queried, "if the emotional needs for plenitude that the revolution had awakened within us, had not found a means of satisfaction in the Melodrama?"[64] The new art, he assured his readers, was a luminous presence for contemporary humanity. It "enlightens those with the least discerning eyes; warms the most lukewarm temperaments; regenerates the most arid imagination . . . [and] satisfies all tastes, enchants both sexes, and captivates all ages."[65]

Behind the excessive rhetoric lies a workable historical assessment of the function of the melodrama in postrevolutionary culture that has only recently been taken seriously by literary scholars. The melodrama satisfied the newly awakened taste for public excitement and passionate spectacle that had originally been nourished by revolutionary events. But it also provided a language and ideology that could explain the meaning of these events and make transparent to ordinary citizens the hidden workings of the modern world. Ultimately, the melodrama was an object lesson in revolutionary justice, transposing onto the plane of private life the abstract moral and ideological values of revolutionary politics. It demonstrated the cosmic struggle between the forces of good and evil as it played out within the internalized realm of individual consciousness. It affirmed the inevitable triumph of individual innocence, perseverance, and steadfastness, against the evil machinations of tyrants and villains. In Peter Brooks' words, the melodrama articulated "simple truths and relationships" and "the cosmic moral sense of everyday gestures."[66]

The political implications of the melodrama were equally significant. The new art form was unambiguously democratic and universalist in orientation. It spoke in a popular style that nevertheless had the power to appeal to all layers of society, from the poorest and most uneducated to the middle orders with a certain degree of literary pretension. The unique achievement of the melodrama was to provide all social groups with a common vocabulary and common images for conceptualizing the nature of modern cultural experience. Stereotypes and standardized formulae, which were to acquire a decidedly pejorative connotation in formulations of high art, played an important role in furthering the collective goals of the melodrama. They gave audiences formulaic characters and plot structures that were immediately accessible and required little or no knowledge of the specialized conventions of the classic theater. As the theorist of the melodrama specified, a certain number of stock characters were essential for the melodrama: "a buffoon, a tyrant, an innocent and persecuted woman, a knight, and . . . some domesticated animals."[67] The tyrant, who embodied absolute corruption and pure evil, was "placed in the melodrama to try the patience and virtue of his victims."[68] After much suspense and the extremes of vicissitude, the outcome of the melodrama was a foregone conclusion: "the tyrant will be killed at the end of the play, virtue will triumph, and the knight will marry the innocent and unhappy woman, etc."[69]

It is precisely through its formulaic conventions that the melodrama was able to give a voice to the emotions of ordinary people who faced the tribulations of a destabilized historical world. At its core, it contained a radical ethic of individual emancipation that was subversive of traditional social order and political authority. The melodramatic hero and heroine were invariably of uncertain birth and ambiguous social status, and they ultimately triumphed over illegitimate power, personified by the villain or the tyrant. It is true that at the end they often regained an exalted social position from which they had been unjustly deprived, but the significance of their actions, nevertheless, resided in their personal fortitude and inner reserves of strength. The central truth of the melodrama revolved around the sanctity of individual consciousness and interiority—defined in terms of virtue, patience, perseverance, sensibility, and honesty—which prevailed over external misfortune and evil. The virtuous knight was ultimately the incarnation of the new individual born of the French Revolution. He was the self-conscious citizen and the sentimental hero in one, who "carries the civil code in his pocket and a sword in his hand, so that he may learn on the one count what he must defend on the other."[70]

For young bohemians, concerned with the emancipation of passion, imagination, and artistic liberty, the appeal of the melodramatic tradition is not surprising. Gautier and his fellow bohemians saw in it a quintessentially modern form of imagination, which had repudiated the tyranny of classical tragedy and comedy and had opened the path to a truly modern form of cultural expression. Beyond the melodrama's aesthetic qualities, however, were its broader philosophic and ideological implications that went to the heart of the young Romanticists' conception of modernity. The melodrama appeared to them as the heroic epic of the modern world that promised to fulfill, at least on the cultural level, the emancipatory and democratic ideals of the French Revolution. Indeed, it embodied the hidden, populist roots of Romanticism and helps explain the deepest reasons for the bohemians' defense of Romanticist art.

The melodrama was the first site for the alliance between radical artists and popular culture that was to become the hallmark of all avant-garde aesthetics in the modern period. Gautier made this point quite explicit in a review written in 1845, praising the broad appeal and aesthetic range of the melodrama. "The public at the Porte Saint-Martin," he wrote of the major theater associated with the melodrama, "is of a particular character, especially on the opening night of plays; it is artistic, educated and popular at the same time; it is composed of society people and naïve spectators, of journalists and wags." The fare of the melodrama was equally inclusive, presenting a wide range of styles and tastes. "Such an ideal," he concluded, "is not to be looked down on and even Hugo and Dumas attained it only three or four times."[71]

Radical artists' deep-seated affinities with the melodrama did not take place in a social or ideological vacuum, however. The transformation of such affinities into a distinctively modernist cultural posture and aesthetic identity occurred in the crucible of external events that eventually discredited the melodrama as a modern art form. In other words, the aesthetic self came into existence only after the melodrama had been marginalized and rendered irrelevant by bourgeois culture. The changes became apparent from the late 1820s in the form of public calls for a more sober theatrical tradition based on an ethic of prudence and moral responsibility. "The time is not far off," intoned a reviewer in Le *Figaro* in 1831, "for a reaction to set in against the overflow of the marvelous and the fantastic in favor of common sense."[72] During the 1830s, it became increasingly fashionable to decry the violence and vulgarity of the melodrama. The theatrical excesses of the melodrama contradicted the ideology of progress and reason that was gaining ground among middle-class citizens. As Frances Trollope put it in 1835, the melodramas performed at the Porte Saint-Martin were at odds with "that universal diffusion of knowledge" that was the characteristic trait not only of the French, but also of the civilized world in general.[73] By the 1840s, the melodrama had acquired the reputation of being a debased form of entertainment that lacked artistic merit. Even former defenders of popular commercial culture, such as Jules Janin, turned against its extravagant formulas. The melodrama, Janin wrote, "cannot be too much loaded with events, accidents, sudden changes of fortune, revolutions, deaths, births, terrors, and convulsions of every kind, to please the taste of their habitual spectators."[74] Not only was the melodrama aesthetically discredited, but it became morally suspect as well, being seen as the chief source of violence among working-class youths. Janin, in fact, established a direct link between the melodrama and the criminal population of Parisian jails, who had, "at an early age frequented those immoral shops, where comedy and melodrama sell, for the lowest possible sum, their lessons of infamy and vice."[75]

The discredited world of the melodrama was symbolically opposed by a new kind of theatrical spectacle, the comédie-Vaudeville, that had been growing in popularity since the 1820s. The comédie-Vaudeville was unambiguously identified with the newly enriched and increasingly respectable commercial middle classes. It appealed, wrote Jules Janin, to the "intermediate world" between the masses and the aristocracy, and found its most enthusiastic support on the "neutral ground" of "the Chaussé d'Antin and finance."[76] A caricature of Henry Monnier's, published in 1831 in the humor magazine *La Caricature,* presents the supporters of the new theater in less circumspect terms; they were seen as the very incarnation of philistinism.[77] Under the title "Théâtre de Vaudeville," are depicted four substantial and unfashionably dressed figures chatting in the foyer of the theater. The two men on the left seem to be engrossed in business negotiation, while a distinctly stout and unattractive woman looks on with interest, and a hatted male figure in a garish striped vest stares out at the spectacle around him with apparent suspicion and disapproval. A more unlikely audience for aesthetic appreciation or refined judgment could not be imagined than Monnier's figures. (Figure 9)

The plots of the comédie-Vaudeville were constructed to appeal to such audiences. They were characterized by close fidelity to contemporary life, by an ethic of prudence and pragmatism, and above all by a kind of moral puritanism that was becoming a dominant feature of bourgeois life. The comédie-Vaudeville succeeded in being relevant, entertaining, and morally uplifting at the same time. Unlike classical tragedy, pointed out Lady Sydney Morgan, a shrewd observer of the contemporary Parisian scene, the

Figure 9. Henry Monnier, *Théâtre de Vaudeville*. From *La Caricature*, 14 July 1831, no. 37. Courtesy of the Boston Public Library, Print Department.

new theater did not demand the kind of "profound and reflective attention" that an aristocratic audience "who had passed the morning in idleness" could provide. The comédie-Vaudeville was amusing and practical and, thus, perfectly suited to the needs of "a merchant who has spent the day in the counting-house, or to the lawyer who is jaded with attendance in the courts."[78]

The acknowledged master of the new genre was the playwright Eugène Scribe, variously characterized as the Christopher Columbus of middle-class culture, the dramatist of the everyday and the conventional,[79] or simply, the arch-Philistine.[80] The epithet that all would have agreed on, however, was "the greatest amuser of the age."[81] According to Lady Morgan, Scribe's comedies "drew crowded audiences, assembled to laugh equally at the classicists and romanticists, whose opinions and disputes were exhibited with much humor and truth."[82] After attending one of Scribe's plays about the unhappy consequences of a young girl marrying against the wishes of her father, she commented approvingly:

> Not all the tragedies of all the classical dramatic writers of France could draw such fast-falling and unconscious tears, such natural half-stifled sobs, as this piece excited the night we first saw it at the Théâtre de Madame. Yet nothing can be imagined of more ordinary occurrence, than the consequences of a marriage in which temporary inclination is gratified at the expense of reason and propriety. We witness such things every day, and they form part of the stock-pieces of our table talk. The effect, however, makes it appear miraculous that such material should have remained unworked and unappreciated.[83]

The popular enthusiasm surrounding Scribe's plays strongly recalls the reception of the melodrama earlier in the century. Indeed, the comédie-Vaudeville could lay claim to being a quintessentially modern genre for much the same reasons as the melodrama had. Like the melodrama, it was a "realistic" and therefore a "modern" form of theater, since it, too, focused on contemporary events and experiences and appealed to individual sentiments and emotions. Moreover, the comédie-Vaudeville, too, had broken from the formal rules of classical comedy, established by Molière and others, and had invented a truly contemporary form of entertainment in tune with the needs of the age.

Yet, the Vaudeville's vision of modernity, its social and ideological truths, were of a fundamentally different nature from those of the melodrama or the Romantic drama. The melodrama identified the modern with dynamic change and an eschatological politics; the Vaudeville, with stability and middle-class values. The melodrama defined the innermost truths of individuality in terms of passion, emotional and physical excess, the struggle against injustice; the Vaudeville saw the exemplary modern self in terms of moderation, common sense, and conformity to social norms. The heroes of the melodrama were placed in an allegorical universe of historical adversity and were engaged in a cosmic battle between the forces of good and evil; the characters of the comédie-Vaudeville functioned in realistically conceived drawing rooms and country estates and were concerned with the daily conflicts of social life. Even the marriage ceremony, with which both the melodrama and the comédie-Vaudeville formulaically concluded, had different moral implications. In both cases, it is true, social harmony was reestablished through the affirmation of the role of the domestic family. But, in the case of the melodrama, this social harmony rested on the valorization of the autonomous, moral self; while in the Vaudeville, on the collective values of the social hierarchy. As Janin perceptively put it, Scribe's plays did not end with the girl of obscure birth who marries the great lord, but, on the contrary, "takes in hand the defense of the opposite opinion, and writes the *Mariage de raison,* to prove that the son of a general would be very foolish to marry the daughter of a soldier."[84]

The ultimate significance of the comédie-Vaudeville lay in its ability to imaginatively define a collective vision of the modern that was relevant for the age; to reinvent a pattern of social and personal ideals that resonated with the experiences of a middle-class, commercial civilization. This phenomenon, however, went hand in hand with the inevitable devalorization of the melodrama and the romantic drama, whose vision of the modern came to be associated with either social degradation or irrelevance. Honoré Daumier, the great chronicler of the age, depicted this development in his caricatures of the 1840s and '50s. One drawing, from 1846, *A la Porte Saint-Martin,* identifies the melodrama with an unsavory audience of hulking shapes, out of whose midst rises an emaciated, ape-like figure, transfixed in a hypnotic trance, whose gaze is directed to the stage. (Figure 10) A second lithograph, from the 1850s, entitled *Le Vaudeville et le drame* depicts a parallel process of devaluation, associated this time with the Romantic drama. The top panel of the drawing, obviously referring to the Vaudeville, shows an enraptured audience, with vivid gestures, mouths

Figure 10. Honoré Daumier, *A la Porte Saint-Martin*. From *Charivari*, 6 February
1846. Courtesy of the Boston Public Library, Print Department.

half-open in admiration or amusement, and handkerchiefs in hand to wipe
away tears of empathy. The bottom panel, dedicated to the Drame, paints
a sea of nodding heads, bored faces, and occasionally horrified expressions, which convey a collective mood of alienation and indifference.
(Figure 11)

The comédie-Vaudeville's growing popularity among the respectable

Figure 11. Honoré Daumier, *Le Vaudeville et le drame* (The Vaudeville and the drama) (1855). Courtesy of the Boston Public Library, Print Department.

middle classes stamped the fate of bohemianism as a cultural enterprise. The triumph of the Vaudeville caused the erosion of the social spaces that had defined and given legitimacy to the bohemian's heroic vision of modernity. The new theatrical tradition could lay claim to being more up-to-date, more truly expressive of contemporary life, than the Romantic drama and the melodrama. In the eyes of the mainstream, it had become the legitimate embodiment of the culture of modernity. This undeniable fact undermined, if not the emotional appeal of the colorful and heroic world of the melodrama, certainly its viability as a direct model for bohemian performance and parodic echoing.

According to Dick Hebdige, subcultural styles become reincorporated into mainstream culture in two different ways: they are either transformed into fashion, or are redefined as deviant or exotic behavior. In the case of bohemianism, both processes came into play. By the middle of the 1830s, bohemian medievalism was becoming fashionable among the well-to-do and the stylish. To be *au courant,* meant wearing clothes that suggested some medieval or fanciful motif, often taken from current theatrical productions; and to furnish one's home with heavy, ornate pieces, suggestive of medieval images.[85] At the same time, however, bohemians became objects of satire in mainstream journals, which both exaggerated their eccentricity, and deflated their seriousness. Probably the best-known of these humorous parodies of bohemianism was a series of articles published in Le *Figaro* in late 1831 under the title of "Jeunes Frances."[86] Bohemians were singled out in these articles for their artistic pretentions, their bizarre clothes, and their exotic tastes in food and interior decoration. The typical Jeune France, wrote the anonymous journalist, had a tendency to "weep at romantic verses, go into convulsions before primitive colors, faint at the sound of free verse, and fall dead before the sight of pure vermilion."[87] Moreover, he deliberately rejected the costumes of ordinary people: "On the contrary, he would blush to be like others. But he stands up for the common man because the common man is spontaneous, unpolished, dramatic, straightforward, colorful, and bearded."[88] The dwelling of the Jeune France was also presented as a mixture of fantasy and morbid exoticism, with stuffed crocodiles hanging from the ceiling, preserved fetuses adorning the mantelpiece, and hammocks used in place of beds.[89] Even in his culinary tastes, the Jeune France was bizarre, showing a preference for "boar's head, wild roe steak, peacocks with large wings, cologne, comfit dishes and drinking bowls." In this, as in everything else, the Jeune France was driven by the dictates of fantasy over taste or good sense, which allowed "metaphor to triumph over appetite."[90]

In 1833, Gautier wrote a rebuttal to these articles in a series of parodic short stories entitled *Les Jeunes France*. As parodies of parodies, Gautier's stories were a brilliant counteroffensive that used conscious exaggeration to deflate the original attack and to deflect its ridicule from the young artists back onto the philistine critic. But Gautier's humorous saga about the eccentricities of his protagonists had more far-reaching implications as well. It provided an unusually acute analysis of the erosion of the bohemian project within the context of bourgeois modernity. *Les Jeunes France* was ultimately an exploration of the fate of imagination when placed under the harsh glare of common sense. It represented a tragicomic revelation of the incompatibility of the bohemian gesture with the dominant bourgeois ethos.

The problem found one of its most ironic expositions in the short story "Onuphrius," which focused on the tribulations of a typical bohemian, as seen through the eyes of a philistine. Onuphrius, we are told, was "Jeune France and a passionate romantic" who had shoulder-length hair, dressed in a dark mantle worn in a Dantesque manner, and was fatally addicted to novels, chivalric tales, mystic poetry, and other fantastic literature.[91] Given such unwholesome nourishment, Onuphrius eventually lost his mental stability, developing a tendency to morbid imaginings. By the end of the story, the young artist had succumbed to madness and the incapacity to distinguish fact from fantasy, reality from dream. The moral lesson to be derived from Onuphrius's sad fate was spelled out with mock-serious didacticism. "By becoming a spectator of his own existence, Onuphrius forgot those of others, and the ties that attached him to the world broke one by one."[92]

This cautionary tale about the pseudo-dangers of romantic imagination obviously mocked the fashionable moralism and pragmatism of the comédie-Vaudeville that routinely cautioned against anything that was extreme, unconventional, and impractical. Just as importantly, however, it exposed the fragility of the Romantic gesture itself, which inexplicably lost its inner pathos and vitality when viewed through the alien lenses of practical life. The conclusion of Onuphrius was that the search for fantasy and enchantment, if undertaken in the naïve spirit of the Jeunes France, withered into eccentricity, narcissism, and even pathology in the context of the world of the Vaudeville.

An even more serious peril, however, lay in the ability of the world of the Vaudeville to appropriate the forms of the Romantic gesture and to transform them in its own image. Gautier explored this possibility in his short story "Celle-ci et celle-là" (The Latter and the Former), a parodic account of the romantic hero's futile, and eventually ludicrous, search for passion and heroism in the modern world. The protagonist, Rodolph, decided to realize his aspiration for emotional intensity through the acquisition of a mistress, whose characteristics were meticulously modeled on the pattern of the melodrama or the romance. Rodolph's choice fell on a fashionable married woman, only referred to as Madame de M., whose Spanish beauty recalled *Hernani*'s heroine and immediately captivated the young bohemian. Sexual conquest of Madame de M. served only to dissipate the illusion of romance and ended up provoking in Rodolph an even more acute sense of boredom and a deeper dissatisfaction with everyday life.

This account of the impossibility of recuperating the conventions of the romance in contemporary life was ultimately an allegory about conflicting visions of modernity embodied in the melodrama and the comédie-Vaudeville. The protagonist failed in his search for fulfillment not because of some unique personal flaw within himself or in his mistress, but because of the historic impossibility of the enterprise he was involved in. Under modern conditions, Gautier implied, the heroic gestures of the Romance and the melodrama were inevitably transformed into drawing room farce. Thus, Rodolph not only failed to become a Romantic hero, but found himself metamorphosed into a character from the comédie-Vaudeville. "There was," he mused after his all-too-easy seduction of Madame de M., "absolutely nothing artistic in the scene that has just been played, and far from making a fifth act of a play, it is worthy of being represented in a vaudeville; he was angry with himself for having so badly dealt with such a beautiful subject, and for having failed to bring passion into such a promising situation."[93]

Rodolph's story concluded with the decision to turn away from the dazzling but illusory attractions of Madame de M. and valorize more tangible charms of Mariette, his pretty servant girl who had long loved him. The shift in Rodolph's erotic investment indicated a major cultural reorientation as well, involving the repudiation of exotic fantasy in the interest of everyday experience. The heroic ethic of the melodramatic tradition was finally admitted to be an unattainable dream, which first turned into the sham of bourgeois comedy and then into the pretensions of middle-class high culture. Rodolph's exemplary story, Gautier informed his readers, needed to be read as a modern morality tale in which the futile aspirations for Romantic transcendence were finally abandoned for the tangible joys of every-day reality.

Gautier's parodic short stories in *Les Jeunes France* marked a turning point in the history of early bohemianism. It signaled the exhaustion of the efforts of young Romanticists to constitute a performative subculture based on the values of the melodrama. Their mock-heroic attempts to transform everyday life into heroic adventure had proven ineffectual in the face of social reality. As Gautier ruefully admitted in an unusually self-revelatory aside, he and his generation had been mistaken in placing such confidence in symbolic actions. They had to accept the fact that "an individual pos-sessed of a beard, a moustache, hair à la Raphael, several daggers, a manly heart, and a slightly olive complexion, was not necessarily superior in at-tractiveness to a fat grocer, greasy, freshly shaven, and daily guillotined by his cravat."[94]

The ultimate implication of Gautier's observation was the acceptance of the nonidentity between life and art. It meant the final rupture with the totalizing impulses of Romanticism and the melodrama, which had hoped to heal the fragmentation of modernity through aesthetics. If the melo-drama and Romanticism had tried to create identity between life and art through "interiority and sentimentality,"[95] bohemianism attempted the same task through the aestheticization of life. The failure of this project, however, did not mean the end of bohemianism as a cultural force. It simply marked the beginning of its transformation and reincarnation in forms more appropriate to the changed circumstances of the modern world.

The separation between life and art found concrete realization in Gau-tier's personal life in 1836, when he abruptly ended his bohemian existence and accepted a post as permanent collaborator at Emile de Girardin's *La Presse*. For the rest of his life, Gautier would have a double identity: as a poet of exquisite, but little-read verses; and as a journalist of influence, widely known for his art criticism,[96] theater reviews, salons, literary essays, and travel accounts.[97] Gautier was not the only young Romanticist of the 1830s to assume an important position within the cultural establishment of the July Monarchy and the Second Empire. Many other members of the former Jeune France became successful theater directors, newspaper edi-tors, literary reviewers, or industrial entrepreneurs. Others, however, failed to translate their early artistic enthusiasms into successful careers and either died early or dropped out of sight.

The melodrama as the site of cultural renewal and modern heroism did not disappear from the cultural landscape, however. Its distinctive values and passionate gestures were to live on in the radical aesthetic project of modernism, whose mission found its earliest formulation in Gautier's *Mademoiselle de Maupin*. Although never popular among the general public, the novel was enthusiastically received by contemporary writers like Baudelaire and Balzac. Both authors admired the book for its stylistic virtuosity and its uncompromising affirmation of the purity of art.[98] Significantly, they failed to thematize the text's complex relationship to the tradition of the melodrama, whose form it both parodied and transformed into an aestheticist icon. The omission was not for lack of traces explicitly linking the novel to the melodramatic tradition.

Indeed, as drama critic, Gautier remained deeply invested in the melodrama as a potentially viable art form under modern conditions. In a highly revealing review of 1845, he thematized the continued relevance of the melodrama for contemporary authors. "We humbly confess," he wrote, "that for many years, our fondest ambition has been to write a melodrama." There were, however, seemingly overwhelming obstacles in the way of this aspiration. For one thing, the melodrama lacked a codified aesthetics that could act as a guide to the aspiring melodramatist. "What poetics can one consult, what rules follow, what authority relate to?" Gautier asked rhetorically. "No Aristotle has provided precepts for this type of composition; its aesthetics and architecture are not spelled out anywhere. What qualities should a good melodrama possess? . . . Epic poems and tragedies are created according to well-known recipes; but all the critics and grammarians have backed off before the difficult task of writing the theory of the melodrama." The problem was only compounded if the modern writer attempted to study the style of the early masters of the melodrama and imitate their secrets. Such action would only result in pedantry and archaism, Gautier concluded. "Language has changed since these great masters and a work of art composed in the dialect that they used would not be understood without a glossary, something that is a serious inconvenience for the stage." Paradoxically, the very characteristics that Gautier presented as an obstacle to modern imitators of the melodrama became the source of its ongoing vitality and validity. As Gautier concluded, precisely because the form of the melodrama could not be copied, its spirit could be perpetually rediscovered and adapted to the exceptional experiences and fantasies that contemporary life presented to the vigilant observer.[99]

Mademoiselle de Maupin, perhaps Gautier's most important testimonial to the truth of this generalization, was a parodic reworking of the conventions of the melodrama for the purpose of reaffirming the relevance of passion and beauty in the modern world. The story itself was based on a historical personage, a certain Mademoiselle d'Aubigny, who dressed as a man, fought duels, and had all kinds of adventures before dying in a convent in 1707. The cross-dressing heroine of popular legend found incarnation in a successful novel of 1829 by Henri de Latouche, *Fragoletta,* and it is almost certain that Gautier's paradigmatic text of modernist aesthetics was a reformulation of this melodramatic work.[100] Gautier's version of the story, however, had complex and far-reaching cultural implications that went far beyond its original model.

How did *Mademoiselle de Maupin* function as a modernist melodrama? How did it transform the cultural type of the Jeune France into the aesthetic persona of the modernist artist? In order to answer these questions, the novel needs to be subjected to a more serious and systematic analysis than its fanciful contents would seem to warrant. Literary critics have remarked on the generically heterogeneous nature of *Mademoiselle de Maupin,* which mixed the conventions of the sentimental novel, the picaresque, and the Romantic theater in a seemingly indiscriminate manner.[101] These diverse styles, however, were organized around a more ancient literary genre, that of the allegorical journey, and it is this form that defined the underlying cultural meanings of the narrative. The hero of this quest, the chevalier d'Albert, was the bohemian artist, identified by his love for unconventional costumes, his addiction to novels and travel accounts, and his longing for passionate adventure. Like his fictional predecessors in *Les Jeunes France,* d'Albert, too, began his journey in the frivolous setting of Paris drawing-room comedy, where he first met and courted his mistress, Rosette. He ended, however, in the fantastic world of a Gothic château, whose balustrades and artificial moats clearly gestured toward the theatrical world of the melodrama. Yet, this was no longer the empirical world of popular theater, but, rather, the disembodied realm of the imagination. Significantly, d'Albert attained this world only after the failure of external sight and the awakening of internal vision.

Like most allegorical quests, d'Albert's story, too, was organized around a narrative of obstacles and emotional difficulties that the hero needed to surmount in order to reach his true identity as aesthetic hero. The catalyst and the symbolic center of these obstacles was the mysterious figure of Mademoiselle de Maupin, who made her appearance in the story after the romance between d'Albert and his mistress, Rosette, had settled into a stalemate and the couple had moved to the idyllic setting of Rosette's

Gothic chateau. Appearing in the guise of a youthful and athletic knight, who, nevertheless, radiated female beauty, Madeleine/Théodore was a true androgyne, who united "the body and soul of a woman [and] the spirit and strength of a man . . ."[102] For d'Albert, she immediately assumed the aspect of ideal beauty that he had always sought, but did not find, in modern life. Yet, she did not function in the narrative as the traditional symbol of transcendental beauty. A focus of accelerating sexual rivalry between d'Albert, who loved her as a woman, and Rosette, who saw her as a man, Mademoiselle de Maupin was a force of destabilization in the novel. She brought into question all existing social conventions, moral norms, and sexual identities that still operated in the world of Paris drawing rooms. The principle of beauty that she represented was based on the unstructured energies of life, rather than the idealized vision of traditional art.[103]

For d'Albert, the love of absolute beauty, which he experienced as sexual attraction to a man, created a shattering moral and psychological crisis. It was the beginning of a journey beyond good and evil, whose stages were associated with social isolation, moral degradation, and psychological self-loss. As his crisis deepened, d'Albert's figure became explicitly allied with the villain of the melodrama, who had also been driven by obsessive lust and illicit sexual passion. Unlike the melodramatic villain, however, d'Albert's existential experience of evil had a creative outcome. It resulted in his eventual rebirth as aesthetic hero, who had merged the identities of virtuous knight and usurping villain into a new kind of self that was defined, not by stable social and moral truths, but by the self-generating energies of art. The moment of integration was symbolized by a night of passion with Mademoiselle de Maupin, who revealed herself to be a woman, only to disappear from d'Albert's life forever. The physical possession and loss of Mademoiselle de Maupin brought to a resolution d'Albert's allegorical quest. Having gained initiation into the secrets of absolute beauty, he could become the spokesman of the truths of art and creativity in a secular and utilitarian world where these had become alien realities.

The aesthetic state at the end of d'Albert's allegorical journey was clearly a reconstitution of the ethic of the melodrama. D'Albert had internalized the passion and energy of the melodramatic hero and transformed these into the imaginative truths of the aesthetic self. In the process, he not only gave new legitimacy to the message of the melodrama, but also helped create a novel cultural type, the modernist artist, who was philosophically as well as spiritually distinguished from the mere bourgeois entertainer.

The meaning of this gesture was unusually complex and went well beyond the conflict with bourgeois art that had triggered it. For in resurrecting the theatrical genre of the melodrama, the modern artist was also reaffirming the Promethean promise of an earlier moment of cultural modernity that was increasingly being pushed to the periphery of modern life. Paradoxically, even while looking backward to the outdated tradition of the melodrama, the aesthetic self became the pioneer of a more thoroughly modern form of subjectivity that was not available to the bourgeois self. Liberated from the external pressures of moral conventions and social conformity, the aesthete was in a position to valorize the hedonistic pleasures of beauty and passion; as well as the critical potential of irony and self-reflexivity. He was, above all, empowered to affirm and protect the autonomy of the creative self in the face of the encroaching conformism of modern life in ways that the cultural bohemian had been unable to do.

The autonomy of the aesthete was far from being absolute, however. The modern artist, as Gautier and the cultural avant-garde of the 1830s conceived of him, was neither a figure of transcendental aesthetic authority possessing the mantle of canonical high art, nor the quintessential professional inhabiting an autonomous intellectual field.[104] He was, rather, a speaker of parables and allegories whose task was to translate the esoteric truths of aesthetic experience within a secular and desacralized world.[105] His role as allegorist made the modern artist both distinct from, and yet, an integral part of the modern marketplace. He had the ability to proclaim the absolute superiority of art over other commodities, but not the power to prevent its ultimate transformation into the image of the commodity.

Gautier explored the paradoxical implications of this situation through an ironic parable with which he concluded his Preface to *Mademoiselle de Maupin*. The parable contextualized his aesthetic project and marked out the complex role that the modern artist was to assume within the increasingly commodified cultural marketplace of the nineteenth century. Assuming for the last time the role of the cultural bohemian, Gautier launched an ironic diatribe against the mass circulation newspaper that had, supposedly, interposed itself between author and reader and had sapped the vitality of direct experience. Gautier's polemic was, of course, a deliberate parody of conservative critics, whose familiar condemnation of popular culture found a radical reformulation in his hands. Rather than rejecting newspapers because of their moral laxity and frivolousness, Gautier accused them of not being lax and frivolous enough. "We don't know what pleasures the papers deprive us of," he lashed out. "They take the virginity of everything; . . . They deprive us of the surprise in the theatre, and tell us all the endings in advance; they deprive us of the pleasure of the chat, tittle-tattle, gossip and slander, . . . They instill ready-made judgments into us in spite of ourselves, and they bias us against things that we should like."[106] Rejecting this increasingly standardized world, Gautier conjured up an alternate environment for the presentation of *Mademoiselle de Maupin* that nostalgically recalled the colorful medieval idiom of the melodrama.

The publication of his novel, he declared, would be proclaimed by "twenty-four mounted heralds, in the livery of the publisher, with his address on their backs and breasts." Bearing banners with the title of the novel embroidered on them, each herald would be preceded by a drummer and a kettle-drummer who would cry out the publication date of the novel and the excellent qualities of its author. This colorful spectacle, recreating an idealized medieval marketplace, was obviously meant to suggest the inherent superiority of Gautier's novel over other commodities being advertised on the pages of the mass-circulation newspaper. Indeed, he humorously predicted, his unique form of publicity would awaken so much interest in his novel that it would "sell five hundred copies a minute," "new editions would appear every half-hour," and "a picket of municipal guards would have to be posted at the door of the shop, controlling the crowd and preventing any disturbance."[107]

Figure 12. Benjamin Roubaud, *Grand chemin de la postérité* (The Highway of the Future) (ca. 1842). Courtesy of the Boston Public Library, Print Department.

Gautier's assumption of the style of a mock epic served to both deflate and also valorize his aesthetic project. It repudiated all efforts to elevate aesthetic truths above the commercial marketplace as both futile and irrelevant. The creations of the modern artist could not be differentiated absolutely from other commodities. In the final analysis, their aesthetic beauty was only a form of exoticism whose function was to increase their desirability in the marketplace, not to separate them from other commodities. His advertising strategies for *Mademoiselle de Maupin* turned out to be, he confessed, only slightly superior to "a three-line announcement in the *Débats* and the *Courier Français,* between the elastic belts, the crinoline collars, the feeding-bottles with incorruptible teats, Regnault paste and cures for the toothache."[108]

At the same time, however, Gautier's implicit message about the fate of his parodic novel and of aesthetic modernism in general was one of affirmation, rather than of defeat. For the market was not the sole arbiter of cultural relevance and value for Gautier and his fellow artists in the 1830s. The market, indeed, was only an aspect of a deeper and broader current of popular modernity that the true artist was still able to plug into and claim for his own in his efforts to create an art that was alive to its time. A lithograph of 1842 powerfully suggested this notion of a cultural modernity that was essentially distinct from, though inclusive of, the market (Figure 12).

The lithograph by Benjamin Roubaud, was entitled *The Highway of the Future* (Grand chemin de la postérité) and depicted the modern literary camp as a motley procession of authors and critics, following the lead of Victor Hugo, who holds aloft the banner of Romanticism with the satiric inscription: "Ugliness is beauty" (Le laid c'est le beau). Roubaud's literary pilgrims were clearly united in their common allegiance to the aesthetic canon of Romanticism, even as they were divided by their different styles of conveyance and travel toward the future. Victor Hugo is mounted on a winged stallion and is closely followed by such writers of imagination and fantasy as Gautier, Lamartine, Cassagnac, Eugène Sue, Balzac, Alfred de Vigny, Gozlan, and M. and Mme. Ancelot. A second cluster of writers is headed by the author of comédies-Vaudevilles, Eugène Scribe, who, in obvious reference to Sainte-Beuve's article on the "industrial literature," is mounted on a railway locomotive. A third group, symbolized by a cabriolet, consisted of actors, pantomime artists, and other popular entertainers, who made no pretense to literary status, but who, nevertheless, enjoyed the unquestioned privilege of being part of the modern camp. Distinctions between "high" and "low" culture, between respectable and commercial production, did not seem an important part of Roubaud's classificatory scheme. It is true that he acknowledged the existence of commercially successful authors, but these were randomly distributed throughout the modern camp, and humorously depicted through Lamartine's huge bag of money or Dumas' status as a colporteur, carrying a pile of printed books on his back.

The distinction that interested Roubaud, and presumably contemporary audiences to whom the lithograph was addressed, was not the relationship of the individual authors to the market, nor even their fame or talent, but rather, their common espousal of the creed of modernity, defined as a radicalized and popularized version of Victor Hugo's aesthetics of the grotesque. Within this camp, the aesthetic modernism of Gautier and his followers had an honorable place, immediately behind Hugo's winged chariot. The source of their authority and legitimacy came, indeed, not from their difference and autonomy from this matrix of modernity, but from their embeddedness within it.

3

The Flâneur and the Phantasmagoria of the Modern City

In 1849 the association between bohemia and the artist's life became publicly consecrated through Henry Murger's spectacularly popular musical play, *La vie de bohème*. Gautier's review of the opening night performance was characteristically generous, though not without a hint of reservation. Murger, he acknowledged, had successfully created an image of bohemia that resembled in many aspects the one Gautier himself had participated in fifteen years earlier. Murger's tableau of this fragile world, "with its joyful miseries, its generous follies, its tender errors and its charming failings," was, Gautier admitted, a "work of true and general interest" despite its "capricious appearance."[1] Gautier's polite review, however, did not entirely repress the fact that he considered the sentimental play somewhat outdated. It was Murger's more understated work as an obscure journalist that Gautier seemed to value. "The advantage of journalism," Gautier ventured, "is that it brings you into the midst of the crowd; humanizes you by constantly giving you a measure of who you are; and preserves you from the infatuations of solitary arrogance; it is a fencing game that provides training and flexibility."[2]

As Gautier's review implied, by the 1840s the symbolic spaces of popular bohemia had shifted from the realm of theatrical spectacle to the more sober world of journalism. The genuine representatives of this new kind of bohemia were to be Balzac, Baudelaire, and other urban writers who came of age during that decade. In his 1868 introduction to Baudelaire's collected works, Gautier made this affiliation explicit. The former hero of the "Battle of *Hernani*" saluted Baudelaire as the foremost representative of the "young generation that followed the great generation of 1830." Baudelaire was, Gautier elaborated, the true heir of the earlier bohemia, who successfully reformulated the meaning of artistic identity at mid-century. He was the incarnation of the "dandy who had strayed into bohemia, without, however, giving up his rank and manners and that cult of the self that characterizes the man imbued by the principles of Brummel."[3]

The cultural affinities between the bohemias of the 1830s and 1840s are not immediately obvious. Indeed, at first glance the two seem to be direct opposites of each other. If the older bohemians had been flamboyant performers, who assumed theatrical costumes to visually represent their presence on the urban stage, the younger generation were self-effacing spectators or flâneurs who intentionally blended in with the crowd. If the former had expressed their modernity through medieval and oriental exoticism, the latter cultivated deliberately understated clothing that avoided all signs of artistic extravagance or singularity. These different strategies, however, grew out of shared cultural preoccupations and aesthetic pressures, created by the growing literary marketplace and the increasingly fragmented urban landscape.

The inner continuities between the Romantic bohemians and the flâneurs can be traced back to contemporary observations of the two types. As early as 1831, an anonymous feuilleton on flânerie described the secession from Romantic bohemia by a small minority of artists who wished to reverse roles with them. Romantics and flâneurs, suggested the author, performed opposing functions in the "vast theater" of modern life. While the former donned extravagant costumes and fought for leading roles in the limelight, the latter were inspired with "the thought of assuming the attractive life of the flâneur," and became observers of contemporary life.[4] Narcissism and exhibitionism, it seems, gave way to seriousness and self-restraint as the minority exchanged the individualistic excesses of Romanticism for the social restraint and impersonality of the flâneur.

The flâneur, as Priscilla Parkhurst Ferguson reminds us, was not a novel invention of the 1840s. In fact, he had been a popular figure of Parisian urban literature throughout the early nineteenth century.[5] It was only in the decade of the 1840s, however, that the type assumed central significance as the symbolic embodiment of the modern artist. According to the journalist Elias Regnault, the new breed of artists made their appearance on the boulevards of Paris in the early 1840s. "There has been a reaction toward good taste in recent days," he announced in 1841. "With the exception of a few stubborn cases, the man of letters now shaves, combs his hair, and dresses in the fashion of all civilized bipeds."[6] Regnault's ironic characterization of this new kind of artist was echoed by Charles Baudelaire. "The times are past," he observed in his Salon of 1846, "when every little artist dressed up as a grand panjandrum and smoked pipes as long as duck-rifles."[7] The true artist of modernity, Baudelaire continued, dressed in the black dress-coat and frock coat of bourgeois fashion and had turned his attention to the problem of "modern beauty and modern heroism," as observed in everyday life, current fashion, and urban experience on the pages of the popular newspapers.[8]

Unlike his colorful predecessor, the somber flâneur has received a great deal of critical attention from literary and cultural theorists in recent decades.[9] He has, in fact, become an iconic figure, who is often cited as the quintessential embodiment of urban culture and modernity. Despite his central cultural status, however, considerable ambiguity still surrounds the figure. As Keith Tester remarked in a collection of essays devoted to the flâneur, "the precise meaning of flânerie remains more than a little elusive."[10] Tester's observation is borne out by the fact that contemporary discussions have produced as many images of the flâneur as there are conceptions of the modern. The flâneur has variously been depicted as the privileged bourgeois male, who surveys and dominates the social spaces of the modern city;[11] but also as the destabilized masculine self, whose identity fragments under the pressure of metropolitan existence.[12] He has been analyzed as the prototype of the detective, who anticipates the modern social scientist and the urban investigator.[13] But he has also been represented as the democratized urban consumer, who first participated in late nineteenth-century mass culture.[14] Perhaps most frequently, the flâneur has been identified with a certain kind of fluid, aestheticized sensibility that implies the abdication of political, moral, or cognitive control over the world.[15]

These proliferating contemporary images highlight important aspects of the flâneur, but they also obscure the original historical context of flânerie. As Walter Benjamin usefully reminds us, "the social basis of flânerie is journalism," by which he meant not merely the practice of writing for newspapers, but more generally, of participating in the world of urban popular culture that was linked to the mass circulation newspaper.[16] The flâneur's deliberately understated external appearance gains its full, ironic significance from the fact that it was also the uniform of the modern journalist, who was forced to compete in an increasingly crowded and uncertain cultural marketplace.[17] It is worth looking a little more closely at the details of this figure, since it gives access to the true circumstances of flânerie and mid-century bohemia.

In a lengthy essay on the physiology of the modern man of letters, the journalist Elias Regnault provided the following portrait. "There is no class in society," Regnault began, "that is so numerous, so varied, so heterogeneous as that of the man of letters: there is no trade that contains so many currents, camps, and rivals. Poets, historians, philosophers, novelists, dramatists, journalists, feuilletonists, vaudevillists, all crowd, jostle, grope, badger, and crush one another."[18] What animates this motley and contentious crowd is the spirit of egotism, ferocious ambition, and struggle for position, in which only a very few can succeed and most are destined to be defeated. The fate of the modern literary man, wrote Regnault, is to oscillate between social and economic extremes that allow for no intermediate stages. His is "a life of absolute glory or obscurity, of misery or opulence. It is possible to believe that in the time of Horace a golden mean could exist for the man of letters; but in our century this is nothing but a beautiful dream. The writer either vegetates or shines, is either an unhappy artisan or a powerful monarch."[19]

The moral implications of this competitive literary environment were considered disastrous by Regnault. It debased both the character, as well as the way of life, of the man of letters. While struggling for recognition and a reputation, he pointed out, the young writer is servile and opportunistic; once successful, thanks to a lucky accident or the caprice of the market, he becomes arrogant and overbearing. Even the domestic arrangements of the modern writer do not escape Regnault's censure. The man of letters, he ironically remarked, despises marriage in the name of individual freedom and nonconformity; yet, he practices the strictest form of monogamy in his relationship with his mistress, who rules over him more tyrannically than any legal wife could. "And do not believe," Regnault added, "that this woman, whose bondage he accepts for perpetuity, is one of those ravishing sylphs whom you encounter in his writings . . . The man of letters' ability to choose a woman is no superior to that of the grocer; he is dominated like the grocer; he is cheated like the grocer."[20]

There is, however, one realm, where the modern writer escapes the pettiness and degradation of ordinary life. The moment he steps out of the circle of his personal concerns and domestic entanglements into the public arena, Regnault affirmed, the man of letters is elevated into a noble being.

As a private self, he may descend "to the level of the most vulgar medi-ocrities; but when he employs himself in the enlarged milieu of the social sphere, he grows in proportion to his efforts and scales the heights of his thought above the material world that had condemned him to be a man."[21] All his moral and practical shortcomings abruptly cease in the public realm, where the man of letters fulfills a civic and religious function unavailable to any other profession in society. Despite his dependent and humiliating position in the marketplace, Regnault concluded, the modern writer needs to be regarded as among "the powerful of the earth, apostles of new des-tinies, missionaries of the future. The miracles of the Pentecost are renewed: the Holy Spirit has descended with tongues of fire, and from the forehead of the writer spreads the burning sign of redemption."[22]

How can we explain the paradox at the core of Regnault's portrait? Why did he present the modern writer as both a degraded producer for the market but also the unquestioned hero of modern life? What attributes could justify the admittedly ironic use of religious imagery in connection with flânerie? Regnault provided no direct answers to these questions. This is hardly surprising, for the peculiar heroism of the modern flâneur was part of everyday knowledge that needed no explication for contemporary audiences. It found expression in the textual formulae and visual conven-tions through which the figure was represented in Parisian popular culture. For the modern observer, the cultural meanings of flânerie can, thus, be recovered only through these often obscure and contradictory codes con-tained in popular representations of the type. It is to these conventions that I now turn.

As we have already seen, external appearance was central to definitions of the flâneur, who was invariably depicted in a black frock coat and top hat, with a cigar in one hand and a walking cane or umbrella in the other. (Figures 13, 14) The association of the flâneur with the correct public apparel of the urban bourgeois gentleman was, however, charged with meanings that were themselves embedded in the codes of middle-class life. The disappearance of color and fantasy from the public appearance of men in the early nineteenth century has been frequently commented on by historians of fashion, who have linked the phenomenon to the symbolic economy of bourgeois culture. According to Philippe Perrot, the charac-teristic conformism of bourgeois male attire served to symbolize a new way of life, based on "modesty, effort, propriety, reserve, and 'self-control,' which were the basis of bourgeois 'respectability.' "[23] John Harvey, too,

Figure 13. Depiction of the flâneur. Illustration from Auguste de Lacroix, "Le Flâneur," in *Les Français peints par eux-mêmes: Encyclopédie morale du dix-neuvième siècle,* vol. 4 (Paris: L. Curmer, 1841), 63. Courtesy of Brown University Library.

Figure 14. Another rendering of the flâneur. Illustration from Auguste de Lacroix, "Le Flâneur," in *Les Français peints par eux-mêmes: Encyclopédie morale du dix-neuvième siècle,* vol. 4 (Paris: L. Curmer, 1841), 65. Courtesy of Brown University Library.

interpreted the reigning bourgeoisie's overwhelming investment in the color black as a sign of the "larger spiritual politics of the time," which was inseparable from the need for emotional, social, and sexual control at a time of intense social and cultural stress.[24]

What has often been ignored by historians is the fact that the flâneur's conventional costume did not slavishly duplicate bourgeois social and cultural norms. It was rather a parodic echo of these dominant codes, whose ironic mimicry allowed the flâneur both to blend in with contemporary life and yet to differentiate himself from it. The flâneur, as contemporary accounts emphasized, managed to be exotic and heroic in spite of his bourgeois exterior. His passionate and imaginative qualities were celebrated by artists like Baudelaire, who saw the quintessential flâneur in Honoré de Balzac, "the most heroic, the most extraordinary, the most romantic and the most poetic" of all the fictional types he had given birth to.[25] In his "Notice" of 1868, Gautier, too, linked flânerie with poetic and expressive qualities that remained legible in spite of the flâneur's conventional appearance. For Gautier, Baudelaire was the perfect embodiment of the type, whose impeccably groomed exterior nevertheless radiated "a certain aura of exoticism that was like the far-away perfume of countries more beloved by the sun than ours. They say that Baudelaire had traveled for a long time in India and this explains everything."[26]

The flâneur's assumption of the characteristic costume of the bourgeois male was, ultimately, more than ironic masquerade. It also implied a creative revision of the possibilities of public identity offered by modern society. The flâneur's obligatory black dress coat provided the modern artist with a new kind of public role that Baudelaire explicitly associated with the heroic possibilities of modernity. The true flâneur, he wrote, was in search of "poetic and marvelous subjects" and the "epic side of modern life."[27] In the final analysis, the flâneur's deliberately understated black apparel was a theatrical costume in the same way that the outrageous historical outfits of an earlier generation of bohemians had been. His somber black frock coat was the external sign of the colorful persona of the melodramatic hero, who projected the passionate intuitions of the popular stage onto the everyday realities of the urban landscape. In both cases, costume symbolically defined the performative nature of artistic identity in the context of the modern city.

This complex transposition of qualities explains why the flâneur, in direct contrast to his bourgeois counterpart, could be regarded as an explicitly public actor and performer whose true home was the physical land-scape of the city. Verbal accounts invariably placed him on the boulevards, arcades, parks, restaurants, and cafes of the city and emphasized how un-thinkable the flâneur was in interior spaces such as salons and even thea-ters, unless it was the foyer, where he could observe the audience. He was frequently portrayed in contemporary accounts as an amiable storyteller who happily shared his knowledge of the city with whoever approached him. "He talks willingly," wrote one writer, "he is within the reach of any and all, he does the honors of his beloved city with ease."[28] "If you are at leisure," enjoined another, "approach the flâneur. Everything can serve as an occasion to enter into conversation with him . . . What a number of things he teaches you! Under what unexpected aspects will such a guide present to your eyes the panorama that surrounds you!"[29]

The flâneur's public persona transcended all class, professional, and do-mestic affiliations that were the markers of bourgeois identity. As one phys-iologist explained: "Before crossing the threshold of his door, the flâneur is a man like any other: a retired general, a professor emeritus, a former lawyer, a diplomat on half-pay . . . The moment he touches the ground of the pavement, inhales the dust of the boulevard, or the odor of the Seine, he enters into action and it is there that we seize his figure."[30] The dramatic transformation of the flâneur from private into public self created a kind of intoxication and emotional excess that strongly recalled the melodra-matic gestures of the popular theater. This central fact about flânerie was playfully illustrated by a chronicler of the phenomenon. When the strug-gling writer or painter goes out into the street, "he is no longer the same man. His head is raised, his chest dilates, his legs feel lighter, life re-ascends to his cheek, hope to his heart . . . At this moment, he has forgotten every-thing; his wife, if he has a wife (but more often the lounger is not married), his creditors, his work, his ambition, his genius, everything, even himself. If he were ill, he would forget his malady, while lounging."[31]

The flâneur's deep affinities with the exotic heroes of the melodrama were, however, scarcely visible to the ordinary or uninitiated observer. His heroic stature and epic vision could not be directly acted out, but became internalized and transformed into aspects of inner life and consciousness. This is why the flâneur as a public figure lacked all recognizable physical traces that would have distinguished him from others. Like modern life itself, the flâneur was anonymous in his outward appearance. Anonymity to the point of invisibility was, in fact, the distinguishing marker of the flâneur as a formulaic character of popular culture. Whereas all other urban types betrayed their identities through small nuances of personal appearance, social habit, or professional conduct, the flâneur alone remained illegible as a type. His ability to perceive the world was accompanied by the inability of the world to perceive him. So central was this paradox to the construction of the flâneur as a public and heroic figure that it deserves to be examined at greater length.

The difficulty of differentiating the true flâneur from his superficial likeness was not only the starting point, but also the essential content, of all physiologies of flânerie. "Let us not confound the knave with the flâneur," cautioned a writer, "the difference lies in the nuances."[32] "Nothing is more common than the name, nothing is rarer than the real thing," warned another.[33] "We do not prostitute the title of flâneur," observed a third expert, "by attaching it to those more or less ridiculous imitators, who walk all day, their idleness both tiresome and irritating."[34]

Potentially, any social type could be mistaken for the flâneur, and the list of false flâneurs was theoretically endless. The lawyer, for instance, "who misses the hour of his trial, because he stopped in front of the displays of the Pont-Neuf, the theater of Polichinelle, or the shop of Lerebours; the doctor who let pass the hour of his consultation, while exhausting a political question with a painter whom he encountered on the Pont des Arts; these are idlers, but never flâneurs."[35] If a dilettantish interest in the arts disqualified the professional from flânerie, so did the opposite tendency to overspecialization. Indeed, the busy and self-important professional, who "buzzes in all the corners of Paris to the annoyance of honest citizens," was by definition incapable of the art of flânerie.[36] So was the proletarian, best exemplified by the ragpicker, "who lives gaily from day to day, without luxury, without worry, without aspiration to fortune."[37] The tourist with guidebook in hand, attempting to measure and systematically visit all the monuments of the city; the family man taking a stroll with his wife and daughter; the shopper seeking the most succulent melons; were just a few of the carefully delineated false flâneurs, who inhabited the world of physiologies concerned with flânerie. Their function was to document, through their very concreteness, the elusiveness of the true flâneur.[38]

The flâneur's physical indistinguishability was, in fact, inversely related to the visual markers of ordinary social types in the city. The more illegible he appeared, the more legible became the social and professional identities of others. The flâneur had deliberately abandoned the role of the Romantic bohemians of the 1830s, but only in order to redirect the limelight on the lives of ordinary people around him and to render the everyday details of their activities as visible and dramatic as if they were performed in a theater. The striking modesty of this gesture was only apparent. For in the guise of an observer who could not be observed, the flâneur occupied a privileged, even transcendental, position within urban modernity. He rose above the fragmented world of social types and became a cultural archetype, with access to the totality of urban culture, unavailable to other characters. The flâneur, in fact, was the only figure in Parisian popular culture who could render the labyrinthine urban landscape legible and meaningful to contemporaries.

By all accounts, the flâneur was able to accomplish this feat through his virtuosity as urban observer. Critical opinion since Benjamin has frequently associated the flâneur with visuality, but usually in a negative sense, as the direct consequence of inhabiting a commodified urban culture, where the commodity had transformed all reality into spectacle.[39] As Benjamin put it, the world of the commodity "permeates [the flâneur] . . . blissfully like a narcotic that can compensate him for many humiliations. The intoxication to which the flâneur surrenders is the intoxication of the commodity around which surges the stream of customers."[40] In the contemporary physiologies, however, the flâneur's power of vision was presented, not as an illusion, but as an exceptional and potentially heroic achievement that helped humanize the urban landscape and overcome the inherent illegibility of the modern world. In fact, the flâneur's ability to see while not being seen was the essential source of his heroism, the central attribute of his public character.

On the most basic level, the flâneur's skills as urban observer gave him access to, and intimate familiarity with, even insignificant detail usually overlooked by more casual observers. "Nothing escapes his investigatory gaze," wrote one physiologist, "a new display in the window of this sumptuous store, a lithograph that is shown in public for the first time, the progress of a construction site that one had thought interminable, an unaccustomed face on this boulevard, whose every inhabitant and frequenter is known to him, everything interests him, everything is a text for observation in his eyes."[41] In the flâneur's perceptive vision, what appeared incoherent and meaningless gained focus and visibility. He brought alive and invested with significance the fleeting, everyday occurrences of the city that ordinary people failed to notice.

The flâneur's expert knowledge of the city involved, however, more complex skills than systematic and dispassionate observation. It was accompanied, by all accounts, with a discriminating taste that allowed him to differentiate genuine quality from charlatanism in the goods and commodities that he observed in shop windows. In other words, he brought to the task of urban flânerie not simply the classifying skills of the natural scientist, but also the inner sensibility and moral compass of the sentimental hero. The point is well illustrated by the behavior of the flâneur in an array of different public spaces. When in the arcades, for instance, he was never distracted, we are told, by second-rate displays of plaster statuettes, but instinctively headed for "the most recent caricature of Daumier," or the latest lithographs of Gavarni.[42] In the Salon or the museum, the true flâneur was alive to the subtlest details of a painting that ordinary observers passed over.[43] Baudelaire used this distinction between genuine insight and superficial observation in his "The Painter of Modern Life," where he differentiated the artist of modernity from the bourgeois art consumers in the museum. While the former was alive to the modern beauty of the city, the latter "walk rapidly, without so much as a glance, past rows of very interesting, though secondary, pictures, to come to a rapturous halt in front of a Titian or a Raphael," which they had become familiar with from lithographs.[44]

The differentiation between the genuine taste of the flâneur and the stereotyped habits of the philistine helps explain the flâneur's positive attitude to all expressions of the urban environment, including its commercial and popular aspects. The true flâneur could perceive the inherent distinction and elegance of even the most mundane manifestations of urban life, since he was independent of external authorities or tastemakers. This sense of autonomy and innate taste in the face of even problematic aspects of city life is well illustrated by his behavior in the restaurant, which was often the object of criticism and sarcasm in popular depictions of the time.[45] He had sophisticated culinary tastes, we are told, but these were always accompanied by moderation, since flânerie and obesity were considered incompatible states of being. The flâneur was both knowledgeable and at his ease, knowing how to enjoy, as well as assert control, over the new environment of the consumer culture. He was the incarnation of the discriminating connoisseur as opposed to the random shopper; of the gourmet, as opposed to the glutton. He was aware of the siren sound of the commodity, but it seems he was never seduced by it.

Ultimately, however, the flâneur's exceptional insight into urban modernity could not be fully explained by scientific skills or natural taste. It was his gift of imagination that allowed him to penetrate beneath the surface appearance of things and to discover their hidden essence. Unlike the common observer, a historian of flânerie pointed out, the flâneur had access "to unknown connections, to unperceived insights, to an entirely new world of ideas, reflections and sentiments, which suddenly gush forth under the trained eye of the observer, like a hidden spring under the probe of the geologist."[46] The special quality of the flâneur's perception lay in the fact that he could imagine objects and phenomena within larger contexts that remained inaccessible to ordinary observers. The point was graphically illustrated through the contrasting behavior of an ordinary bourgeois and a flâneur in front of a shop window displaying a new piece of cloth. When the bourgeois passes the window, he briefly and casually surveys it with the thought that perhaps his wife might like it, and then passes on. By contrast, the flâneur remains transfixed before the same object for hours, engaged in complex reflection about the fashion trends indicated by the cloth, about the factory processes that went into its making, about the far-off places where the raw materials originated. What had appeared as an isolated, and self-contained commodity to the common observer, was transformed by the flâneur's imagination into a coherent story of exotic adventure and heroic creation. It had given rise "to a hundred type of reflections which the other spectator did not even suspect; it gave him the opportunity for a long voyage in the imaginary world, that brilliant world, the best and above all, the fairest of all possible worlds."[47]

In his influential physiology of flânerie, *The American in Paris,* Jules Janin also referred to the qualities of imaginative vision, which allowed the flâneur to penetrate behind the physical appearance of phenomena, in an effort to distill their human and emotional qualities. Only the flâneur knew, Janin stressed, that "Paris is not merely an assemblage of houses, palaces, temples and fountains, it is also a world of passion and ideas; the time is past, for the traveler to think his task accomplished when he has told his readers: 'The Bourse is a fine building, situated at the end of the Rue Vivienne.'—Now-a-days, one must—apropos of the Bourse, for instance—tell, not only of what the walls are composed, but what passions inhabit these walls, and how these evanescent fortunes are made and lost."[48]

At this point the actual source of the flâneur's much-vaunted public identity becomes fully apparent. It was his literary and artistic skills that allowed the flâneur to render the urban scene transparent to contemporary observers. Unlike the Romantic bohemians of the 1830s, who had been public performers in a literal sense, acting out their cultural agendas before the astonished eyes of their fellow urbanites, the flâneurs of the 1840s were novelists and journalists, who occupied a symbolic and mediated public space, made available to them by the commercial press and the mass media. Behind the impeccably groomed and anonymous public façade of the flâneur, there lay concealed the private face of the professional man of letters. The flâneur was none other, confided one physiologist, than a writer of "novels of manners or philosophic works." Indeed, the essence of flânerie was "the distinctive character of the true man of letters."[49]

Significantly, there was a potential conflict between the flâneur as public figure and as popular writer or artist. This is betrayed by the fact that physiologists referred only rarely and obliquely to the essential duality of the flâneur's function in modern life. The writerly and artistic side of flânerie could not readily be incorporated into the traditional formulae of flânerie, because the two images implied antithetical and unreconciled elements of modernity. The flâneur as urban symbol was public, anonymous, and democratic; the flâneur as literary man was private, individualized, and grandiose. For this reason, attempts to visualize the explicitly creative or writerly side of flânerie often found expression through a different iconographic tradition from that of the ordinary flâneur.

One of the most interesting and coherent examples of this tradition can be found on the title pages or the end pages of the multivolume collection of urban vignettes *Les Français peints par eux-mêmes,* published serially in 1841. The images depicted the artist-flâneur in his various guises as storyteller, novelist, journalist, editor, or artist. At times, he appeared as the long-haired painter, with sketchpad in hand, observing an array of smaller characters who crowd in all around him.[50] (Figure 15) At other times, he was shown in the pose of the contemplative reader by the fireside, with the shadowy products of his imagination peering in on him from behind the drawn curtains.[51] (Figure 16) Occasionally he was pictured as a journalist with pen and notebook in hand, intently surveying the cluttered studio of an artist, who is seated in front of an easel and is observed in turn by a friend.[52] (Figure 17) Yet again, he was shown as a seated figure in an imaginary forest, with a bushel of miniscule characters by his side, whom he picks up with his outstretched hand as they wind their way down the forest path beside him.[53] (Figure 18)

Figure 15. Frontispiece from *Les Français peints par eux-mêmes: Encyclopédie morale du dix-neuvième siècle*, vol. 3 (Paris: L. Curmer, 1841). Courtesy of Brown University Library.

These portraits of the creative process involved in flânerie are noteworthy for a number of reasons. Perhaps most strikingly, they placed the artist-flâneur in an imaginary landscape or an interior space that was no longer explicitly related to the empirical landscape of the modern city. Direct social observation seems to have given way to inner contemplation in these portraits. The flâneur, moreover, was depicted as a gigantic and all-powerful figure, whose size was out of all proportion to the puny creations of his imagination. No longer simply the amiable and unassuming story-teller of the general chronicles of flânerie, the artist-flâneur appeared in these images as a God-like presence exercising benevolent domination over the social world of modernity.

In order to understand the source and nature of these heroic aspirations, as well as the inner contradictions that would neutralize them in less than

Figure 16. Endpiece from *Les Français peints par eux-mêmes: Encyclopédie morale du dix-neuvième siècle*, vol. 4 (Paris: L. Curmer, 1841). Courtesy of Brown University Library.

a decade, one needs to turn from iconic images of the flâneur to the urban realists themselves who invented the figure. For flânerie was, as I have already implied, not just a cultural identity but a particular kind of textual and visual practice that came into existence in the course of the 1840s and was explicitly associated with the world of the novel and urban realism.

This popular urban culture was, as historians of the phenomenon have pointed out, far from homogeneous.[54] Its characteristic expressions ranged from the simple feuilleton, often published anonymously in the mass-circulation newspapers, all the way to Balzac's serial novels, conceived as a comic epic of modern civilization. In between were to be found a whole range of literary and artistic genres that were more or less unique to the 1840s and '50s and did not always survive into the latter half of the century. One of the most characteristic literary forms of the period were the pan-

Figure 17. Endpiece from *Les Français peints par eux-mêmes: Encyclopédie morale du dix-neuvième siècle,* vol. 2 (Paris: L. Curmer, 1841). Courtesy of Brown University Library.

orama essays, which were collectively authored vignettes of Parisian life and characters, bound in multivolume deluxe albums and conspicuously displayed in bourgeois homes.[55] Even more wildly popular were the so-called physiologies, which consisted of pocket-size illustrated booklets about social stereotypes, sold to a mass audience at one franc apiece.[56] During the decade of the 1830s and 1840s, caricatures also assumed a specifically modern form, focusing for the first time on the social satire of everyday life and on ordinary characters and professions. These found commercial outlets in book forms as well as through such widely-read humor magazines as *La Caricature* and *Le Charivari*.

Despite differences of style and appeal, however, the boundaries between these realistic genres of urban representation were remarkably porous.

Figure 18. Endpiece from *Les Français peints par eux-mêmes: Encyclopédie morale du dix-neuvième siècle,* vol. 1 (Paris: L. Curmer, 1841). Courtesy of Brown University Library.

Balzac wrote not only novels but also panorama essays and physiologies, the latter being his special invention.[57] Daumier was not only a caricaturist but also an illustrator of physiologies, and his "Robert Macaire" figure made its appearance in 1841 in the form of both a caricature series and a physiology. Physiologists quoted freely, not only from each other, but also from novelists,[58] while novelists borrowed self-consciously from the social types created by physiologists.[59] More generally, all these genres resorted to a common fund of images and references, as well as to a familiar style of address, which presupposed the same cultural and historical setting.

The common denominator that united novelists, essayists, physiologists, and caricaturists in the 1840s was their often-stated commitment to depicting the history of everyday life. They characteristically referred to themselves as "historians of manners" (historiens des moeurs), whose mission was to provide for future generations an accurate picture of the everyday events and ordinary characters of contemporary life. This is how Jules Janin explained the central purposes of panorama essays, in his Introduction to the nine-volume encyclopedia of Parisian social and moral types, *Les Français peints par eux-mêmes*. The aim of the volumes, he claimed, was to leave for posterity an accurate picture of "who we were and what we did in our time; how we dressed; what clothes our women wore; what our houses, our habits, our pleasures were; what we understood by that fragile word, subject to eternal changes, that is called beauty."[60]

Historians of manners pointed to the unprecedented nature of the modern experience and challenged artists to invent new aesthetic forms appropriate to contemporary needs and sensibilities. Baudelaire gave memorable expression to this impulse in his Salon of 1846, where he meditated on the impossibility of recreating in the modern period those collective masterpieces that had characterized the great traditions of classical ages. Although frequently read as an expression of nostalgia and regret, Baudelaire's statement was actually a celebration of the creative potential of modern life. As he put it, the decline of classical models was not the result of the "decadence" of the present age, but the sign of the emergence of a new vision of beauty, "intrinsic to our emotions" and to the special circumstances of contemporary urban life. The themes appropriate to modernity, he insisted, were to be discovered "in private subjects" and in "the pageants of fashionable life" that were being explored by the popular literature of the day. In his words, "the *Gazette des Tribunaux* and the *Moniteur* prove to us that we have only to open our eyes to recognize our heroism."[61]

The juxtaposition of the potential heroism of the modern age with the anachronistic heroism of classical antiquity became the central rhetorical trope and literary formula that historians of manners returned to over and over again in their various attempts at self-definition and self-justification. In his 1842 Introduction to *La comédie humaine,* for example, Balzac reproached the chroniclers of Egypt, Persia, Greece, and Rome for leaving behind only a "dry and repellent list of facts" and for failing to provide for posterity "a history of manners." He conceived his own function as historian of modernity in terms of correcting the failings and limitations of the ancients. "With much patience and courage," he explained, "I will succeed in creating for France in the nineteenth century, the book that we regret that Rome, Athens, Tyre, Memphis, Persia, India, have unhappily left unwritten about their civilization."[62] Jules Janin also took classical authors to task for their failure to inquire into the problems of people's everyday habits and customs. All they have left for posterity, he complained, were "accounts of sieges, battles, towns captured and overthrown, treatises of peace and war, and all kinds of deceitful, bloody and futile things."[63] The same theme can be found among writers of physiologies who regularly evoked the dichotomies of the ancients and moderns in their own efforts to rewrite the history of modernity in a more popular and accessible form. As the anonymous author of the *Physiology of the Smoker* (Physiologie du fumeur) put it, "The great events of history are not wars and revolutions, which affect only a certain class of society and which interest humanity only at certain bloody and turbulent points: instead of revolutions, speak to me of changes affecting private life, of the inventions and discoveries that influence customs, habits, and the happiness of each individual."[64]

It is worth pausing for a moment to examine what these urban writers actually meant by the concept of the "history of manners," since the formula was far less innocent and transparent than it appears on the surface. Indeed, as Georg Lukács pointed out, the very idea that ordinary life, everyday events, and common characters were worthy of being recorded and described as historical phenomena implied a revolutionary attitude to modern life.[65] This attitude, however, cannot be fully explained, as Lukács thought, in terms of some abstract insight into the historicity of contemporary events that was automatically given to individuals. On the contrary, the historical consciousness of the early nineteenth century was mediated by popular cultural forms that defined for ordinary people the meaning and implications of modernity as a cultural experience. Histories of manners were, I would like to argue, deeply implicated in, and indebted to, the melodramatic and sentimental traditions that saw human affairs in terms of underlying moral patterns, ethical conflicts, and passionate experiences that existed under the surface of reality and awaited the creative energies of the artist to be made visible and tangible. Thus, when urban writers defined themselves as historians of manners, they meant something far more ambitious than the mere task of recording the "everydayness" of modern life.[66] They conceived of themselves as the self-appointed chroniclers of modernity whose accounts lifted ordinary events beyond the fleeting moment of the present and exposed their epic possibilities. Their repeated invocation of everyday life transcended mere realism. Theirs was a wager and a challenge that modernity contained heroic potential and would outshine the ages of classical antiquity.

Contemporary critics of Balzac frequenth pointed to this broader philosophic agenda implicit within his conception of realism. As a favorable reviewer put it in 1833, "Among all our young writers, it is M. de Balzac who has best understood the alliance between literature and philosophy; his numerous writings show the imprint of exalted philosophic ideas that all converge on one goal."[67] According to a conservative observer, the same mixture of philosophy and factuality rendered the work of Balzac and his allies dangerous and immoral. For his goal was, claimed the critic, to use the cover of facts "to enthrone vast philosophic conceptions that embrace our entire society and tend to materialize our soul by proclaiming the absolutism of the senses."[68] The fundamental dualism of Balzac's work was frequently referred to by critics, who saw him as equally divided between reality and fantasy, philosophy and science, realistic descriptions and flamboyant hallucinations.[69]

These epic ambitions of the historians of manners were not without a subcurrent of anxiety and uncertainty, however. They found complex expression in a series of caricatures by Daumier that exposed the underside of contemporary visions of modernity. Entitled "Ancient History" ("L'Histoire ancienne"), the caricatures were published serially between 1842 and 1843 in the leading humor magazine of the time, *Le Charivari*. The images depicted the revered figures of classical antiquity in deliberately deheroicized roles and social situations. Mythological figures, gods and goddesses, and literary heroes, were pictured in the guise of familiar bourgeois types, acting out the rituals of private life in what had become the anachronistic costumes of classical culture. Thus, the legendary female warriors, the Amazons, were portrayed as modern bluestockings, whose bookish and quarrelsome features played on contemporary ambivalences about the nondomestic woman. (Figure 19) The sword of Damocles was transferred above the head of a contemporary restaurant patron, about to order from an obsequious and obviously untrustworthy waiter. Despite his toga and antique appearance, the figure was the very incarnation of the uncertainties of the modern consumer, about to embark on a dubious adventure with the restaurant industry, whose reputation of adulterated food was notorious at the time. (Figure 20) The abduction of Helen that caused the eruption of the Trojan War was transformed into an allegory of modern feminism in which it is Helen who abducts a cigar-smoking and emasculated Paris. (Figure 21) The reunion of Ulysses and Penelope was transformed from an epic event of public significance into a private scene of an ordinary bourgeois couple conversing in bed. (Figure 22)

On one level, these satirical drawings obviously represented a challenge to what had come to be experienced as the tyranny of the ancients over the moderns. Their intention was, in part at least, to overthrow their authority and to ridicule the attempt of contemporary culture to clothe itself in the costumes of the past. This was how Baudelaire read the meaning of "Ancient History," which he considered among the most important achievements of Daumier's art.[70] It was, Baudelaire commented, "an amusing blasphemy, with a useful role to play." The series provided, in his opinion, "a dramatic paraphrase of the celebrated verse: 'Who will deliver us of the Greeks and Romans?' " By daring to present the ancient ideals in "all their ridiculous ugliness," Daumier caused indignation among many, Baudelaire concluded, but those, "who do not have a great respect for Olympus and for tragedy were naturally overjoyed."[71]

Daumier's deheroicized images, however, did more than expose the inadequacies of the classics. They also left in doubt the character of the moderns. For the bourgeois figures that masqueraded in the costumes of the ancients hardly presented admirable alternatives to the classics. Their inability or unwillingness to appear in contemporary clothing implicitly brought into question the capacity of the modern world to create images of its own heroism. It raised uncertainties about the nature of modernity and its ability to generate cultural traditions of its own. If antiquity had expressed itself through its military prowess, its public ceremonies, its aristocratic gestures, how could modernity display its own unique form of greatness? Was a heroic public life possible for a civilization whose habits were anchored in domestic and private relations and whose values were defined by commercial and professional activities?

Figure 19. Honoré Daumier, *Les Amazones* (The Amazons). From *Charivri*, 3 April
1842. One of a series of fifty images by Daumier entitled "L'Histoire
ancienne" (Ancient history), published in *Charivari* 22 December 1841–
5 January 1843. Courtesy of the Boston Public Library, Print Department.

These images went to the heart of contemporary anxieties about modernity. What was at stake was the privatization of experience and the erosion of transparency in modern culture.[72] Probably the most familiar refrain of the period was the illegibility of life and experience in the contemporary city. It was repeatedly likened to a maze or a labyrinth that

Figure 20. Honoré Daumeir, *L'Epée de Damocles* (The sword of Damocles). From *Charivari*, 12 June 1842. One of a series of fifty images by Daumeir entitled "L'Histoire ancienne" (Ancient history), published in *Charivari* 22 December 1841–5 January 1843. Courtesy of the Boston Public Library, Print Department.

Figure 21. Honoré Daumier, *L'Enlèvement d'Hélène* (The abduction of Helen). From
        Charivari 22 June 1842. One of a series of fifty images by Daumier
        entitled "L'Histoire ancienne" (Ancient history), published in *Charivari* 22
        December 1841–5 January 1843. Courtesy of the Boston Public Library,
        Print Department.

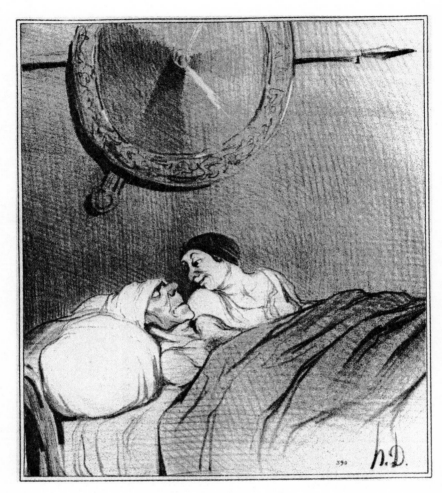

Figure 22. Honoré Daumier, *Ulysse et Pénélope* (Ulysses and Penelope). From *Charivari* 26 June 1842. One of a series of fifty images by Daumier entitled "L'Histoire ancienne" (Ancient history), published in *Charivari* 22 December 1841–5 January 1843. Courtesy of the Boston Public Library, Print Department.

provided no coherent pattern or logical design. The motif of the labyrinthine city emerged not only in such contemporary best sellers as Eugène
Sue's *Les mystères de Paris* and Alexander Dumas's *Les Mohicans de Paris,*
but also in many of the physiologies and panorama essays of the day.
Almost without exception, these focused on the disturbing experience of
blurred or disrupted vision that accompanied rapid growth in the city.
According to "The Physiology of the Streets of Paris" (Physiologie des rues
de Paris), the emergence of new streets in the middle of old neighborhoods
had become so common that "the birth of a street is no more remarkable
than that of a child." What rendered this kind of rapid urban expansion
disturbing was the fact that the names assigned to these streets no longer
reflected their individual histories, their physical aspect, or the type of
commerce being conducted there. They had become indecipherable, and
failed to evoke "any resonance, any sympathy among the people."[73] Balzac
referred to the same lack of transparency not so much in connection with
the streets of the city, as the people encountered in them. Under the old
regime, he wrote, "one could tell who people were from their outward
appearances and demeanor, even from their clothes," whereas contemporary life had produced a world of "infinite nuances," where identity was no
longer publicly available.[74] Jules Janin used a political metaphor to characterize the sense of fragmentation and incoherence that seemed to be the
universal experience of modernity. The *ancien regime,* he speculated, had
been defined by two centers of social experience, the court and the city,
whose codes and relationships were transparent to everyone. Modernity,
by contrast, had shattered "into so many small republics, each of which
have their own laws, customs, jargon, heroes, political opinions in place
of religious beliefs, ambitions, faults and loves."[75]

The problem of "visibility and invisibility, clear seeing and 'blurred'
seeing" is, as Christopher Prendergast reminds us, the central aesthetic and
epistemological question of realism, a literary-cultural concept that has had
a long, if troubled, relationship with modernist criticism.[76] Though frequently dismissed, the concept has, in Prendergast's words, "an uncanny
capacity for springing Lazarus-like back to life, returning again and again
to the agenda of discussion."[77] It is, of course, Georg Lukács who is most
closely associated with debates about realism and modernism, and it is to
his theories that we need to return in order to understand the complex
preoccupations and temporary solutions that characterized the historians
of manners or everyday life in the 1840s. Lukács linked nineteenth-century

realism with the philosophic concept of totality or the ability to envision the multiplicity of modern experience within an overarching historical frame or process. This comprehension, in turn, was dependent on the concept of the type or the typical example, conceived as a microcosm representing the whole. For Lukács, the type gave access to the epic qualities of modern life precisely by depicting "the decent and the average, rather than the eminent and all-embracing."[78]

Historians of manners were to repeatedly invoke the idea of the social type in their own efforts to render urban culture transparent and familiar to its participants. Though their particular usage of the concept of the type was not identical with that of Lukács, it clearly filled similar functions. Nineteenth-century artists and writers derived their ideas about the type from the tradition of seventeenth- and eighteenth-century physiognomies, which had first systematized the correspondences between external physical features and inner spiritual qualities.[79] Yet, as Jules Janin pointed out, the use of types by contemporary Parisian writers in the 1840s had no precedent in the past. It was a novel undertaking, he argued, meant to give expression to the unprecedented nature of modernity. "Whoever speaks of *type*," he wrote, "speaks of a complete character, a model man, a curious thing. Paris is full of types, or rather of singular minds, of original characters, out of which a good book might easily be made."[80] As Janin's remarks implied, types provided generalized models, which made visible specifically modern characters not customarily included in canonical representations of art and literature. Types were collective portraits, giving expression to the various social and occupational groups that had emerged in the modern city of the 1840s. The bourgeois, the lawyer, the physician, the bluestocking, the grisette, the student, the journalist, the porter, the grocer, the fashionable woman, were only a few of the familiar social types that emerged in the universe of the novel and urban literature in the 1840s.

Perhaps no one gave more self-conscious and eloquent testimony to the importance of social types for the historian of manners than Balzac, who structured his 1842 Introduction to *La comédie humaine* around the concept. As he made clear here, the importance of the social type lay in the fact that it could potentially provide a scientific classification for society and thus help systematize our understanding of the human world in the same way as the natural sciences had systematized the animal world. The exemplary figure for the historian of manners was the naturalist Buffon, whose classification of zoological species was to serve as a model for an analogous classification of the human species. "The difference," Balzac pointed out, "between a soldier, a worker, an administrator, a lawyer, an idler, a scholar, a statesman, a merchant, a sailor, a poet, a poor person, a priest—though more difficult to define, are just as marked as the differences that distinguish the wolf, the lion, the ass, the raven, the shark, the seal, the ewe, etc. There have existed, there will always exist, social species, just as there are zoological species. If Buffon had done a magnificent job of representing in one book, the collection of zoology, is not a similar book waiting to be written about society?"[81]

Balzac was far from unique in feeling that the example of the natural sciences would cause "the undifferentiated surfaces of modern urban existence to reveal their systematic meaning."[82] All the physiologies and panorama essays made the same claim, often accompanied by mock-heroic gestures that both parodied and emulated the canonical narratives of science. As the author of the "Physiology of Physiologies" ("Physiology des physiologies") put it, the writers of physiologies intended to make amends for the insufficiencies of Buffon and Cuvier, who had failed to include man within their scientific treatises. "Thanks to these little booklets, formed by science and wit," he declared, "mankind will be better classified, better divided, better subdivided than his relatives the animals."[83] Creating types and classifying them according to social categories represented a kind of modern ethnography, whose purpose was to achieve a comprehensive picture of contemporary humanity. So laborious and extensive was the task, pointed out Janin, that, in the case of the panorama essays, it was necessary to subdivide the project among multiple authors, who could bring their particular expertise to the vast panorama of modern life. The ultimate purpose of all these efforts was to discover the principle of unity at the core of modernity, or as Balzac put it, "to surprise the hidden meaning in the midst of this immense assemblage of figures, passions, and events."[84]

This epic enterprise whose goal was nothing less than to match and surpass the achievements of the classics remained unfulfilled and unfulfillable. The culture of everyday life remained stubbornly resistant to the synthesizing and generalizing impulses of science. Modernity, as manifested in the urban landscape, could be disciplined and transformed into apparent homogeneity, but it could not be rendered transparent and public in the way the ancient polis had been. This is why critics and historians have often pointed to the epistemological and moral instabilities inherent in representations of everyday life in the 1840s.[85] The sheer diversity and heterogeneity of these forms undermined any possibility of creating a "panoptic vision" of modernity. As Margaret Cohen put it, the popular urban texts of the 1840s failed to "generate . . . referential stability through their narrative practices. The reader must decide for himself or herself how to sort through representational anarchy, how to negotiate texts whose representational codes and referential claims differ widely, how to read through these codes to the reality they represent."[86]

Historians of manners seemed to realize on some level the internal contradictions of their project and sometimes even problematized them explicitly. Balzac, for instance, supplied a critique of his conception of social types in the very text where he articulated its most ambitious claims. As he put it in the Introduction to *La comédie humaine,* the difficulty was that the analogies between the social and the natural worlds were not exact. Social types differed from zoological species, Balzac admitted, in at least two important respects: gender and material culture. Among animals, the female species was more or less identical with the male and did not require separate typification, but in the social world this was far from the case. "In Society," Balzac wrote, "woman is not just the female version of the male," but an entirely different species, whose identity cannot be derived from that of her husband. Woman's nature was not just biologically determined, but also the result of social conditioning and cultural construction that had an inner logic of its own. To illustrate the point, Balzac pointed out that, "the wife of a merchant is sometimes worthy of being that of a prince, and sometimes that of a prince is not equal to that of an artisan."[87] But human beings differed from the animal species also in the possession of personal property. While animals were essentially invariable and predictable in their actions, human beings differentiated themselves through "their habits, their clothing, their speech, their dwellings," which varied enormously depending on occupation, social status, and degrees of wealth.[88]

Balzac's meditation on the unique horizons opened up by the history of manners also signaled its inevitable failure. Popular urban realism, defined as the depiction of everyday life grounded in notions of totality, would not survive into the latter half of the nineteenth century. The novel itself was to be transformed in the course of the 1850s, but characteristic forms of the genre, like the physiology and the panorama essay, almost completely disappeared from the cultural scene by the late 1840s. With the loss of legitimacy of these popular forms, the figure of the flâneur also became problematic. His original mission, to become a public figure and the authorized interpreter of a potentially heroic modernity, could not be sustained. Put differently, the flâneur's representations of everyday life could not, in the final analysis, transcend the fragmentations of the modern city and the compromises of the cultural market. The demise of the flâneur as a public figure also signaled the end of the bohemia of the 1840s. As Albert Cassagne put it, "In 1848 bohemia no longer constituted the avant-garde of artists; it was rather an arrière-garde, outmoded and in disarray, painfully following the lead of others."[89]

There was, it is true, a brief attempt to revive the flâneur as a public figure during the Revolution of 1848. But the failure of this effort only serves to illuminate the deeper cultural causes of the flâneur's demise. In May 1848, a short-lived radical republican journal was founded in Paris, with the resonant title of *Le Flâneur*. As the lead editorial on the title page of the journal proclaimed, the enterprise of the traditional flâneur, associated with a leisured, urban way of life, was "centuries out of date." Yet, it continued, a more modern form of flânerie was, nevertheless, possible with the transformation of the flâneur into a republican patriot: "we maintain that the flâneur can and should think about his rights and duties as a citizen. These are demanding times and require of us all our thoughts, all our time; let us by all means be flâneurs, but let us do it as patriots."[90] The political enterprise of *Le Flâneur* was only an evanescent phenomenon, abruptly terminated by the defeat of the revolution and the consolidation under Louis Napoleon of a semi-authoritarian regime. Republican politics could not ultimately recreate a viable public culture where a new, politicized version of the flâneur could flourish. Baudelaire's brief flirtation with republican politics in 1848 and his subsequent turn to aesthetic concerns faithfully reflected these developments in the broader culture.

Susan Buck-Morss has observed that the "era of origins" of flânerie has been irretrievably lost with the Parisian arcades of the 1840s. From the contemporary perspective, she elaborated, only fragments remain of the original flâneur, whose traces are "more visible in his afterlife than in his flourishing."[91] I would modify Buck-Morss' astute observation by adding that it was not only the decline of the physical spaces of the arcades that explains the fragmentation of the flâneur as a cultural type, but also the dissolution of the cultural horizons that brought him into existence in the first place. The flâneur was, after all, the characteristic product as well as the unacknowledged creator of the urban texts of the 1840s that aspired to produce comprehensive and epic histories of modernity.

The conditions for this heroic enterprise were to disappear, as Buck-Morss pointed out, with the world of the arcades and with the political hopes of 1848. In its place was to emerge a new, narrower, explicitly scientific, textual, and visual practice that assumed the programmatic title of Realism. The word itself had been used sporadically as early as the 1830s to describe the works of Balzac, Stendhal, and even Hugo. But it was only in the period between 1846 and 1851 that the idea of "réalisme" and "réaliste" gained currency as an important critical category.[92] With the founding of the journal *Le Réalisme* in 1856 and the publication of Champfleury's volume of essays *Le Réalisme* in 1857, the concept became established as the canonical modern artistic practice.

The doctrine of Realism implied a number of principles that were spelled out and codified by its advocates. It meant the exact imitation of nature; the exclusion of the artist's personal point of view; an emphasis on the material rather than the spiritual aspects of nature; a disdain for "style," "elegance," and "convention"; the rejection of idealism, imagination, and fantasy; and perhaps most important of all, an insistence on contemporaneity and truth in description. Implicit in this literary code was a new vision of modernity that radically simplified earlier definitions. Whereas modernity in the 1840s had a broadly synthetic connotation that united the scientific attitude with passionate, ethical, and epic values, modernity in the 1850s came to be exclusively associated with a decontextualized and abstract science.

The modern artist as reconceptualized by canonical Realism was no longer a complex and historically embedded creature, caught in the dialectical tension between the present and the past; but rather, a radically individualized self that had declared its independence from all historical traditions and collective affiliations. As Fernand Desnoyers put it in a manifesto of Realism published in December 1855: "Realism says to people: we have always been Greeks, Latins, Englishmen, Germans, Spaniards, etc., let us be ourselves, even if we may appear ugly. Let us write, let us paint, only what we see, what we know, what we have lived. Let us be neither masters nor students! Strange school, isn't it? One which acknowledges neither masters nor students, one whose only precepts are independence, sincerity, and individualism."[93] The emphasis in this declaration was on emancipation from the past and on the affirmation of the uniqueness of the present. Notably absent from this pronouncement was the complex rivalry with the ancients that had provided the epic dimension of the historians of manners. In the eyes of its militant advocates, Realism had succeeded in making modernity autonomous, and the past irrelevant.

Daumier captured the type of the artist as Realist at the very moment when he assumed the place of the flâneur as the representative artist of modernity. In a witty caricature of 1849, he depicted the Realist as a painter standing in front of an easel, copying his self-portrait from a mirror placed at a right angle to his easel. (Figure 23)[94] The title of the image, *Un Français peint par lui-même* (*A Frenchman Painted by Himself*), invited comparison with the artist-flâneurs of the early 1840s, who had produced the multivolume panoramic essays, *Les Français peints par eux-mêmes* (*The French Painted by Themselves*). Unlike his predecessor, the new type of artist was no longer a heroic and fecund creator, surrounded by his teeming fictional progeny. He was reduced to the lone and isolated individual, peering insistently into a mirror that was his only link to external life. The complex notion of urban observation, associated with flânerie, was replaced by a mechanical idea of visuality, which excluded imagination and subjectivity as valid categories of perception.

The prototype of the artist as Realist was the scientist, who pursued his aesthetic goals in a lonely and single-minded way that presupposed detachment, not only from all personal prejudice, but also from all social and cultural ties as well. The kind of determination required of the Realist had little to do with the playfulness, irony, and worldliness of the flâneur of the 1840s. As Champfleury spelled out in a programmatic letter published in *Le Figaro,* "Any man who does not possess enough courage to become a kind of encyclopedist, who is incapable of absorbing all the scientific and moral tendencies of his age, should give up on the idea of writing a novel. He needs to incorporate in his studies a profound concentration, an indifference for all political, artistic, and religious fashions, a fine ear, an acute eye, a naïve intelligence, ceaseless labor, an iron will, a robust or sickly constitution. This is the ideal type of the novelist which only a few ever succeed in approximating."[95]

Champfleury's depiction of the modern artist as scientific observer explicitly repudiated the public function of the artist-flâneur as urban observer. The Realist consciously avoided the fleeting and superficial aspects of modern life in the city, focusing instead on its deeper physical and moral laws. He also implicitly cut his ties with popular culture of all kinds by establishing his credentials as a serious scholar, rather than a mere storyteller or a carnivalesque performer. In 1857 Sainte-Beuve gave an exem-

Figure 23. Honoré Daumier, *Un Français peint par lui-même* (A Frenchman painted
by himself). One of a series of four images by Honoré Daumier entitled
"Scènes d'ateliers" (Scenes from the studio), published in *Charivari*
January 1848–April 1850.

plary description of such an artist in his famous review of Flaubert's *Madame Bovary*. "In many places and under many different forms," he declared, "I detect symptoms of a new literary manner: scientific, experimental, adult, powerful, a little harsh. Such are the outstanding characteristics of the leaders of the new generation. Son and brother of distinguished surgeons, M. Flaubert handles the pen like others the scalpel. Anatomists and physiologists, I meet you at every turn."[96]

Realism's powerful claims to avant-garde status in the 1850s did not go unopposed, however. Indeed, it was Flaubert's *Madame Bovary* that provided the occasion for a repudiation of the doctrine of Realism in the name of an alternate artistic ideal suggesting the continuation by new means of the culture of flânerie. The challenge was posed by Charles Baudelaire, whose review of *Madame Bovary* in 1857 suggested a reading of Flaubert's novel that was directly at odds with that of Sainte-Beuve. Rather than seeing *Madame Bovary* as the latest example of the Realist school, Baudelaire considered it to be a parody of Realism that self-consciously used the techniques of objectivity and impersonality to reaffirm the values of imagination, passion, and picturesque beauty banished by Realists from the practice of modern art. *Madame Bovary* was, Baudelaire insisted, "a wager, a real wager, a bet, like all works of art" that true beauty could be created out of the most commonplace and trivial material at the disposal of the artist: from an incident of provincial adultery recorded on the pages of the daily newspaper.[97]

Baudelaire's review is of particular interest to the cultural historian, since it graphically illustrates the nature of the transformation of the cultural environment in the middle of the nineteenth century. "The last years of Louis-Philippe," Baudelaire complained, "witnessed the final explosions of a spirit that could still be stimulated by the play of the imagination."[98] Within the span of a few years, two radically different literary and artistic sensibilities found themselves juxtaposed to each other. On the one side was the defunct world of flânerie, associated with the epic aspirations of the historians of manners. On the other side was the new ethos of Realism, associated with the values of science and progress. Baudelaire did not hesitate to declare his opinion of this new literary school. Realism was, he declared, "a repulsive insult flung in the face of every analyst, a vague and elastic word which for the ordinary man signifies not a new means of creation, but a minute description of trivial details."[99] It was in opposition to Realism that a new version of the flâneur and a new definition of flânerie was to emerge on the cultural scene of the 1850s.

"The painter of modern life," as Baudelaire called this resurrected flâneur, reaffirmed the idea of modernity as epic experience anchored in a hidden unity at the core of a fragmented civilization.[100] Yet the avant-garde flâneur could no longer fully identify his sense of modernity with the actual empirical city of Paris, nor could he celebrate it in the social types and everyday life he observed in the urban landscape. He stood in silent opposition to Hausseman's monumental urban renewal project, which was transforming Paris into a rational, predictable, visually coherent, but emotionally alienating urban landscape.[101]

The very concept of modernity as a synthetic project that could unify science and imagination, everyday life and history, ethical values and emotional excess, fractured during the 1850s. The flâneur's avant-garde incarnation became the uniquely endowed defender of the values of imagination against a narrowly scientific conception of modernity. Baudelaire gave memorable expression to this new, purely aesthetic vision of modernity in his passionate polemic against photography, which he saw as the incarnation of the destructive potential of modern science. Progress and Poetry, he wrote in his "Salon of 1859," were two ambitious men, "who hate one another with an intrinsic hatred, and when they meet upon the same road, one of them has to give way."[102] The ideal of flânerie had fragmented into incompatible visions of modernity, which faced each other without any possibility of reconciliation. For the 1850s, the problem had become, not how to distinguish the true flâneur from the mere idlers, but how to differentiate the genuine painter of modernity from the mere photographer or the scientific realist.

Baudelaire's seminal essay of 1858, "The Painter of Modern Life," was structured precisely around this problematic. Generally regarded as the most important definition of the artist-flâneur of the mid-nineteenth century, Baudelaire's essay has received a great deal of critical attention over the years. Yet, a certain enigma surrounds both the form of the text and the identity of its hero, Constantin Guys. The account seems to belong to an "indefinite genre," wrote Jessica Feldman, which was part "tale, philosophic essay, prose poem, 'Salon,' novella, biography and operetta," but which most resembled the autobiography or the Wagnerian *Gesamtkunstwerk*.[103] Equally puzzling is the status of Constantin Guys, the rather obscure lithographer and foreign correspondent, as the exemplary artist of modernity, especially when compared with seemingly more appropriate figures such as Manet.[104]

The difficulty of defining "The Painter of Modern Life" and Constantin Guys in terms of canonical aesthetic conventions is not surprising. For the prototype of both the essay and its protagonist were to be found in the defunct physiology and the popular flâneur of the 1840s. Like the original physiologists, Baudelaire, too, aspired to a comprehensive or epic depiction of modernity; and like his predecessors, he, too, made the flâneur the heroic incarnation of this possibility. Unlike the physiologists, however, Baudelaire could no longer assume that the ultimate meaning of modernity could be distilled from the physical manifestations of everyday life or urban existence. He could duplicate only on the level of analogy and metaphor the original project of the physiologists.

The centrality of analogy in Baudelaire's vision of modernity has frequently been examined from a strictly aesthetic point of view, but rarely from that of social and cultural practice. Yet, as he noted in "The Painter of Modern Life," the aesthetic realm was not simply an embodiment of the "eternal and the immutable," but also the reflection of the "ephemeral, the fugitive, the contingent."[105] In other words, it was analogically linked to both the timeless realm of transcendental forms, as well as to a historical world of urban modernity, as defined by popular culture. This analogic relationship between the cultural and the aesthetic realms was explicitly suggested in the opening chapters of "The Painter of Modern Life," which juxtaposed the oeuvre of Daumier, Gavarni, and Balzac with the more specialized and esoteric creations of Constantin Guys. The former had given rise, Baudelaire explained, to "the sketch of manners, the depiction of bourgeois life and the pageant of fashion, while the latter produced a series of dazzlingly original drawings, appreciated by art-lovers but ignored by the general public."[106]

That Constantin Guys constituted the aesthetic double of the popular flâneur was unmistakably suggested by his close association with the formulaic definitions of flânerie. Like the original flâneur, he too was an urban creature, whose "passion and . . . profession are to become one flesh with the crowd." He too was essentially a public self who had "set up house in the heart of the multitude." Perhaps most revealingly, he too was a "passionate spectator" who was "at the center of the world, and yet remained hidden from the world."[107] Yet, these familiar formulae did not have the same function in the world of avant-garde flânerie as they did in the world of popular flânerie. In fact, they not only linked the avant-garde flâneur with his popular counterpart, but also served to differentiate him from him.

This could hardly be otherwise, since the figure of the avant-garde flâneur was constituted in fundamentally different ways from the popular flâneur. Rather than being a type, defined by codes applicable to all members of the class, the avant-garde flâneur was a unique individual, who represented a principle of differentiation and originality. His identity was based, not on typification; but on masks, disguises, and incognitos, through which he defined his empathetic identification with modernity. At times, he was a child, able to see "everything in a state of newness;"[108] at times a savage or barbarian, drawing with an instinctive and untrained genius; at times a courtesan, displaying her charms through the world of fashion and artifice; but perhaps most often, a dandy, embodying the principle of "personal originality" and aristocratic discipline in an age of democracy.[109] Whatever façade he chose to assume, the avant-garde flâneur was always composed from the outside, rather than from within, oscillating between "the vaporization and centralization of the Self."[110] This kind of mobile, centerless self was capable of the multiplication and intensification of experience precisely because it had the capacity to relate to the world through multiple façades. The flâneur's subjectivity, wrote Baudelaire, was "a mirror as immense as the crowd itself; or a kaleidoscope gifted with consciousness, responding to each one of its movements and reproducing the multiplicity of life and the flickering grace of all the elements of life."[111] Ultimately, masquerade for the avant-garde flâneur was identical with the life of imagination, through which he transformed "the world of categories" into "a world of analogy."[112] Liberated from the weight of empirical reality, he assumed the function of the original creator. Such a consciousness, Baudelaire explained, "decomposes all creation, and with the raw materials accumulated and disposed in accordance with rules whose origins one cannot find save in the furthest depths of the soul, it creates a new world, it produces the sensation of newness."[113]

The avant-garde flâneur's heroic stature was, thus, directly related to his radical creativity, to his god-like ability to refashion himself and the world in ever-new forms. It is worth comparing the nature of this creativity with that of the popular flâneur's, who had also been represented as a superhuman figure, invested with the monumental task of creating modern culture anew. The activity of the popular flâneur was however, still linked to an empirically definable modernity that was presumed to exist independently of the artist. By contrast, the avant-garde flâneur's version of modernity no longer existed as an objective reality. It came into existence only after the empirical world of appearances had been radically dismantled, broken into its component parts, and newly reassembled as a work of imagination. Modernity had ceased to be a social text, that waited to be deciphered by the urban writer, and became an aesthetic construct, that needed to be freshly created through the artist's imaginative act.

Not surprisingly, the avant-garde flâneur's version of urban modernity was fundamentally different from that of the popular flâneur. It was no longer concerned with the teeming variety and multiplicity of social types, and it made no attempt at creating a panorama of modern life. Instead, it was deliberately selective in focus and aestheticizing in technique. In the case of Constantin Guys, for example, Baudelaire tells us that a new, harmonized urban landscape was created in his sketches, which distilled such idealized images of the city as "fine carriages and proud horses, the dazzling smartness of the grooms, the expertness of the footmen, the sinuous gait of the women, the beauty of the children, happy to be alive and nicely dressed."[114] (Figure 24) The city ceased to be a labyrinth or a mystery, whose overall meaning would be revealed and decoded through the description of the urban observer. It had become, instead, the site of heightened experience and of a particularly modern form of beauty, revealed through flashes of insight that were mediated through the aesthetic vision of the artist. As Baudelaire took pains to point out, in this revised and radically aestheticized vision of modernity, reality had become synonymous with the concrete surfaces of urban life, as displayed in the world of artifice, fashion, and decoration. The artist's true subject was in "the outward show of life" and "the pageantry of military life, of fashion and of love," which were displayed in the "capitals of the civilized world."[115]

Rather than trivializing the creative mission of the modern artist, this shift of focus and meaning actually expanded its potential. Cultural modernity, as redefined by the avant-garde flâneur, became synonymous with the imagination, and liberated from the concrete social realistics of Paris or even Europe. It is worth noting that the popular flâneur had still taken it as axiomatic that Paris, or at any rate Europe, was synonymous with modernity and that he could not exist anywhere else in the world. The avant-garde flâneur, as personified by Constantin Guys, no longer did so. Presented as a man of the world and as a great traveler, Guys felt at home in all parts of the globe. Indeed, according to Baudelaire, he spent as much time in Bulgaria, the Crimea, and Spain as in Paris or London. Such faraway places, "ministered lavishly to the eye of M. G.," we are told, offering "tableaux vivants," "uniquely picturesque fragments," and "exotic details" to the practiced eye of the artist of modernity.[116] In the guise of the exotic, modernity could even more readily be discovered in the non-European world of the Orient and the Middle East, than in the metropolitan centers, because these places provided more varied and more intense stimulation to the imagination of the artist.

The aestheticizing vision of the modernist artist had been liberated from the constraints of geography, social condition, and national traditions. He had become a truly cosmopolitan figure, whose imagination enabled him to inhabit, not only the city, but in the entire globe. The avant-garde flâneur's capacity to transform reality into exotic vision and expressive artifact

Figure 24. Constantin Guys, *Meeting in the Park*. Pen and brown ink, with gray, blue, and black wash. Courtesy of the Metropolitan Museum of Art, Rogers Fund, 1937.

was paradoxically in tune with a dynamic, modern Europe that was at the cusp of massive imperial expansion. Despite his passionate opposition to the world of politics, science, and industry, the particular identity that the avant-garde flâneur forged for himself proved remarkably compatible with the tendencies of the modern world.

Yet, the heroism of the avant-garde flâneur was also a deeply ambiguous achievement. He gave voice to the heroic potential of modernity, but only as abstract beauty, not as social truth. His world had expanded to include the entire globe, but it also contracted to the closed and autonomous realm of aesthetic creation. His heroism was no longer that of the public chronicler of modern life, but that of the esoteric artist of modernity. The peculiar combination of greatness and resignation that defined his role in society found a perfect embodiment in Baudelaire's definition of the dandy as "an out-of-work Hercules!"[117] The kind of public and collective tasks that would have befitted the energies of a Hercules were no longer available to the modern artist. But, in an essential sense, the artist of modernity did remain a Hercules; through imagination and creativity, he succeeded in forging an aesthetic vision of modernity that could not be realized in the empirical realm.

Baudelaire's celebration of the heroism of modern life was never without ambiguity, but the full complexity of his ironic vision emerges only in the context of his overall conception of modernity. He hinted at this broader perspective in the opening lines of "The Painter of Modern Life," where he briefly juxtaposed the esoteric originality of M. Guys with the more robust gifts of "the painters of manners," in whose ranks he included lithographers such as Daumier, Gavarni, Deveria, and others; as well as novelists such as Balzac. What united all these artists was their shared experience of urban modernity, where trivial life and "the daily metamorphosis of external things" required of the artist speed of execution and sensitivity to the passing moment.[118] As Baudelaire noted, this was a contingent, destabilized universe, where the artist had become an integral part of the dynamic realm of popular commercial culture.

Baudelaire was to explore the special qualities of this culture in his fragmentary writings on caricature, where he explicitly identified aesthetic modernity with the world of comedy and laughter. Of the several pieces he wrote on the subject, it is perhaps his essay "On the Essence of Laughter and, in General, on the Comic in the Plastic Arts" that provides the most important clues about his ideas on the subject. The essay, on the surface a rather abstract meditation on the meaning of humor in human affairs, was actually a highly personal and idiosyncratic philosophic confession in which he equated modernity with a fallen and demonic universe that no longer offered the possibility of innocence or unself-conscious identification with nature. This was a world of pride, egotism, and vanity, where laughter was provoked by the sight of another's misfortune and weakness, which turned out to be, "almost always a mental failing." Such laughter, Baudelaire remarked significantly, was invariably founded on "the idea of one's own superiority," and was therefore "the clearest tokens of the Satanic in man."[119]

It is impossible to avoid the impression that Baudelaire was recapitulating here the vision of the Parisian literary market that Regnault had already presented in 1841 in connection with his physiology of the modern man of letters. Baudelaire reinforced this idea by juxtaposing the world of the comic with an earlier culture of Romanticism, whose characters, he argued, were incapable of laughter. In an imaginary scenario, Baudelaire pictured the "great and typical figure of Virginie, who perfectly symbolizes absolute purity and naiveté," suddenly transported into the bustle of contemporary Paris. Virginie, "still bathed in sea-mists and gilded by the tropical sun," decides to stroll through the Palais-Royal, where her eyes fall, at a glazier's window, on a table of caricatures, "full-blown with gall and spite, just such as a shrewd and bored civilization knows how to make them." The encounter with modern urban culture results in a "shudder of a soul," a "sudden folding of the wings," which signaled Virginie's fall from innocence. "No doubt," Baudelaire prophesied, "if Virginie remains in Paris and knowledge comes to her, laughter will come too."[120]

Baudelaire placed the flâneur squarely within this profane world of laughter and entertainment, but he also suggested that his participation in this world was more self-reflexive, more paradoxical, than that of ordinary producers. The artist's laughter was a sign of his suffering and his consciousness of his double nature, which was "infinitely great in relation to man, and infinitely vile and base in relation to absolute Truth and Justice." The artist who laughs, Baudelaire concluded, "is a living contradiction," because he expressed simultaneously his debased status within modern culture as well as his superiority over it.[121]

Baudelaire's essay on humor, like Gautier's depiction of the publication of *Mademoiselle de Maupin* almost twenty years earlier, suggested a common frame of reference for understanding the nature of aesthetic production in the modern world. The artist of modernity in both accounts inhabited a desacralized universe of fleeting experiences and commercial relationships where he could no longer claim privileged access to transcendental truths. Yet, it is precisely his ability to recognize the paradoxes and contradictions of his condition, and to use irony and parody to give expression to this condition, that constituted the heroic possibilities of modernist art.

4

The Decadent and the
Culture of Hysteria

J. K. Huysmans's controversial novel of 1884, *À Rebours* (Against the Grain), almost single-handedly created the image of the modernist artist that was to define avant-garde identities till the end of the century. The decadent, as the figure came to be called after 1886,[1] was widely depicted as the neurasthenic product of an aging civilization, which had reached a stage of development analogous to that of the Roman Empire in its decline. The new psychological type, claimed Paul Bourget, one of the popularizers of fin-de-siècle decadence, was characterized by "a refined and mournful nervousness, a bitter taste of life, a nostalgic pessimism about life,"[2] already anticipated by the works of Baudelaire, Flaubert, Stendhal, and Dumas, but fully realized only in the contemporary consumers of these texts.

What is the relationship between this decadent type and the mid-century flâneur that Baudelaire did so much to glamorize? More generally still, what is the connection between decadence and bohemia? The answer to both these questions seems deceptively simple. According to traditional narratives, the phenomenon of decadence was directly traceable back to Baudelaire, especially as reinterpreted for the late nineteenth century by Gautier's "Notice" of 1868. It was in this extended essay that Gautier first elaborated the concept of decadence as it applied to Baudelaire's work in particular and to modern artistic production in general. Gautier's starting point was the familiar assertion that the modern historical experience was incommensurable with the ancients, and therefore needed new forms that could give expression to its uniquely complex insights and emotions. "The characteristic feature of the nineteenth century," Gautier stressed, "is not exactly naiveté and it needs to render its thoughts, its dreams and its postulates in an idiom a little more complex than the language of the classics. Literature is like the day: it has a morning, a noon, an evening and a night . . . Does the evening not have its own beauty, like that of the morning?" Decadence, as presented by Gautier, was not exclusively a pejorative concept signaling moral decline and enervation, but rather an affirmation of the unique qualities of modernity. As Gautier put it, "the understanding of modern beauty rejects the antique beauty as not only not available to contemporary artists, but as something lacking subtlety and sophistication—he regards antique beauty as primitive, vulgar, barbaric."[3]

Paradoxically, this familiar definition of aesthetic modernity, which was an integral part of the avant-garde affirmation of everyday life and urban modernity, acquired entirely new connotations in the modern critical tradition. It came to be associated with an esoteric literature of stylistic refinement and psychological nuance, whose defining quality was precisely its estrangement from modernity, its violent opposition to the world of popular culture, urban entertainment, and democratic politics. Exemplified by a handful of writers and artists such as J. K. Huysmans, Stéphane Mallarmé, Paul Verlaine, Barbey d'Aurevilly, Villiers de l'Isle-Adam, Remy de Gourmont, and Rachilde, the decadent self has by definition been seen as an alienated figure detached from his society and his century.[4]

The creators of decadent texts themselves contributed to the process of decontextualization that transposed the decadent into an ideal space and erased his links with his age. Huysmans, for instance, insisted in his 1903 Preface to *À Rebours* that the book was nothing more than an escapist fantasy illustrating the contemporary artist's revolt against the vulgarity of modern life and his distaste for "the American habits of his time." His decadent hero, he elaborated, took flight "to the land of dreams, seeking refuge in the illusion of extravagant fantasies, living alone and aloof, remote from his own country, amid the association called up by memory of more cordial epochs, and less villainous surroundings."[5]

The Preface, however, inadvertently provides glimpses of a different source of origins for the decadent self, which places him centrally within the cultural developments of the fin-de-siècle. Significantly, these alternate images were embedded, not in Huysmans's own analysis, but in his ironic account of the critical reactions to his book. The unconventional novel, it appears, was received with shock and outrage by the establishment. " '*Against the Grain*,' " he recounted in his Preface, "fell like an aerolite into the literary fairground, to be received with mingled amazement and indignation; the Press completely lost their heads; such an outburst of incoherent ravings had never been known before."[6] The novel was criticized on at least three separate counts. It was blamed for its violently anticlassical attitude, which presented the revered figures of Virgil, Horace and Caesar in a negative and even ridiculous light. Its author was, furthermore, accused of hysteria and emotional pathology that threatened the moral health and integrity of society. "Would be critics," Huysmans recounted ironically, "were kind enough to advise me that it would do me a world of good to be confined in a hydropathic establishment and suffer the discipline of cold douches."[7] Perhaps most surprising of all, the novel was repudiated for its unsavory affinities with the world of popular entertainment. In Huysmans's words, "the serious reviews, such as the *Revue des deux mondes,* deputed their fugleman, M. Brunetière, to liken the novel to the vaudevilles of Wallard and Fulgence."[8]

Despite their polemical edge and blatant unfairness, these critical reactions to *À Rebours* are highly instructive. They suggest that Huysmans's paradigmatic hero was not a figment of his imagination, as he claimed in his retrospective Preface; nor an echo of admired predecessors such as Baudelaire, as he reiterated in the actual text of the novel. Rather, the hidden origins of the decadent artist were to be found in the culture of urban entertainment and popular hysteria that were the markers of modernity at the turn of the century. More specifically still, the unacknowledged prototypes of Huysmans's eccentric hero were the radical artists and intellectuals who came of age in the late 1870s and early 1880s, and recreated a new version of bohemian culture, closely affiliated with the cafés and cabarets of the Left Bank and Montmartre. It was within the carnivalesque world of artistic cabarets and literary cafés that the persona of the modern decadent was first conceived as a new embodiment of the culture of modernity. Far from being the bookish and enervated victim of neurasthenia that Huysmans and Bourget portrayed, the original decadent was a parodic and transgressive figure, opposed both to the established order and to official art. His close affiliation with urban spectacle and performance made him the direct heir of the flâneur of the 1840s and the romantic bohemian of the 1830s, who had also been engaged in the task of formulating an explicitly popular and performative vision of modernity.

This decadent bohemia associated with the low culture of urban entertainment is notoriously difficult to bring into focus, and is more or less absent from familiar narratives of late nineteenth-century art and literature.[9] Characterized by André Billy as part of "the minor literary history of the nineteenth century" ("la petite histoire littéraire du XIX siècle"), fin-de-siècle bohemia seems to defy classification in terms of specific literary movements or artistic categories.[10] Most of its members were minor literary figures who created their reputations through carnivalesque performances and outrageous pranks that are, by definition, ephemeral. Even in those cases where individual bohemians left behind autobiographies, memoirs, articles, or sketches, the broader significance of their gestures remains elusive and hard to interpret outside their immediate contexts.[11] It is no wonder that Daniel Grojnowski, the historian of fin-de-siècle popular bohemia, has issued this cautionary remark: "To take an interest in this group of bohemian artists and writers is to risk becoming a collector of anecdotes, an exhumer of minor poets fallen into an oblivion where they might as well harmlessly remain. In their case we must confront fundamental questions: what was their importance in the art and literature of the last century, and what is their importance to us today?"[12]

The answer to this question has to be sought in the elusive concept of "modernity" or "modernism," terms first coined by the avant-garde of the 1850s and rediscovered by the radical artistic generation of the 1880s. Perhaps no other epithet was used more persistently and more ambiguously than these words to describe the activities and personnel of fin-de-siècle bohemia. The young people flocking to bohemian cafés were "violently stricken by modernism," wrote one observer, and "waving the flag of modernism."[13] They were defined, according to another account, by their "rejection of the legends of antiquity and the stories of the middle ages and by the search for the present moment, for the hour that passes with us."[14] The Chat Noir, perhaps the epicenter of decadent bohemia in the early 1880s, hung a sign at the entrance of its premises, commanding customers to "Be modern!" Appropriately, parodic accounts of the Chat Noir referred to the cabaret as a "temple of Modernity" that embodied the very essence of the concept.[15] The meaning of these frequent references, while seemingly obvious to contemporaries, is far from simple or transparent. Indeed, their hidden significance needs to be painstakingly recuperated from the fragmentary, seemingly insignificant traces left behind by popular narratives of the time. Following their lead will take us from the cultural spaces of the artistic cabaret and the literary café, through the medical lectures and demonstrations of the Salpêtrière, all the way to the aesthetic writings and manifestoes of avant-garde artists. The common threads that ran through these seemingly disconnected realms of discourse were the themes of modernity, hysteria, and decadence that constituted interconnected categories for the turn of the century.

The uncontested chronicler of fin-de-siècle bohemia was the poet Émile Goudeau, whose autobiographical account, *Dix ans de bohème,* is comparable to Gautier's better-known "Battle of *Hernani.*" Goudeau was highly self-conscious about the relationship of his generation to earlier versions of bohemia. As he acknowledged in an article of 1879, he and his fellow artists had the ambition to revive "the great literary battles of 1830."[16] To a large extent, they succeeded, and Goudeau's narrative provides unparalleled insight into the ways that the *bohème* of 1878–1888 reclaimed and recapitulated the colorful gestures and parodic performances of its predecessors. Without any question, the founding event that launched the phenomenon and set its characteristic patterns was the convening of the Society of the Hydropathes in October 1878 under the leadership of Goudeau himself. The group held its first meeting in the Café de la Rive Gauche in order to provide Left Bank artists, poets, musicians, students, and actors with a public venue where they could present their own work in front of each other. In many respects, the event duplicated the established formulae and informal atmosphere of the popular café-concerts of the time. The name "Hydropathes" was, in fact, a parodic reformulation of the title of a catchy waltz, whose tune had struck Goudeau's imagination while he was attending a café-concert with friends.[17] (Figure 25)

Goudeau, who was elected first president of the Society of the Hydropathes, established the formal rules and procedures of the society. He and the vice president presided over the meetings, installed behind a large desk that was positioned at an angle from which they could survey the increasingly crowded gathering. When the hall that contained chairs, benches, and small round tables for the consumption of drinks was completely full, messengers were sent from row to row, collecting the names of volunteers who wished to perform.[18] The names were then taken to the president and the vice president, who made up the list of performers for the evening. They attempted, as Goudeau recalled, to construct the program for the evening according to a pleasing or artistic pattern, interspersing, "as much as possible music and verse, happy numbers with sad ones." While this operation was taking place, the audience was engaged in lively conversation, which was sometimes kept to a murmur, sometimes grew to thunderous proportions. As soon as the president's hammer was heard, how-

Figure 25. Georges Lorin (Cabriol), *Emile Goudeau, président des Hydropathes*. Hand-colored photo-relief cover illustration for *L'Hydropathe,* 22 January 1879. Schimmel Fund. Jane Voorhees Zimmerli Art Museum, Rutgers, The State University of New Jersey. Photograph by Jack Abraham.

ever, "silence was established and there emerged one after another poets, monologists, actors or singers, pianists and violinists," who delivered their numbers.[19]

The novelty of these proceedings lay in the unusual performance style that came to characterize their presentations. As Jules Lévy was to describe them decades later, the performers said their pieces "simply, without emphasis, without attempts at quackery, and with a naïve candor full of charm."[20] Goudeau confirmed the unconventionality of these performances, which lacked artistic polish or formal structure. The astonished audience was confronted by "singers of rhymes, who were distinguished by their Normand or Gascon accents, their incoherent gestures or their uncouth carriage." There was about their presentations, he added, "the peculiar savor of the author producing himself in public through the expressivity of his thought."[21]

So successful was the venture of the Hydropathes that in the course of the following months they were forced to enlarge their venues several times and to expand their meetings from once to twice weekly sessions. "The gatherings became enormous," Goudeau remembered. "Three hundred and fifty people were crowded together in a small space, spilling out into the corridor and the kitchen of the hotel."[22] As president of the Hydropathes, Goudeau played a central role in exerting control over their extraordinary séances, which "were sometimes inexplicably tumultuous."[23] and required the physical ejection of unruly participants. Most observers remarked on Goudeau's extraordinary talent for the task of running these artistic happenings. "His southern charm," remembered one participant, "his unexpected and always amusing interventions, the liking he enjoyed everywhere, made him an amazing president, who sometimes had to thunder, but who was always listened to and was capable of calming the storms."[24] Despite the rowdyism associated with Hydropathic gatherings, they quickly gained a reputation for serious artistic innovation and intellectual creativity. Their meetings became, according to Félicien Champsaur, the gathering place for everyone in the Latin Quarter "who thinks, who works, who has dreams and ambitions."[25]

The wildfire popularity of the Hydropathic séances ironically also contributed to their evanescence. They quickly lost their novelty and ability to shock, and the group disbanded in 1881 just three years after its founding. The "incoherent" performance style that they pioneered survived, however, to become a central feature of fin-de-siècle cabaret culture. Perhaps the best-known successor to the Hydropathes was the Chat Noir cabaret, which opened its doors in December 1881, under the leadership of Rodolphe Salis and Émile Goudeau, who assumed editorship of the cabaret's journal, also entitled *Le Chat Noir*. Despite the explicitly commercial nature of the new venture and despite its relocation from the Left Bank to Montmartre, the artists of the Chat Noir continued the traditions established by the Hydropathes. This is hardly surprising, since many of the former Hydropathes continued to collaborate with the Chat Noir and developed even further the implications of their earlier practices. Here, too, parodic performance and expressive self-dramatization were united in a complex mixture of art and entertainment. The role of master of ceremonies, which had been performed by Goudeau in the Hydropathic meetings, was assumed by Salis, who came to be known as the "gentleman innkeeper." Dressed in an eccentric costume that mimicked a military uniform, Salis acted as an intermediary between the artistic performers and the audience, welcoming guests and providing commentary about the diverse acts of his artists. By all accounts, Salis was a charismatic presence who had a central function in the artistic performances of the Chat Noir. His role was compared by one contemporary to that of "the ancient chorus, [who] explains the plays and presents the poets and singers to the audience, without using any text."[26] The peculiarly heady atmosphere of the early Chat Noir was suggested by Coquelin Cadet, the actor-writer, who was to provide one of the most important theories of fin-de-siècle bohemian performance. In the Chat Noir, he observed, Salis brought together "poets, painters, musicians, sculptors, architects, comedians. They served drinks. And the world comes to the Boulevard Rochouard to see these young men smitten by the arts, full of blind paradoxes, a dizzying fantasy, without respect for conventions and the bourgeois, bringing forth in a loud voice flamboyant opinions, singing and reciting verses that overflowed with lyricism and impressionism."[27] (Figure 26)

Significantly, bohemian performances were not restricted to artistic cafés and cabarets. Under the auspices of the former Hydropathe Jules Lévy, the spirit of decadent bohemia found new incarnations in the so-called Incoherent art exhibitions and costume balls of the 1880s. With a subtle sense of symbolism as well as keen business acumen, Lévy initially staged his exhibition in the abandoned shopping arcade, the Galerie Vivienne, which had been the primary haunt of the flâneurs of the 1840s. Later, his venues were relocated to places of popular entertainment such as the Odéon The-

Figure 26. Henri Rivière, *L'Ancien Chat Noir*. (The original Chat Noir). Photo-relief illustration for *Le Chat noir,* 13 June 1885. Schimmel Fund. Jane Voorhees Zimmerli Art Museum, Rutgers, The State University of New Jersey. Photograph by Jack Abraham.

ater and the Folies-Bergères. According to Levy, the inspiration for the Incoherent art movement came to him in the form of a dream. "On Friday 13 of the year 1882," he recounted in parodic echo of one of Murger's fictional bohemians, "I was wakened earlier than usual by the rays of the sun, which filtered through the curtains of my window: at the end of the ray was an idea that lodged in my head and worried me all morning. This idea was simple in appearance, here it is in all its simplicity: 'To make an exhibition of drawings by people who do not know how to draw.' "[28] The exhibitions, which resulted from this far from "simple idea," were carnivalesque inversions of the art establishment, which outrageously parodied, not just the conventions of the official Salon, but also the aesthetics of impressionism. Lévy proved an inexhaustible source of fresh ideas for parody and provocation. Incoherent art exhibitions displayed satiric copies of Salon paintings by Toulouse-Lautrec, as well as monochromic canvases by Alphonse Allais, mocking the impressionists. Just as striking were Incoherent parodies of the Salon's formal proceedings. Incoherents used newspapers, flyers, and personal invitations to advertise their events among the general public; they published catalogues with fictional and satirical biographies of artists; they even went to the trouble of sanctimoniously donating the proceeds from their admission fees to charity. (Figure 27)

Surprisingly, the yearly Incoherent exhibitions of the 1880s proved to be enormously popular. The second Incoherent exhibition of 1883 attracted no fewer than twenty thousand visitors in the month of its existence, between October 15 and November 15. Visitors included "fashionable actresses, famous soldiers, lyric artists, journalists, even the chief rabbi of Paris [who] were astonished in unison."[29] Lévy followed up his exhibitions with the organization of Incoherent costume balls, where invited participants vied with each other in the display of extravagant costumes. The guests, proclaimed a contemporary article, consisted "almost entirely of journalists, painters, sculptors, musicians, comedians and others, [who] employed all their wits to disguise themselves in the most comical way possible."[30]

The seemingly frivolous activities characteristic of fin-de-siècle bohemia inevitably raise questions about the meaning of the bohemian enterprise itself. What were the common cultural roots and aesthetic goals that sustained and energized these outrageous public performances? Why were bohemian cabarets, literary cafés, and parodic art exhibitions so unexpectedly successful with the general public? What was their long-term significance for the future of popular entertainment and avant-garde art? Historians of fin-de-siècle culture have suggested a number of conflicting answers to these questions. According to Jerrold Seigel, the artistic cabarets of the fin-de-siècle, "testified to a new kind of symbiosis between the Bohème and the bourgeoisie" that signaled the triumph of consumerism. "The same changes," he elaborated, "that altered the market for clothing and household goods also changed the relations between cultural producers and their audience. Émile Goudeau's idea that a literary cabaret retaining the aura of Bohemia could serve to introduce aspiring writers and poets to prospective consumers of their work was the cultural equivalent of the department store."[31] However, as Lionel Richard's recent work on cabarets makes evident, just the opposite interpretation of the phenomenon is equally possible. "Toward 1880," he wrote, "a more radical category of bohemians appeared. These were rebels, who deliberately rejected the se-

Figure 27. Henri Boutet, photo-relief invitation for the 1882 *Exposition des Arts incohérents*. Bartman Fund. Jane Voorhees Zimmerli Art Museum, Rutgers, The State University of New Jersey. Photograph by Jack Abraham.

ductions of money and power and refused all compromise with the distractions of the stupefied masses, with the well-being promised to everyone by the 'democratization of enjoyment' and with the homogenization of culture."[32] Charles Rearick, writing of the phenomenon of mass entertainment in the Belle Époque, made a parallel argument from a slightly different point of view. "Montmartre," he wrote, "was an antidote to the pomposity and stiff class rule that reigned elsewhere. In its dance halls and cabarets Parisians could temporarily free themselves from the inhibitions of everyday respectability."[33] Literary and art historians, on the other hand, have tended to see artistic cabarets and cafés as the "noninstitutional showplace" for an emerging and increasingly close-knit literary and artistic community that foreshadowed twentieth-century avant-garde culture. In the words of Phillip Dennis Cate, the activities of the fin-de-siècle bohemia "mark the genesis of essential aspects of twentieth-century avant-garde aesthetics."[34]

These diverse accounts, focusing on the economic, social, and aesthetic implications of the bohemian cabaret, are both compelling and incontestable. Yet, they are also incomplete insofar as they ignore contemporary perceptions and interpretations of these phenomena. For participants who flocked to the artistic cafés and parodic exhibitions of fin-de-siècle bohemia, and for observers who tried to make sense of them, their meaning was not exhausted by the concepts of consumerism, escapism, or even artistic innovation. The significance of bohemian performances for contemporaries lay in their uncanny ability to embody the essence of the modern experience. Bohemia made legible and visible the secrets and hidden characteristics of what it meant to be modern. It bridged, if only for a moment, the gap between meaning and representation that was a constant source of anxiety in a rapidly changing and increasingly complex urban world.

Impressionists, who had been the standard-bearers of modernity throughout the 1870s, were no longer able to fulfill this role. It is true that their well-publicized campaigns against the academic establishment and the Salon system still caused them to be branded as revolutionaries and innovators.[35] Yet, they had also become an integral part of the bourgeois establishment and invariably reflected its norms and values. As Philip Nord has persuasively argued, impressionism and republicanism "intersected in the 1870s. The new painters were in the main men and women of republican conviction . . . [who] entered into republican society, painted its inhabitants, and looked to it for patronage." Their work, Nord continues, reflected the "events and personalities that defined a particular and circum-

scribed milieu. On their canvases can be made out the features of a democratic society under construction, a society inhabited by popular politi-
cians and middle-class hostesses, by Protestants and Jews, by a whole cast
of newcomers to the stage of public life."[36]

The challenge of the bohemian cabaret was, on the most general level,
to a culture of respectability and bourgeois propriety that impressionism
celebrated in the 1870s. For impressionist art was, as Nord admitted, an
essentially utopian vision of the ideal possibilities of bourgeois culture,
rather than its unvarnished expression. It hid or only hinted at the subterranean anxieties and anomalies that unceasingly threatened its harmonious
surfaces. On closer view, the bourgeois interior that was so appealingly
depicted by impressionists was also a claustrophobic space of elite con-
noisseurship and isolated contemplation, which found perhaps its most
eloquent depiction in Edmond de Goncourt's *La maison d'un artiste* (The
House of the Artist). The book, published in 1880, was the story of the
Goncourt brothers' passion for art collecting and interior decorating, whose
fruits were displayed in their famous, antique filled house at Auteille.[37] As
de Goncourt made explicit, these activities were not simply the personal
idiosyncrasies of the two brothers, but broadly symptomatic of their age.
Contemporary life, he pointed out, was a combat that demanded "concentration, effort and work." As a consequence, the individual naturally turned
inward to the four walls of his home to find solace and compensation for
the harshness and competitiveness of modern existence. Such a person's
real existence was "no longer exterior, as it was in the eighteenth century,"
de Goncourt continued, but was defined by the inner spaces of his house,
which he endeavored to make "agreeable, pleasant and amusing to the eye."
Significantly, de Goncourt's vision of the house beautiful was not a celebration of domesticity. In fact, his aestheticized world of art objects seemed
to exclude women and gallantry. "For our generation," de Goncourt confessed, "the mania for bric-à-brac [bricabracamanie] has become a substitute for woman, who no longer excites the imagination of man; and in my
own case I have observed that whenever by chance my heart was occupied,
the object of art held no interest for me." The real significance of de Goncourt's artistic interior was the fetishization of the work of art, which became not only a substitute for women, but also a sedative and a compensation for the inadequacies of modern existence.[38] In the nineteenth
century, de Goncourt concluded, one observes "an entirely new sentiment,
the almost human tenderness for objects, which at the present moment

makes of almost everyone, collectors of art, and of me in particular, the most passionate of all the collectors."[39]

Only against this background of interiorized experience and fetishized art consumption do the carnivalesque performances of fin-de-siècle bohemia assume their full meaning. Bohemians implicitly repudiated the elite art collector described by Goncourt, but also the professional art producer represented by the impressionists. They affirmed, instead, the values of spontaneous experience and direct communication, even if these were at the expense of enduring masterpieces or technical perfection. Indeed, they were even more emphatic than Baudelaire had been in rejecting narrow specialization in art. They went one step further than Baudelaire—who only made his ideal artist a "man of the world"—by ironically affirming the essential role of dilettantism in the creation of modern art. "The Incoherent," wrote Goudeau, "is a painter or a bookseller, a poet or a bureaucrat, or a sculptor, but what distinguishes him is the fact that the moment he surrenders to his incoherence he prefers to pass for what he is not: the bookseller becomes a tenor, the painter writes verses, the editor discusses free trade, all with exuberance."[40]

The implicit contrast between the conventional artist and the bohemian performer was well articulated in Albert Millaud's ironic sketch of the incoherent, which intentionally incorporated the typical bourgeois attitudes toward the figure. "The Incoherent," he wrote in *Physiologies parisiennes* in 1886 "is a worthy young man, an artist by temperament, but still naïve. He is a time-waster who uses his qualities and his talent to discover something funny that will make the public laugh. There may be among the Incoherents some budding Raphaels, some infant Guido Renis, who, although capable of spending three months creating a Holy Family or a Beatrice, prefer to compose a brasserie sketch or a caricature for a ten penny newspaper." His blatant disregard for high art and for all serious accomplishments was, it seems, the central attribute of the Incoherent. It was the source of his essential charm as well as the cause of his merciless censure by conventional observers. "I love the Incoherent," Millaud concluded, "because he does not claim to be regenerating art. He enjoys himself and wants to amuse others, but he makes the mistake of according too much importance to his amusements, which are childish as they are useless, and nothing of which will survive."[41](Figure 28)

Fin-de-siècle bohemians resorted to parodic performance, not only to criticize the official art establishment, but also to affirm their links with

Figure 28. Caran d'Ache, *L'Incohérent.* Photo-relief illustration from Albert Millaud,
   Physiologies parisiennes (Paris: Librairie Illustrée, 1886), 141. Bartman
   Fund. Jane Voorhees Zimmerli Art Museum, Rutgers, The State University
   of New Jersey. Photograph by Jack Abraham.

earlier bohemias that had flourished in the 1830s and 1840s.[42] Jules Lévy was a master of the genre of parody and he used ironic quotation persistently, both to appropriate the achievements of admired predecessors, as well as to distinguish himself from them. The first Incoherent exhibition in 1883 opened with fictional "retrospective sketches" or caricatures that carried the signatures of Baudelaire, Mérimée, Daumier, Eugène Sue, and others. His Incoherent costume balls, which invariably spilled out into the streets of Paris, were also parodic reenactments of the theatrical street performances of the Jeunes France of the 1830s. The parallels with the earlier tradition did not escape contemporary commentators, who remarked that "through these balls, the Incoherents reestablished ties with a carnivalesque tradition that had fallen into disuse."[43]

Rodolphe Salis, too, was partial to historical costumes and exotic interiors that harked back to the characteristic gestures of Romantic bohemia. In his early days as a struggling artist, he made an impression on his contemporaries by recreating the provocative clothing of the Jeunes France. "He stupefied the local inhabitants and passers-by," recounted a contemporary, "with his extraordinary clothes. He donned, in effect, the costume of Don César of Bazan: a felt hat with plume, red cape with a sword on the side, and in this outfit, with pallet in hand, he set himself up in public and began to paint . . . but also to play practical jokes."[44] Salis's affinity for Romantic bohemia found more enduring expression in the pseudo-medieval furnishings and rituals that made the Chat Noir cabaret both famous and notorious. The cabaret was outfitted with massive wooden furniture, illuminated stained glass windows, a huge fireplace, ancient armor, and all kinds of medieval bric-a-brac that recreated a particularly exotic atmosphere. Waiters, dressed in the robes of members of the academy, attended on astonished guests, who were often greeted with complex and ironic ceremonies. The Chat Noir's well-publicized move from its original location on the boulevard Rochouart to the rue Victor-Massé was another example of Salis's genius for theatrical public gestures. This particular performance was especially resonant with meaning, since it was also a direct quotation from the Preface to *Mademoiselle de Maupin,* in which Gautier celebrated the publication of his novel with an imaginary medieval procession. The colorful parade that accompanied the Chat Noir's relocation was equally fantastic, though this time physically, rather than just symbolically, enacted in the streets of Paris. It was, according to a contemporary account, headed by two Swiss guards in ornamental costumes and followed by academicians in official robes, by hunters carrying the coat of arms of the Chat Noir, and brought up in the rear by torchbearers and musicians playing minuets and gavottes. Salis himself was clad in a Prefect's costume and made up the center of the cortege, which was escorted by enormous crowds as it made its way through the outer boulevards of Paris.[45]

These provocative activities of decadent bohemia have often been equated with the desire to shock the bourgeoisie, or alternately, with the intention to create publicity for marginal art movements.[46] While such motivations were unquestionably present, they fail to explain the full complexity of bohemian performances. Fin-de-siècle bohemians were, of course, highly aware of the uses of sensationalism in the modern world and were experts at manipulating the popular press and public opinion for their own purposes. Indeed, they are often regarded as pioneers of techniques of self-promotion that later avant-gardes were to copy with great success. "Publication games," wrote Daniel Grojnowski, "went hand in hand with public meetings, poetry readings, literary and satirical newspapers, cabaret, and caricature—all kinds of 'eccentric enterprises' whose fruitfulness André Breton was one of the first to realize."[47] The flamboyant gestures of decadent bohemia, however, also contained broader cultural agendas that were not necessarily incompatible with self-advertisement. For fin-de-siècle bohemians were not only pragmatists, but also, in a sense, visionaries. They accepted the commercial mass media not only because they considered its existence inevitable, but also because they saw in it the potential for a public culture that could transcend the fragmentation of modern life. At the core of their strivings was a distinct vision of modernity that was identified with the public spaces of the city and was opposed to the privatized anonymity of bourgeois culture.

Goudeau made this explicit in *Dix ans de bohème,* where he pointed out that the café was the extension of the city street and the peculiarly modern incarnation of the public forum of classical antiquity. In self-conscious echo of Baudelaire's vision of flânerie in the 1850s, he argued that "it is necessary to descend into the crowd, to intermingle with the passers-by, to live, like the Greeks and Latins, in the *agora* and the *forum.* Under the rainy skies of Paris, the *agora* and the *forum* is the café . . . The cafés are the places of reunion, where, between two games of cards or dominoes, there take place long dissertations—sometimes confused, hélas!—on politics, military strategy, the law and medicine. What is more, these establishments have replaced the Academy, in whose famous gardens, philosophers walked back and forth, declaiming their inductions and deductions."[48]

Goudeau was not alone in stressing the need to reinvent public culture in the modern world and in associating this enterprise with the cafés and cabarets of the time. Jules Lévy made the same point in 1885, when he declared that the goal of the Incoherents was to cure the boredom and pessimism of contemporary existence by rejuvenating public life. Culture, he complained, had been run over by "a rabble of swells and idiotic public women" while "the intelligent have fled from the public square and stay at home these days, there to be bored at leisure. It is imperative to act and the Incoherents have set the scene in motion."[49]

Once again, there is no simple way to evaluate the nature and character of the public spaces that bohemians brought into existence in the course of the 1880s. Critics like T. J. Clark have been highly skeptical of their implications from a social or political point of view. He conceded that bohemian venues attracted a heterogeneous audience that included artists, students, men of letters, petty officials, actresses, and even at times workers. He also admitted that this mixture of bourgeois and popular clientele seemed to bring about a certain kind of cultural democracy, where "the boundaries of class identity, the very existence of class divisions, seemed to blur and disappear."[50] He objected, however, that the emancipation from class divisions that was spontaneously enacted in the cabaret was nothing more than an illusion or "charade."[51] For bohemia did not erase the economic inequalities, social injustice, or class oppression of modern society. The harsh realities of class society remained as inexorable as ever and were, perhaps, made even more insidious by the illusions that were conjured up to distract people from their real situation.

The problem with such a perspective, which incidentally is not restricted to Marxist-oriented critics such as Clark, is its inadvertent reductionism and its disregard of the autonomous function of culture in the modern world. Indeed, it misses the point of bohemian cultural practices in general, which were relational rather than foundational. Their clearly articulated goal was not to abolish social injustice or to bring about immediate institutional changes in the world, but rather, to transform perceptions and ingrained attitudes to existing realities. Bohemians' primary concern, in other words, was not with the outer world, but with the nature of experience, or with what Raymond Williams had called "structures of feeling" characteristic of contemporary life.[52] Their hope was to transform modernity on the symbolic and experiential level, making it transparent, accessible, and emotionally expressive for ordinary people.

Goudeau's reflections on the exceptional qualities of the Hydropathes' meetings confirms this conception of an inclusive and creative public space. In contrast to the literary salon, he wrote, the Hydropathes were an open forum, where "everyone had the right to appear, the public alone was to be the judge. This was not a coterie, nor a personal enterprise, but a sort of theater of poetry, open to all."[53] The critic Francisque Sarcey, who wrote the first review of the Hydropathes in 1879, made the same comparison between the open meetings of the Hydropathes and closed literary coterie of the establishment. "This large audience," he wrote in December 1878, "is more suitable for sharpening public taste and eliminating flaws than those so-called little chapels of poetry, where everyone takes turns being God, while half a dozen flatterers provide incense, on condition that the favor is returned. These narrow circles keep their windows carefully closed to the larger currents of public opinion. The initiates breathe there a heady, subtle atmosphere, where their talent is in danger of becoming enervated. The precious refinement of these sculptors of verse does not reach the large public, and this is why I am glad to see that our young poets are able to read today their new creations before a large public."[54]

The bohemian cabaret was not an exclusive literary salon, but neither was it a theatrical spectacle. It could more appropriately be compared to an experimental community, whose members were transformed from mere spectators into initiates through a collective experience that all shared and participated in. The cabaret's staged and improvised acts were public enactments of psychic processes and artistic creativity, made visible through the combined art of the actors and the master of ceremonies. These performances were both private and public, just as the characteristic repertoire of the cabaret was "at the same time elitist and popular, familiar but artistic."[55] No wonder that it was impossible to define the public spaces of bohemia in terms of conventional political, social, or even artistic categories. On the rare occasions when an attempt at definition was actually made, the results were farcical. Goudeau's amusing skirmishes with the police over the legal status of the Hydropathic meetings is a case in point, and is worth recounting in some detail.

The Hydropathes' conflicts with officialdom began with local complaints about the noise level of the artistic meetings, which resulted in the appearance of the police. Requested to produce the usual permit required for political meetings, Goudeau protested that the Hydropathes should not be regarded as a political club, but rather, as a theatrical enterprise like the Comédie Française, which ordinarily did not require police permission. Goudeau's attempt to legitimate his bohemian enterprise by assuming the august mantle of the Comédie Française did not work. The Chief of Police insisted on a political definition of the Hydropathes and demanded that Goudeau produce written statutes for his organization. This solution, however, had its own difficulties, which emerged when Goudeau was asked to amend the statutes with a clause specifying that "women are not admitted to the séances of the Hydropathes." Goudeau objected strenuously, pointing out that this would imply the exclusion, not only of the numerous female participants, but also of budding actresses and musicians from the conservatory, whose attendance at the meetings was part of their professional training. Indeed, Goudeau continued, producing his trump card, the exclusionary clause would implicate Sarah Bernhardt herself, who was an honorary member of the Hydropathes. The Chief of Police, unexpectedly sympathetic to these difficulties, resolved the situation by ruling that "Mme Sarah Bernhardt was not a woman but a great artiste," and that the budding actresses were also in a special category, since they were preparing for public careers in the theater. The final agreement reached by Goudeau and the Chief of Police was that the exclusionary clause would be retained in the official rules of the Hydropathes, but that unofficially, women would, nevertheless, continue to be permitted to attend the Hydropathes' meetings.[56]

The story of Goudeau's compromise with officialdom sheds interesting light on decadent bohemia's general relationship with the bourgeois world. On the one hand, it highlights the incompatibilities between the two realms, whose categories could not be juxtaposed without comic consequences. The meetings of the Hydropathes, in other words, were not only outside the categories of bourgeois culture, but directly in conflict with its class and gender codes. On the other hand, however, the story also makes evident that the transgressive qualities of bohemia were not perceived to be so dangerous or threatening as to preclude a compromise solution with the representatives of bourgeois order.

The protocols of this liminal space were codified under the dual categories of "*fumisme*" and the "monologue," which originated in the Hydropathic séances of the late 1870s.[57] The concepts had overlapping meanings, but were not fully synonymous with each other. *Fumisme* referred to the subversive, carnivalesque aspects of bohemia and involved practical jokes, unusual pranks, and elaborate provocations, directed primarily against the authorities and the establishment. The monologue, on the other hand, represented the more formal, aesthetic aspects of bohemia and usually implied a mock-serious lecture or an uninterrupted free-association of ideas delivered by a single individual.[58] Unlike *fumisme,* which was spontaneous and often improvised, the monologue was structured according to the narrative formulae of the short story or the anecdote. As Coquelin Cadet, the official theorist of the monologue put it, "it is imperative for the monologue to have a beginning, a middle and an end; one could not listen to it if it were otherwise."[59]

The conceptual distinctions between *fumisme* and the monologue faithfully duplicated the actual repertoire of the artistic cabaret and the literary café at the turn of the century. *Fumisme* reflected the extravagant gestures of the artist-performers, who enacted their fantasies and emotions in front of the audience; while the monologue corresponded to the activities of the master of ceremonies, who provided a stable narrative frame for the excesses of the inspired actors. *Fumisme* and the monologue were, however, more than simply different aspects of bohemian performances. They were also incompatible aesthetic and cultural principles inherent within the decadent bohemian project itself. *Fumisme* and the monologue gave expression to the inner tensions between pure expressivity and formal narration, between inner experience and outer signification, which had earlier found resolution in the dramatic conventions of the melodrama and the literary form of the popular novel. The polarization between these two artistic principles brought into question the very definition of decadent bohemia as a public space where the inner meaning of modern life could be publicly performed and made transparent. It signaled the potential crisis of nineteenth-century bohemia, defined as a coherent cultural experience made visible and legible through the interpretative activities of artists.[60]

These inherent conflicts, however, were kept at bay, at least for a while, by the common conventions of a particularly vibrant popular culture that united decadent bohemians against the world of high culture. Indeed, the essence of both *fumisme* and the monologue was its ironic relationship to elite culture, whose forms it provocatively echoed. *Fumisme,* according to its theorist Georges Fragerolle, was to wit "what the operetta is to the opera-bouffe, the joke is to the caricature, the prune is to Hunyadi-János water."[61] Through the amusing juxtaposition of opposites, Fragerolle not only equated *fumisme* with the pursuits of low culture, but also valorized it in relationship to its elite counterpart. The disreputable *fumiste,* he insisted, was superior to the respectable man of wit, because his practice was more complex and ultimately more effective in destabilizing conventional culture than that of his opponent. The man of wit was logical and direct, using his powers to openly reduce his opponent to an imbecile. The *fumiste,* by contrast, was illogical and indirect, assuming the identity of the imbecile and thus multiplying the impact of his attack. "In order to pass for a man of wit," Fragerolle illustrated, "it is often enough to be an ass wearing a lion's skin; to be a good *fumiste,* it is often indispensable to be a lion covered with an ass's skin. In the first case, the effect is direct, in the second, it is once, twice, often ten times removed."[62] *Fumisme* was not only more effective than the conventional power of wit, but also more creative in the long run, since it was able to reinvent culture and establish its independent forms. It was, Fragerolle declared, the *l'art pour l'art* of humor, which would replace bourgeois culture in the same way that bourgeois culture had supplanted the aristocracy. Appropriating the famous symbol of middle-class self-assertion during the French Revolution, Fragerolle ended his manifesto with the ironic battle cry: "*fumisme* was nothing, it is everything" (Le Fumisme n'était rien, il est tout).[63]

The monologue found its own theoretician in Coquelin Cadet, whose *Le monologue moderne* (The Modern Monologue) paralleled Fragerolle's parodic manifesto of *fumisme.* Coquelin Cadet was a successful actor in the Comédie-Française, equally known to bourgeois salons and to Montmartre cabarets. So enormous was his influence among his contemporaries that even Mallarmé dreamed of having Coquelin interpret his "Monologue of a Faun" at the Comédie-Française.[64] Coquelin spelled out the implicit continuities between the monologue and *fumisme* by suggesting parallels with the strategies of Romantic bohemians and flâneurs. The *fumiste* was comparable to the Romantic buffoon, who donned "a clown's outfit and a many-colored mask"; while the speaker of monologues was like the flâneur, who assumed "the black suit of the notary [which] lends gravity to these dry jokesters."[65] Consistent with his seemingly conventional appearance, the speaker of monologues parodically enacted the discourses of the formal lecture hall or the conventional theater, even while transforming them into an intimate dialogue with the audience of the cabaret. As Coquelin emphasized, the monologist found his true voice only if he succeeded in approximating the spirit of casual conversation "that one has with a friend who is dear to one and from whom one expects genuine good will."[66] The enemy of all formality and pretension, the monologue was an integral part of everyday life and capable of amusing both children and parents.[67] (Figure 29)

Fumisme and the monologue shared a further characteristic, however, which is difficult to explain simply in terms of the conventions of low culture. Both Fragerolle and Coquelin associated these practices with states of emotional excess, psychological instability, and physical delirium that unmistakably reproduced the symptoms of hysteria. As Coquelin Cadet put it, the monologue was a source of modern humor, where "the unlikely and the unexpected calmly frolic with a serious idea, where the real and the impossible merge in a cold fantasy; the monologue, finally, is a type, whose absolute incarnation is the *Obsession,* and in a deeper and more philosophic vein, the cup-and-ball."[68] Goudeau, too, applied the language of medical pathology to describe the related phenomena of *fumisme* and incoherence. *Fumisme,* he explained, was "a kind of inner madness, which is translated for the outside by a kind of imperturbable buffoonery."[69] Incoherence, he wrote elsewhere, in a parody of contemporary medical usages, can be recognized when "subterranean rumblings are suddenly heard in the skull, shaking the sturdiest walls erected by logic, agitating cells and overturning nucleoli, twisting nerves, and suddenly forcing the entire immobilized brain to begin to dance."[70] The language of hysteria even supplied the secret codes of bohemia that allowed its participants to recognize one another in their incognitos. "The Incoherent," Goudeau illustrated, "walks through Paris like everyone else, he bows to his superiors and shakes hands with his equals; but if perchance he meets a fellow Incoherent somewhere, his body suddenly comes unglued; his forehead, his nose, his eyes, his mouth are transformed into cabalistic grimaces, his arms thrash about strangely, and his legs shake in an extravagant rhythm. This lasts only a moment or two. But these are the Masonic signs by means of which the Brotherhood of Incoherence recognize one another."[71]

Why did bohemians' performances assume and reproduce the specific forms of hysteria? What were the reasons that radical artists and their audiences identified with hysteria and perceived its signs and gestures to be the privileged site of modernity? How did this parodic and performed version of hysteria relate to mainstream visions of a decadent modernity articulated by critics like Paul Bourget? In order to answer these questions, it will be necessary to expand our frame of analysis from the "frivolous"

Figure 29. Coquelin Cadet, *Les Hommes d'aujourd'hui* (vol. 5, 1882, no. 245). Courtesy of Brown University Library.

world of decadent bohemia to the "serious" world of medical psychiatry, especially as defined by Jean-Martin Charcot in the Salpêtrière of the fin-de-siècle.

The centrality of hysteria to the cultural life of fin-de-siècle France has received a great deal of attention in recent years, both from cultural historians and from literary critics.[72] Most agree that the actual medical diagnosis of hysteria, thought to be connected to the malfunction of the uterus, was not a unique discovery of the late nineteenth century. As Martha Noel Evans has pointed out, the disease had a long and complicated history reaching back to antiquity.[73] Yet, this amorphous and symbolically charged malady, always difficult to limit to a specific diagnosis, acquired particularly complicated resonances and connotations in the late nineteenth century. "The sheer accumulation of meanings of hysteria," wrote Mark Micale, "is nothing short of extraordinary. During the later 1800s alone, hysteria was employed as a metaphor for artistic experimentation, collective political violence, radical social reformism, foreign nationalism, and a host of other new and unsettling developments. It became shorthand for the irrational, the willess, the incomprehensible, the erratic, the convulsive, the sexual, the female, 'the Other.' It was a synonym for everything that seemed extreme or frivolous or excessive or absurd about the age."[74] Preoccupation with hysteria reached epidemic proportions during these years, Janet Beiser asserted, assuming the status of a "media event" that fascinated all segments of the population.[75]

Although much of the recent literature on hysteria has focused on gender and sexuality, and to a lesser extent on the professionalization of psychiatry, it is self-evident that hysteria was also an integral component of popular culture. One of the few historians to touch on this aspect of the phenomenon has been Rae Beth Gordon, whose work on performance culture in late nineteenth- and early twentieth-century Paris is exemplary from this perspective. According to Gordon, the body language of hysteria was frequently performed in the song and dance routines of *café chantants* and was later incorporated in the characteristic acting style of silent films. These "epileptic performances," as they were called at the time, exactly duplicated, she claimed, "the same movements, gestures, tics, grimaces, fantasies, hallucinations, and speech anomalies found in nineteenth century hysteria."[76]

Remarkably little has been written about the widespread popularity of these unusual performances. One of the reasons is the automatic contempt that they evoked from elite observers, who saw in them nothing more than a particularly debased form of popular farce. The Goncourt brothers, who attended an "epileptic performance" at the Eldorado, left the following description of the event: "Toward the back a theater stage with footlights; and on it a comic in evening dress. He sang disconnected things, interspersed with chortling and farmyard noises, the sounds of animals in heat, epileptic gesticulations—a Saint Vitus' dance of idiocy. The audience went wild with enthusiasm."[77] It is not hard to recognize in these popular acts the same cultural impulses that found expression in the more sophisticated "incoherent performances" of artistic bohemia. The genres were obviously related to each other, reenacting on different levels the same fascination with the cultural and psychological manifestations of hysteria that pervaded the entire culture.

What may not be immediately obvious, however, is that the model for both kinds of performances was to be found in the medical lectures and live demonstrations of the Salpêtrière, made famous under its charismatic director, Jean-Martin Charcot. The universal appeal of Charcot's lectures at the Salpêtrière was, to some extent, a reflection of the unprecedented prestige and authority of late nineteenth-century physicians and scientists, who were regarded "as heroes of the new age."[78] As Jean Starobinski put it, the small minority of men who met "in the course of Claude Bernard, at the demonstrations of Charcot" were generally seen as the definers of the intellectual climate of the age. They were "accorded the right to solve all problems—moral, social, historical—of which up till then, the philosopher, the theologian believed themselves to be the competent judges."[79]

The pivotal position that the Salpêtrière came to occupy in the cultural life of fin-de-siècle Paris cannot, however, be explained by the predominance of modern science alone. It was also a result of the exceptional personality and self-defined mission of Charcot himself, who transformed the Salpêtrière into a world-renowned institution uniquely identified with hysteria. As a prelude to exploring the cultural implications of this phenomenon, it is useful to start with Charcot's official reputation as one of France's preeminent physicians and scientists, whose prestige was celebrated in André Brouillet's famous painting *Une leçon clinique à la Salpêtrière*. The canvas was displayed in the official Salon of 1887 and was, by all accounts, "immense, theatrical and colorful."[80] (Figure 30) It depicted one of Charcot's famous Tuesday lessons at the Salpêtrière, with Charcot demonstrating the techniques of hypnosis on a supine, half-clad hysterical patient, who was supported in the arms of a close associate, Joseph Ba-

Figure 30. André Broullet, *Une leçon clinique à la Salpêtrière* (A clinical demonstration at the Salpêtrière) (1887). National Library of Medicine, Images from the History of Medicine, Bethesda, Maryland.

binski. The object of Charcot's and Babinski's ministrations was one of the "grand hysterics" of the Salpêtrière, a young woman known as Blanche Wittman, who was capable of producing the classic symptoms of hysteria and was accorded quasi-celebrity status in the hospital. Outside of the elderly nurse, hovering in the background, Blanche Wittman was the only woman in the scene, her flimsy white drapery providing a stark contrast to the black frock coats of the medical men, gathered in a semicircle around her.

Brouillet's painting has become an icon in the history of psychiatry and psychoanalysis,[81] as well as a classic illustration of nineteenth century medical attitudes toward women. The painting is equally noteworthy for another reason, however, that has been less frequently analyzed: this is the fact that Brouillet's image included only a carefully selected part of the audience that habitually attended Charcot's Tuesday lessons. By the 1880s, these were usually held in a vast amphitheater and drew a wide assortment of Parisian artists, intellectuals, and celebrities, among whom women formed a significant constituency. The actual appearance of Charcot's Tuesday lessons was considerably livelier and more heterogeneous than Brouillet's idealized version would suggest. An unofficial portrait of the Tuesday lessons was provided by a contemporary physician, Axel Munthe, whose interest in hysteria eventually brought him into conflict with Charcot. "I seldom failed to attend," he wrote, "Professor Charcot's famous *Leçons du Mardi* in the Salpêtrière, just then chiefly devoted to his *grande hystérie* and to hypnotism. The huge amphitheater was filled to the last place with a multicolored audience drawn from *tout* Paris, authors, journalists, leading actors and actresses, fashionable *demimondaines,* all full of morbid curiosity to witness the startling phenomena of hypnotism almost forgotten since the days of Mesmer and Braid."[82]

Charcot's Tuesday lessons reproduced the same kind of ambiguity that characterized the public meetings of the Hydropathes. Officially, they were considered a closed medical gathering and associated with an almost exclusively male professional audience; unofficially, however, they functioned as a popular spectacle, drawing a mixed audience, whose composition was not very different from that of the Hydropathes' séances, the Incoherent exhibitions, or the Chat Noir cabaret. Indeed, as Rae Beth Gordon has pointed out, under Charcot's stewardship, hysteria became a sensational illness, whose images "must be included alongside images from wax museums, puppet shows, pantomime, and pre-cinematic devices in the cultural series that contributed to the genesis of performance styles in the Parisian cabaret and in early film comedy."[83]

By the late 1880s, the Salpêtrière became a popular tourist attraction, listed in official travel guides to Paris, along with the Chat Noir, the Folies-Bergères, the Jardin des Plantes, and the newly completed Eiffel Tower.[84] The name of the Salpêtrière became a common household word, and the work of its physicians was reported in the daily tabloids.[85] The interchangeability between the medical enactment of hysteria and its cabaret performance was brilliantly satirized in one of Coquelin Cadet's comic monologues entitled "Hydrotherapy." The monologue was published in 1888, a year after the exhibition of André Brouillet's "Un leçon clinique à la Salpêtrière," and was clearly an ironic deflation of the pretentious gravity of the official painting. The title of the monologue, "Hydrotherapy," referred to both the Hydropathes and the standard cure for hysteria, thus establishing an intimate link between bohemia and the Salpêtrière, as well as between Goudeau and Charcot. "All those suffering from nerves, fatigue, jadedness," declared Dr. Béni-Barde, a hybrid between the master of ceremonies and the physician, "all those with poor circulation, who see life black, the neurasthenics smitten by passing agitation, who feel uneasy, only need to gather all the energy they can muster . . . hail a carriage, make an unparalleled effort, and tell the driver the address of Dr. Béni-Barde. There, they will discover joy, a return of faith, happiness, amusement, strength, enthusiasm, a lively eye, a straight and vigorous body, a laughing soul, oblivion to worries, the renewal of good will, the courage to put up with one's mother-in-law. Parisians, my brothers; dear delicate nervous ones, let us become really healthy, let us shower, let us béni-barde ourselves."[86]

Coquelin Cadet's parodic monologue implied more than a simple fusion between bohemia and hysteria or between the identities of Goudeau and Charcot. It also accomplished a carnivalesque inversion of their social roles and cultural functions. In the context of the monologue, it was the bohemian café that became a place of therapy and the Salpêtrière that became a place of entertainment. By the same token, it was Goudeau who assumed the persona of the fashionable physician and Charcot, that of the popular performer. The comic plausibility of such role reversal suggests a greater affinity between the two universes of discourse than traditional interpretations of fin-de-siecle art or medicine suggest.

Charcot's role in sensationalizing hysteria has been the subject of controversy among both contemporaries and later commentators. Critics have accused Charcot of bad faith and have implied that he single-handedly invented hysteria as a theatrical and artistic spectacle. According to Axel Munthe, for instance, the Salpêtrière demonstrations had gotten out of hand, turning into "stage performances," and into "an absurd farce, a hopeless muddle of truth and cheating." Although he admitted that there may have been genuine instances of hypnotism and somnambulism among Charcot's cases, he added that, "many of them were mere frauds, knowing quite well what they were expected to do, delighted to perform their various tricks in public, cheating both doctors and audience with the amazing cunning of the hysterics."[87]

Contemporary caricatures of Charcot, such as Albert Millaud's depiction in *Physiologies parisiennes,* reinforced this skeptical view of Charcot's science. Transparently disguised as Dr. Carot, Charcot was accused of vicariously seducing the women of Paris, magically transforming them into neurotic types called "Carolines." "It appears," Millaud explained, "that M. Caro, like certain exotic plants, emanates a certain magnetism, which works on individuals of the female sex. Not everyone succumbs, but all are susceptible."[88] The skepticism of contemporaries has been continued by recent critics such as Georges Didi-Huberman, who has argued unambiguously that "hysteria as conceptualized at the Salpêtrière in the latter half of the nineteenth century" needs to be seen, not as a part of medical history, but rather, "a chapter in the history of Art."[89]

Charcot's disciples and associates, on the other hand, have strenuously resisted these accusations, insisting on the integrity of Charcot's scientific achievements, and maintaining that the exclusive association of Charcot's name with hysteria was a distortion and an exaggeration. As his biographer, George Guillain has pointed out, Charcot's clinical practice included men as well as women, and extended over a large variety of neurological and organic illness besides hysteria. He even produced statistical evidence to support this position, showing that in the course of one year, the diagnosis of hysteria at Charcot's Tuesday clinics "was made 244 times in 3,168 consultations."[90]

The problem with such polarized accounts is that, even while they explain certain aspects of Charcot's clinical practices, they fail to address the larger question of Charcot's astonishing influence on the general culture of his time. For Charcot was not simply a medical pioneer whose concerns were circumscribed by the professional protocols of psychiatry and neurology. He was also a cultural innovator of genius who touched on some of the deepest longings and fantasies of his age. As Mark Micale perceptively pointed out, "[t]he history of hysteria in particular has in a real sense been two histories, one medical and the other popular."[91] While the two histories cannot, and probably shouldn't, be separated from each other, they do need to be placed within a broader cultural and symbolic framework that transcends the empirically defined contexts of fin-de-siècle medicine and politics. For Charcot's ability to shape and define the popular discourse of hysteria was ultimately the expression of cultural trends that he was, both by temperament and by training, unusually well suited to articulate and popularize.

Neither a charismatic charlatan, nor a dispassionate scientist, Charcot could probably be more usefully regarded as an example of the nineteenth-century synthesizer, for whom science still held the solution to the mysteries of both the biological and the historical worlds. He saw in the Salpêtrière a microcosm of modernity and in the achievements of medicine the power to illuminate and to heal the dissonances between the inner and outer worlds so dramatically exemplified by the patient material in the hospital. Indeed, Charcot's unique relationship to the Salpêtrière has frequently been commented on by observers. For most physicians, it seems, the ancient and chaotic mental institution was simply a temporary rotation in their routine training as physicians. For Charcot, however, it was nothing less than a treasure trove of psychological types waiting for description and classification. "Charcot," reflected one observer, "envisioned a systematic categorization of the masses of Salpêtrière residents. With this experience, the core features of numerous disorders and the variants would later be defined. This process, the methods of archetypes and variants, became one of the foundations of Charcot's teachings."[92]

Given such assumptions about the integrative powers of science, Charcot's much-contested role as popularizer of hysteria appears far less idiosyncratic. In fact, his commitment to scientific observation and classification paralleled the literary project of urban flânerie, transposed to the institutional context of the Salpêtrière. If the flâneur had used his powers of observation to transform the confusion of metropolitan existence into urban narratives, Charcot applied his clinical gaze to explicate the mysteries of the human organism through his lectures and case histories. Both urban and medical systematizers were united by the common aspiration to create visual images and coherent narratives capable of transforming privatized and fragmented experiences into meaningful public spectacles and collective representations. It is perhaps not surprising that contemporaries tended to apply specifically urban and spatial metaphors to describe Charcot's presentations of neurological abnormalities. These were characterized as "panoramic" visions that made the different features of illnesses apparent "in a vast synoptic tableau that the spectators could appropriate in the bat of an eye."[93]

Reminiscences by former students and disciples tend to support this view of Charcot as a double-voiced or hybrid figure who combined the roles of artist and scientist in ways reminiscent of the urban flâneur of the 1840s. One of the most telling accounts came from Sigmund Freud, who had observed Charcot's methods during an extended research trip to Paris in 1885. "He was," wrote Freud in a posthumous tribute in 1893, "not a man of reflection, a thinker: he had the nature of an artist; he was, to put it bluntly, a *visuel,* a man who saw. This is what he taught us as a working model. He looked again and again at the things he did not understand, in order to deepen day after day the impression that it made on him, until an insight about them suddenly came over him. Then before his mind's eye, the apparent chaos of the continuous repetition of the same symptoms gave place to order . . . One could hear him say that the greatest satisfaction that a man could have is to see something fresh, that is to recognize it as new; he constantly drew attention to the difficulty and the value of this kind of 'vision.' "[94]

Freud's characterization of Charcot as a *visuel* was to be frequently repeated in later accounts. Henry Meige made this the central theme of his interpretation of Charcot in a book entitled *Charcot, artiste.* Behind the stern exterior of Charcot's official scientific image, Meige maintained, was to be discovered the temperament of the artist, who used drawings, illustrations, personal mimicry, and eventually photography, as integral parts of his medical teaching. Charcot's artistic affinities began, it seems, in early life, when he experienced a conflict between pursuing the profession of painting or medicine. Although he eventually chose medicine, he retained a vivid interest in the art of caricature throughout his life. According to Meige, his early sketches, depicting social types such as the dandy, the bohemian, and the novice, displayed a remarkable talent for burlesque and parody.[95] This same talent was seen by Guillain to be the explanation for Charcot's remarkable intuitions as a clinician. "What we can conclude," he wrote, "is that at the first glance he was able to recognize some oddity or other of the human habitude. Now to be able to discern a comic anomaly and to project it in relief, that is the very essence of the art of caricature. But aside from the comic, does not the physician's art have as one of its goals the discovery of physical anomalies and making them perceptible to others? That is why it is not presumptuous to say that Charcot's talent for drawing caricatures served him well in his profession as a clinician."[96]

Perhaps nowhere did Charcot demonstrate more dramatically the synthesis between clinical skills and artistic intuitions than in his famous Tuesday lessons at the Salpêtrière. Unlike his Friday lectures, which were carefully scripted and rehearsed and exclusively based on patients who had already been diagnosed by Charcot, the Tuesday lessons were impromptu performances, where Charcot demonstrated his diagnostic skills on unfamiliar cases. This difference between the two teaching styles signified more than a pragmatic adaptation to different pedagogic needs. It also implied a shift in cultural register from the formality of the academic lecture to the spontaneity of the informal seminar or working session. The popularity of Charcot's Tuesday lessons was due not only to the famous theatricality of their subject matter, but also to the deliberately accessible tone of Charcot's address, whose clarity, simplicity, and visual appeal were repeatedly commented upon. (Figure 31)

Charcot assumed in these sessions the role of an informal, even colloquial, interlocutor, patiently guiding his auditors through the complexities and invisible labyrinths of neurological illness. His lectures resembled in many respects detective tales or mystery stories in which the famous physician shared his perplexities and solutions with his audience. Hysteria was, of course, the greatest mystery of all, which Charcot had first encountered in 1862, when he returned to the Salpêtrière as an attendant physician and professor. "I was befuddled as I looked at such patients," Charcot confided in a typical lesson of February 1888, "and this impotence greatly irritated me. Then one day, when reflecting over all these patients as a group, I was struck with a sort of intuition about them. I said to myself, 'Something about them makes them all the same.' "[97] In this seemingly casual summary, Charcot touched on the core of his hysteria diagnosis that enabled him to transform the disease from a medical puzzle into a phenomenon of general cultural relevance. Hysteria, Charcot implied, was a disease, whose bewildering variety could be traced back to a common core or an archetype.

Charcot did more than simply explicate the mysteries of hysteria, however. He also provided physical proof of its symptoms. What made Charcot's lectures spectacular and a source of attraction for fashionable

Figure 31. Charcot, *A l'amphithéâtre de la Salpêtrière* (In the lecture hall of the Sâlpetrière). Illustration from *Nouvelle iconographie de la Salpêtrière* (1898). National Library of Medicine, Images from the History of Medicine, Bethesda, Maryland.

Paris were his live demonstrations of the hysterical attack, which were artificially induced and publicly enacted by an actual patient, drawn from Charcot's outpatient clinic or from the regular inhabitants of the Salpêtrière. On a signal from Charcot, the attack was triggered, either through hypnosis or by touching one of the patient's "hysterogenic points." Charcot then provided the audience with a detailed narrative that explained the unfolding stages of the attack. A typical hysterical attack was divided into an epileptoid phase, when the patient recapitulated the symptoms of epilepsy; a phase of exotic movements, which often included the characteristic arching of the back; and finally, a hallucinatory or emotional phase, in which the patient could give way to both terror and joy. (Figure 32, 33, 34, 35) As Charcot pointed out, these stages were not necessarily apparent to the untrained observer. Distinguishing and identifying the actual sequence of the hysterical attack required the expert eye of the trained physician, who was able to distill from the concrete, empirical manifestations of the disease the general archetypes valid for all cases of hysteria. "There are as many as 20 variations," Charcot informed his audience, "but if you have the key to the archetype, you immediately focus on the disease and can say with confidence that in spite of the many possible variations, all these cases represent the same disease."[98]

Charcot's use of the archetype to solve the mystery of hysteria recapitulated the flâneur's social typologies, which had played an equally central role in the urban narratives of the 1840s. Just as the social type made visible and classifiable the heterogeneity of the modern city, so the archetypes of hysteria rendered transparent and predictable the irrationality of the human organism. Pierre Janet described Charcot's use of the type in terms that recall Balzac's own conception of the role of social types in the realist novel. For Charcot, Janet wrote, the type "is a collection of symptoms which depend on each other, which are arranged hierarchically, which can be classed into limited groups, which clearly distinguish themselves by their nature and combination from characteristics of related illnesses."[99] Again in close analogy with urban realism, Charcot's project of scientific classification through the use of the type was inseparable from the faculty of visuality and realistic reproduction. "If you want to see clearly," Charcot instructed his audience, "you must take things exactly as they are . . . in fact all I am is a photographer. I describe what I see."[100] Charcot was speaking quite literally, as well as metaphorically. In 1875, he instituted the "Service photographique de la Salpêtrière" (Department of Photography

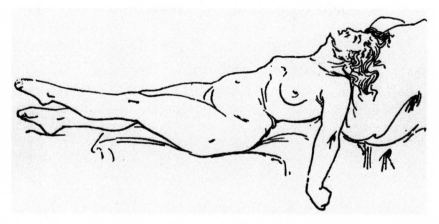

Figure 32. The epileptoid phase of the classic hysterical attack. Illustration from J.M. Charcot and Paul Richer, *"Les Démoniaques dans l'art" suivi de "La Foi qui guérit" de J. M. Charcot,* Introduction by Pierre Fédida, afterword by Georges Didi-Huberman (Paris: Macula, 1984; orig. pub. 1887), 93.

Figure 33. The phase of exotic movements of the classic hysterical attack. Illustration from J.M. Charcot and Paul Richer, *"Les Démoniaques dans l'art" suivi de "La Foi qui guérit" de J. M. Charcot,* Introduction by Pierre Fédida, afterword by Georges Didi-Huberman (Paris: Macula, 1984; orig. pub. 1887), 93.

of the Salpêtrière) under the directorship of Albert Londe, who made photography an integral part of the study and classification of hysteria.[101]

Despite their striking parallels with the cultural project of flânerie, it is still difficult to read these accounts of the Tuesday lessons without a sense of unease and discomfort. From our current perspective, at any rate, Charcot's transformation of hysteria into a theatrical spectacle that deliberately provoked, publicly displayed, and visually recorded, the hysterical attacks of mostly poor, working-class women appears morally problematic if not outright misogynistic. The demonstrations of hysteria have an air of voyeurism and showmanship that was only exacerbated after the 1870s with the introduction of hypnotism and photography as a regular part of the proceedings. Indeed, it could be argued that the clinical practices instituted by Charcot at the Salpêtrière were inseparable from modern tech-

Figure 34. The emotional phase of the classic hysterical attack. Illustration from J.M. Charcot and Paul Richer, *"Les Démoniaques dans l'art"* suivi de *"La Foi qui guérit" de J. M. Charcot,* Introduction by Pierre Fédida, afterword by Georges Didi-Huberman (Paris: Macula, 1984; orig pub. 1887), 99.

nologies of control and surveillance that Foucault was to theorize a century later. Martha Noel Evans summarized this position when she pointed out that "Charcot's periodization of attacks and the photographs he took mutually reinforced each other in producing an effect of stasis and control over the untamed, tumultuous fits of hysteria."[102]

It takes an effort of historical imagination to recognize that Charcot and his audiences experienced the Tuesday lessons in entirely different terms and categories than did later observers. Significantly, these dramatic demonstrations were perceived not simply as amusing or sensational, but also as instructive and inspirational. Charcot's project, in other words, was identified with broadly defined intellectual, philosophic, and spiritual concerns that transcended the realm of popular entertainment, but also that of professional medicine. Charcot aspired to a vision of totality, something consistent with his definition of himself as a generalist, rather than a narrow specialist. He saw his particular field of neuropathology as the least specialized realm of medicine, that was committed to the study of the totality of the human organism. On the occasion of his inaugural address on being

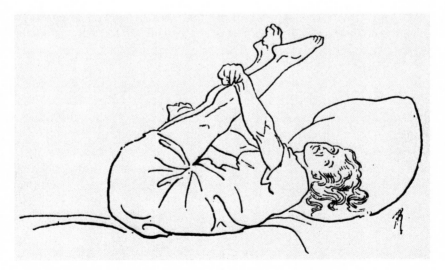

Figure 35. The terminal phase of the classic hysterical attack. Illustration from J.M. Charcot and Paul Richer, *"Les Démoniaques dans l'art" suivi de "La Foi qui guérit" de J. M. Charcot,* Introduction by Pierre Fédida, afterword by Georges Didi-Huberman (Paris: Macula, 1984; orig. pub. 1887), 101.

appointed Professor of Clinical Diseases of the Nervous System in 1882, he spelled out this conviction. "In the field of neuropathology," he claimed, "we need not fear any danger of being drawn into a narrow groove of overspecialization, because neuropathology is becoming today one of the broadest disciplines now in existence. It is the one that is growing the most rapidly, and the one which requires the most general knowledge of those who wish to engage in it and cultivate it."[103]

Charcot's public mission, however, went considerably beyond this image of the neurologist as the medical generalist. As his Salpêtrière demonstrations of hysteria made evident, his function as a physician was only incidentally connected to the cure of hysteria. He was even more concerned with the task of demonstrating its "readability" to as large a public as possible. In other words, Charcot and his audience perceived in the hysterical attack not just a sign of pathology, but also a revelation of the inner mysteries of the human organism itself. They saw hysteria as the spectacular performance of the passions and hallucinations of the inner life, made public and visible through the mediation of the artist/physician. Hysteria was the site of universal truths about human life that were ordinarily hidden from empirical view.

Only in light of this broader intellectual and philosophic perspective does it become fully understandable why Charcot was so insistent on detaching the diagnosis of hysteria from its exclusive association with female pathology and in generalizing it as a universal condition beyond the clinical realm. In this, Charcot's analysis of hysteria recapitulated popular assumptions circulating in the larger culture. As Jacqueline Carroy-Thirard has pointed out, by the latter half of the nineteenth century, the symptoms of hysteria had come to be associated with male writers and artists as well as with women. "Hysteria," she wrote, "became a source of identification, pointing to the dilemmas and delights of the experience and creation of literature; it was a necessary symptom that was cultivated in ambivalence."[104] Both Baudelaire and Flaubert were self-confessed hysterics, and Flaubert explicitly associated his solitary life and writerly habits at Croisset with the clinical symptoms of hysteria. "The sensibility becomes immensely exalted in such a milieu," he wrote to George Sand. "I have heart palpitations for no reasons at all (something, by the way, that is understandable in an old hysteric like myself). For I maintain that men are hysterics just like women and I am one of them. When I was working on *Salammbô*, I read the 'best authors' on the subject and I recognize all my symptoms."[105]

The effort to generalize and universalize the phenomenon of hysteria took Charcot in surprising directions. He extended the diagnosis of the disease even to members of the working classes, who were presumed to be exempt from pathologies of the emotional life connected with indiscriminate reading, solitary introspection, and excessive fantasy. "It is conclusively demonstrated today," he wrote in a joint article with Richer, "that hysteria is not peculiar to the female sex. Young men, men of all ages, including workers, whose habits are not intellectual and whose exterior has nothing effeminate, can become the prey of the disease of the nerves."[106]

Charcot's conception of hysteria eventually even included religious phenomena and historical manifestations. He was to argue that medieval images of demonic possession and religious ecstasy were actually cases of hysterics, who were depicted in the midst of the different stages of the hysterical attack. The medieval artists who recorded these enactments of hysteria in engravings, tapestries, and statues were described by Charcot as "primitive caricaturists," presumably resembling their modern counterparts in the medical establishment of the Salpêtrière. "For them," Charcot wrote, "ecstasy is an expressive pose, a pure attitude of passion. All their efforts are to represent, to render exterior, an interior and internal phenomenon; in a word, to objectify through physiological traits and bodily gestures, that which happens in the region of the soul inaccessible to vision."[107]

Hysteria had ceased to be a medical event for Charcot and his associates. It had become an allegory of the inner life, whose passions and mysteries found scientific representation through the clinical drawings, photographs, case histories, and lectures of the Salpêtrière. Like the realistic novel, whose formal structure it recapitulated, hysteria was both a performance and a narrative. It was composed of the dramatic gestures of the "grandes hystériques," who skillfully enacted the different stages of hysteria, and of the narrative formulae of the observing physician, who applied the concept of the archetype to make sense of the phenomenon. Charcot's concept of hysteria attempted to bring about an aesthetic fusion between the passion of the hysterical patient and the knowledge of the physician. It was an experiment whose goal was to transform the anarchic manifestations of her symptoms into visual and narrative images comprehensible to the world at large.

The subterranean conjunctions between radical art and popular hysteria become explicit at this point. For fin-de-siècle bohemian artists, hysteria was a privileged phenomenon that affirmed the passionate and expressive potential of the self in modern culture. The modernity of hysteria lay precisely in its theatrical character, which symbolically reestablished the severed bonds between individual and public life. The hysteric as represented in the Salpêtrière was by definition a public figure who performed the drama of her inner life in a setting that transcended the interiorized spaces of domesticity or the artistic interior. Rather than projecting her emotions onto a fetishized work of art, she was identified with them, her body becoming, quite literally, an incarnation of her symptoms. She succeeded in overcoming, if only for a brief period, the alienation between life and art that tortured nineteenth-century aesthetes. It is for this reason that, more than forty years later, Surrealists would celebrate hysteria as the "greatest poetic discovery of the late nineteenth century." Hysteria, they elaborated, was "not a pathological phenomenon and should, in all cases, be considered as a supreme mode of expression."[108]

There was, however, a further reason for the centrality of hysteria in late nineteenth-century aesthetic imagination. Hysteria was not just the public performance of passionate experience, but also an allegory of the modern artistic enterprise as defined by the protocols of early nineteenth-century realism. The actions of the hysterical patient and the attending physician, like those of the bohemian *fumiste* and monologist, were symbolic reenactments of the novelist as hero and observer of modernity. Their combined gestures reproduced the cultural universe of the novel, imagined as a totality of the modern experience and recreated through the bohemian cabaret and the medical demonstration. What was ultimately at stake in the theatrical spectacles of bohemia and the Salpêtrière was the ambition to reaffirm the transparency and legibility of the modern world through the interpretative activities of the artist.

This general enterprise could not be sustained. By the late 1880s and early 1890s, the celebrity status of hysteria, along with the prestige of the Salpêtrière and the bohemian cabaret, came to a relatively abrupt end. The simultaneous decline of hysteria as a medical event and as an artistic gesture was interrelated, of course. To some extent, it was due to the inevitable exhaustion of the creative energies of these movements; as well as to a change in popular fashion that had originally sustained them. The failure of popular hysteria also lay, however, in an insoluble paradox at the center of the entire project. For in the long run, the effort to create coherent narratives of the inner life through the simultaneous performance and interpretation of the phenomenon proved an impossible undertaking. The gestures of the hysteric subject and the narrative of the physician remained theoretically distinct in the same way as the performances of the *fumistes* and the free association of the monologist. Ultimately no viable bridge, no logical and inevitable correspondence, existed between the inner and the outer worlds, between gestures and signification. The culture of hysteria was based on flawed premises that could not stand up to the pressures of empirical experience.

This inner inconsistency was noted early on by opponents of Charcot such as Axel Munthe, who pointed to the moral and medical problems implicit in the Salpêtrière lessons on hysteria. The so-called "grandes hystériques" were often frauds, he revealed, who imitated the prescribed phases and gestures of the hysterical attack out of cynical calculation or sheer exhibitionism. According to Munthe, Charcot's famed demonstrations of hysteria were based on an implicitly coerced relationship between patient and physician that could not ultimately explain the genuine causes of hysteria. Using the same line of argument, one could add that the apparent unity of the bohemian cabaret also depended on consciously manufactured illusion that had no grounds in everyday experience.

By all accounts, Charcot himself began to have considerable misgivings about the cultural and medical status of hysteria, to whose explication he had devoted most of his life. "Our conception of hysteria has become obsolete," he confided to a companion shortly before his death in 1893. "A total revamping of this area of neurological disease is required."[109] At roughly the same time, bohemia also began to lose its status as a site of avant-garde innovation and provocation. The Chat Noir was challenged and eventually replaced by competitors that copied its practices in ever more elaborate and commercially successful forms. The Incoherent exhibitions and costume balls also lost their radical cachet, and by 1889 were upstaged by the newer and more spectacular attractions of the Universal Exposition. The final disintegration of Incoherence was pronounced by a journalist in 1891: "Incoherence has had its heyday. Eccentricity that is too outrageous is dead . . . this year will see the last of the Incoherents. May they rest in peace."[110]

Perhaps nothing sheds more light on the precipitous decline of hysteria as cultural symbol than the transformation of Charcot's image in the expressionist film, *The Cabinet of Dr. Caligari,* conceived by two pacifist intellectuals during the First World War, serves to illustrate the point. The film was an allegory of the hypnotic power of rulers over their subjects, but it was also an explicit denunciation of the abuses of hypnotism and psychological suggestion when practiced by unscrupulous physicians. In the film, Dr. Caligari, bearing an uncanny resemblance to Charcot, is presented as an evil genius, who becomes fascinated by medieval descriptions of hypnotism and, in an act of scientific hubris, assumes the identity of the legendary Dr. Caligari. Like Charcot, the fictional Dr. Caligari proceeds to practice his dangerous and esoteric art in the fairground of the city, where a credulous audience is drawn under the hypnotist's spell. After he wreaks havoc among the population through the murderous actions of his medium, Cesare, the true identity of Dr. Caligari is eventually revealed. He is discovered to be none other than the respected director of a mental institution that resembles the Salpêtrière. The attempt of the hero to unmask the infamous Dr. Caligari has inconclusive results. In fact, the film has two endings, with the original showing the raving Dr. Caligari being led away in a straightjacket; and the second depicting the accusing hero being placed in a straightjacket under the ministration of Dr. Caligari himself. Whichever version one chooses to focus on, the the interpretation of hypnosis in the film is unambiguous. Within less than a generation of Charcot's death, the formerly respected medical practice had acquired an entirely negative connotation as a sinister instrument of mass manipulation.

The phenomenon accurately reflects the transformation of popular ideas about hysteria itself after 1890. Its earlier associations with the parodic and transgressive energies of bohemia faded and it came to be linked with abstract notions of historical decline and degeneration.[111] The hysteric self, celebrated in the 1880s as the incarnation of passion and emotional excess, lost its privileged status in the culture. The hysteric became synonymous with the enervated modern self who had turned inward to the private realm of fantasy and had lost all links with everyday life and popular culture. Indeed, the very idea of hysteria as a metaphor for artistic renewal and cultural regeneration disappeared from mainstream public discourse, which increasingly identified hysteria with social and cultural pathology reflecting the inner exhaustion of Western modernity.

Perhaps no thinker played a more central role in reformulating the cultural meaning of hysteria at the fin de siècle than the poet-critic Paul Bourget. Bourget's singular achievement was to establish a direct connection between hysteria, modernity, and decadence by erasing the mediating

function that bohemian culture had played in the public performance of
hysteria. In Bourget's hands, hysteria became a sign of social anomie and
moral dissolution that needed to be countered with discipline and religious
values if modern society was to survive. There is considerable irony in
Bourget's role as the spokesman for bourgeois moralism. For he had himself
been an intimate member of the world of bohemia that he later denounced.
During the late 1870s and early 1880s he regularly attended the Hydropathic séances, and was on friendly terms with key participants such as
Goudeau and Champsaur. From their descriptions, Bourget emerges as an
anomalous figure both drawn to and repelled by the exuberance of the
environment that was to provide him with his chief source of evidence for
the decline of modern civilization. Félicien Champsaur perceptively
summarized the nature of Bourget's ambivalence. The poet's passionate
"modernisme," wrote Champsaur, made him a friend and ally of the Hydropathes, but his innate dandyism always constituted an invisible barrier
between himself and the uproarious world of bohemia.[112] Goudeau reaffirmed this diagnosis in an even more nuanced portrait of Bourget, which
only barely hinted at his sense of betrayal at Bourget's eventual defection.
The young poet's instinctive attraction for the refinements of aristocratic
society and the fashionable world was, according to Goudeau, an expression of "an enormous need to get away from the real world composed of
bohemians." It was Bourget's "profound taste for worldliness," Goudeau
wryly explained, that "happily saved him from all sorts of eccentricity." Yet,
Goudeau was careful to add that Bourget's discomfort with bohemia was a
complicated kind of escapism that had a spiritual and intellectual as well
as a social component. Ultimately, it was "not at all a sign of snobbism but
a profound taste for a special kind of modernity" that explained Bourget's
actions. The source of this attitude, suggested Goudeau, was to be found
in the exemplary practice of Barbey d'Aurevilly's dandyism, in whom
"Bourget was fortunate to discover . . . a master." Bourget's companions
among the Hydropathes were less generous in their assessment. They parodied him, apparently, as the future Sainte-Beuve who was destined to
become the great critic of their generation.[113]

The prediction proved to be prescient, for Bourget did, indeed, fulfill a
role analogous to that of Sainte-Beuve. Like Sainte-Beuve, he also repudiated the expressive energies of popular bohemia and reinterpreted it according to the tastes and needs of middle-class audiences. In a series of
influential essays, eventually published as *Essais de psychologie contempo-*

raine (Essays on Contemporary Psychology), Bourget presented a collective portrait as well as a moral analysis of late nineteenth-century decadence that became a standard in all contemporary discussions of the questions. Bourget's essays focused on canonical literary figures such as Baudelaire, Flaubert, Dumas, and Stendhal, but his real interest lay in the younger generation, who, by reading the modern masters, had been rendered decadent and unfit for the moral and collective struggle of existence.

Bourget evoked this symbolic reader in the 1883 Introduction to his *Essais de psychologie contemporaine,* in the guise of a studious and introspective adolescent, absorbed in one of the very books under investigation in the volume. Oblivious to the pleasures and beauties of the outside world, the young man found a more intense source of experience in literature than in actual life. "He crosses entirely into the world of his preferred author," Bourget explained. "He talks to him heart to heart, man to man. He heeds his advice about how to enjoy love and practice debauchery; about how to seek happiness and to endure sorrow; about how to envisage death and the shadow world beyond the tomb . . . These texts introduce him into a universe of sentiments hardly perceived until then. From this initial revelation, the road to imitating these sentiments is a short one and the adolescent does not hesitate to take it."[114]

It is impossible not to recognize in this portrait of the fin-de-siècle decadent the characteristic traits of the hysteric, well-known to contemporary readers of popular novels and medical tracts. Indeed, Bourget's analysis of decadence faithfully recapitulated the medical diagnosis of hysteria, as it had been established and popularized by Charcot's lectures at the Salpêtrière. Significantly, however, Bourget recontextualized hysteria from the realm of popular entertainment to that of high art. He then pathologized it by linking it with the supposed moral crisis and psychological dysfunction of contemporary youth. And finally, he historicized it by embedding it within a metanarrative of social and cultural decline that reversed the evolutionary philosophy of scientific Darwinians. The result was a powerful new theory of modernity that both reflected the anxieties of the time and also provided an antidote for them. Hysteria in Bourget's hands became both a diagnosis of contemporary malaise and a therapy for the reassertion of moral standards and social discipline in fin-de-siècle culture.

Bourget in effect reversed Charcot's interpretation of the meaning of hysteria by seeing in it not the transparency and interpretability of individual emotional life, but rather the excessive individuation and privatization of society. Modern individualism, in turn, represented for Bourget the loss of the cohesive energies of collective life. "By the word decadence," Bourget summed up his conclusions in the 1899 Preface to the *Essais de psychologie contemporaine,* "is implied the state of society that produces too few individuals suited to the work of collective existence. A society needs to be compared to an organism . . . the social organism enters into decadence the moment that the individual life expands in importance, due to the influence of acquired well-being or heredity."[115] Bourget implicitly acknowledged earlier theories of decadence, by admitting that, artistically at any rate, the state of hyper-individualism to which modern society had succumbed was capable of creating superior art.[116] Nevertheless, his real concern was with the moral and social implications of this process, which Bourget considered devastating to the future health of civilization. "The proof is," he illustrated, "that from one end of Europe to the other, contemporary society presents the same symptoms of melancholy and dysfunction, inflected by the nuances of race. A universal nausea about the inadequacies of the world permeates the hearts of Slavs, Germans and Latins alike. Among the first, it is manifested in the guise of nihilism, among the second in pessimism, and among us, in solitary and bizarre psychological types." Bourget assumed apocalyptic language in his assessment of the future. "Slowly and surely," he warned, "a belief in the bankruptcy of nature emerges, which is in danger of becoming the sinister faith of the XX. century, unless a renewal, which can hardly be other than a religious renaissance, does not save an overly rationalized humanity from the fatigue of its own intellect."[117]

These culturally conservative conclusions eventually led Bourget to the religious and political right. It would be wrong to conclude from this, however, that Bourget's cultural vision was inherently reactionary. Indeed, Bourget's theory of decadence was so influential precisely because it bridged ideological differences and lent itself to different, often antagonistic, interpretations.[118] For conservatives of various stripes, the appeal of Bourget's essays was obvious, for they directly linked contemporary social and individual malaise with the decline of religious and moral absolutes. But Bourget's analysis was equally compatible with the outlook of progressive and liberal elites. It provided them with a scientific diagnosis and moral antidote for a range of disturbing phenomena, including popular culture, consumerism, feminism, avant-garde art, and anarchism, which were all perceived as interrelated threats to the stability of the established order. It is little wonder that decadence became one of the central myths of modern social science at the turn of the century.

Possibly the single most influential popularizer of the theory was the psychiatrist Max Nordau, whose polemical book of 1892, *Degeneration,* reached a mass audience throughout Europe. Nordau, who was by training a psychiatrist, was in many respects the direct antithesis of Charcot. While Charcot aestheticized the medical category of hysteria, transforming it into a cultural phenomenon, Nordau medicalized the cultural debate about decadence, rooting it in physiological causations. He argued for a direct causal link between the manifestations of popular culture, consumerism, experimental art, and nervous disorder. "The physician," he wrote, "especially if he has devoted himself to the special study of nervous and mental maladies, recognizes at a glance, in the *fin-de-siècle* disposition . . . the confluence of two well-defined conditions of disease, with which he is quite familiar, viz. degeneration (degeneracy) and hysteria, of which the minor stages are designated as neurasthenia."[119]

Paradoxically, Bourget's theory of degeneration had profound relevance for avant-garde artists as well; though in their case the cultural implication of the phenomenon was directly reversed. The figure of the decadent became a symbol, not of the pathological individuation of modern life, but rather of its excessive conformism to inherited literary and cultural norms that blocked creative energies. Probably the most important formulator of this radical position was J.-K. Huysmans, (Figure 36) whose notorious novel *À Rebours* (*Against the Grain*) became the manifesto of fin-de-siècle avant-garde identity.

Through a convenient coincidence, Bourget and Huysmans were personally acquainted with each other. Bourget had written a favorable review of a collection of Huysmans's art criticism in which he identified the young writer with the very phenomenon he was engaged in typifying in his own essays on modern decadence. There is in Huysmans's writing, Bourget wrote in 1883, "a refined and mournful nervousness, a bitter taste of life, a nostalgic pessimism about life, to which, for my part, I am particularly sensitive . . . It is part of a literature of decadence and subtlety, whose troubled idealism nevertheless has its contemporary poetry, or to use the term found in the title of this review, its modernity."[120] The grateful young author wrote back immediately to thank Bourget for the favorable review. He ended his letter with a reference to a "bizarre novel" he was working on at the moment that was directly influenced by Bourget's essays. "I hope you

Figure 36. Eugène Delâtre, *Portrait of Huysmans* (1894). Color aquatint, 32.4 × 24.1 cm?. Jane Voorhees Zimmerli Art Museum, Rutgers, The State University of New Jersey. Photograph by Jack Abraham.

will like it," Huysmans concluded, "because I think of you often, especially in connection with certain chapters on orchids and the combination of perfumes, on furniture and on painters."[121] The "bizarre novel" to which he was referring was *À Rebours*.

In his autobiography, Huysmans confessed that he wrote the novel with relatively modest goals and with a limited audience in mind. He was, he explained, addressing only a dozen persons, and "fashioning a sort of hermetic book which would be closed to fools."[122] Instead, he ended up producing a cult book that became the "flagship of the Parisian avant-garde,"[123] and the "breviary of an entire generation."[124] Almost within a month of its publication, in July 1884, Barbey d'Aurevilly welcomed *À Rebours* as a representative text reflecting the spirit of the age: "M. Huysmans's hero— and the heroes of novels that we write are always to some extent ourselves—is a sick person like all the novelistic heroes of this sick age. He is a captive of the neurosis of the century. He hails from Charcot's hospital."[125] Within two years of its publication, the controversial novel had generated two avant-garde journals, *Le Décadent* and *La Décadence,* which were both modeled on Huysmans's decadent hero, Des Esseintes. Recalling Huysmans's cultural impact, Paul Valéry wrote: "One thing cannot be emphasized enough and that is the enormous effect of Huysmans on the young people of my generation . . . Huysmans prepared without any question the transmutation of naturalism into symbolism."[126]

Despite consensus about the centrality of *À Rebours* for artistic innovation at the turn of the century, it is difficult to treat the novel as a conventional manifesto of the avant-garde. *À Rebours* was not a programmatic text that spelled out a specific aesthetic agenda for the future. It was, rather, a dramatic, often ironic, exploration of the literary and culture ideals of the recent past that were already losing their hold on Huysmans's generation. David Weir perceptively remarked on this when he pointed out that *À Rebours* was "an a posteriori formulation" that paradoxically "announced as new [what] is really over or almost over."[127] Huysmans's project was, in fact, a reenactment, a celebration, and ultimately a devastating critique, of a bohemian culture whose decline could already be predicted by the mid-1880s.

Huysmans provided no direct evidence for the intimate relationship between *À Rebours* and contemporary bohemia. The book was, in the words of a critic, an "immense mystification, a prodigious *'fumisterie'* of the artist, who amuses himself enormously at the expense of the vulgar."[128] *À Rebours* seemed to recapitulate the formula of the modern artist's withdrawal into an aestheticized interior that Edmond de Goncourt had thematized in *La maison d'un artiste*. (The House of an Artist).[129] The real sources of Huysmans's inspiration, however, lay outside this familiar frame, a fact that was reflected in the scandal that the book caused among respectable circles. Huysmans's hero, Des Esseintes, was not a collector of art objects, nor was his house on the outskirts of Paris an aristocratic version of the "house beautiful." On the contrary, Des Esseintes was, as conservative critics instinctively realized, a theatrical performer, a male version of the "grande hystérique" of the Salpêtrière; who conceived of his retreat to Fontenay as an aesthetic experiment comparable to the Salpêtrière or the bohemian cabaret. Its purpose was to create an artificial setting, a laboratory environment, where a perfect correspondence between emotional states and physical effects could be brought about.

For the "qualified reader," there were a number of clues that would have betrayed this hidden agenda. Perhaps most tellingly, the theme of hysteria was pervasive in the account, reflected both in the setting and in the state of mind of the hero. The domestics whom Des Esseintes employed to take care of his needs at Fontenay were described as hospital attendants, who were "trained to the methodical habits of wardsmen at a hospital, accustomed to administer at stated hours spoonfuls of physic and doses of medicinal draughts."[130] Des Esseintes himself was a classic case of the hysteric, displaying the full catalogue of symptoms customarily associated with the disease. So accurate, in fact, were Huysmans's descriptions of hysteria, that Victor Segalen, a physician and an admirer of *À Rebours,* actually raised the question whether Huysmans had ever studied medicine. To this, Huysmans answered, "Never, though always curious about medical matters and profoundly attracted by the intensity of their notions."[131]

Huysmans's text also evoked themes typically associated with the contemporary cabaret and café concert. His frequent references to acrobats, ventriloquists, Pierrots, and other curiosities of popular entertainment betrayed an intimate familiarity with, as well as appreciation for, the world of cabarets and café concerts.[132] Indeed, as Grojnowski remarked, his narrative recapitulated the well-known cultural formulae of the café concert, which consisted of "a string of numbers, as spectacular as possible" whose goal was to "provoke and satisfy the curiosity of the public."[133] *À Rebours,* like the acts of the artistic cabaret, lacked a conventional plot or character development but consisted of a patchwork of heterogeneous texts—some serious, some frivolous—which could have been rearranged in any order without seriously affecting the overall effect.

Perhaps the most revealing clue about *À Rebours's* cultural affiliations was contained in the title of the book itself. Ostensibly, *À Rebours* referred to the fashionable philosophy of artifice and pessimism advocated by Schopenhauer and his followers. But it also parodically echoed the uproarious banquet held by the Incoherents at the close of their first exhibition in October 1882. As any reader of *Le Chat Noir* magazine would have known, where the event was reported in full detail, the banquet was organized according to the carnivalesque credo of the exhibition and proceeded in reverse order, that is "à rebours," by beginning with dessert and ending with the hors d'oeuvre.[134] Huysmans's novel was also a performance of the aesthetic and theoretical possibilities of artifice, that set about its task by reversing the natural order of life and art.

In order to appreciate the full implication of Huysmans's exemplary text, however, it is important to see it as more than a parodic reenactment of the world of fin-de-siècle bohemia. Even while recapitulating decadent bohemia's characteristic gestures and parodic spirit, Huysmans also provided a diagnosis of its flaws and a prognosis of its demise. Significantly, he did so by linking the cultural crisis of bohemia with the literary exhaustion of the novel. As he pointed out in his Preface of 1903, *À Rebours* was originally conceived as a critique of the conventions of the modern novel in general, and of Naturalism in particular, which had become emptied of creative energy by the 1880s. "Invent what one chose," Huysmans illustrated, "the story could be summed up in half-a-dozen words—to wit, why did Monsieur So-and-So commit or not commit adultery with Madame This or That? If you wished to be distinguished and stand out as a writer of the most polite taste, you made the work of the flesh take place between a Marquise and a Count; if on the other, you wanted to pose as a popular author, a writer knowing what's what, you chose a lover from the slums and the first street girl to hand. Only the frame was different."[135] Huysmans's goal, as he explained to Zola immediately after the publication of *À Rebours,* was to find a way out of this creative impasse. "The desire that filled me," he recounted, was "to shake off preconceived ideas, to break the limitations of the novel, to introduce into it art, science, history; in a word not to use this form of literature except as a frame in which to put more serious kinds of works."[136]

There were a number of ironic twists to Huysmans's quest for personal renewal and artistic liberation from what had become the *cul-de-sac* of the novelistic universe. Perhaps the most important in terms of his own personal development was the fact that it was to lead him into an even deeper spiritual crisis, which was to find resolution only after his conversion to Catholicism in 1892. Less obvious, but equally important, was the fact that Huysmans's attempt to clarify and transcend the literary crisis of the novel could only be undertaken through the seeming detour of confronting the cultural phenomenon of hysteria. Indeed, hysteria formed the central theme and essential problematic of *À Rebours,* whose plot revolved around the hero's increasingly ambiguous experience with the disease. By demonstrating the fundamental incompatibility between hysteria as a cultural metaphor and as a physiological condition, Huysmans's narrative simultaneously undermined the cultural foundations of hysteria, the theoretical premises of urban realism, and the existential validity of the bohemian project.

It is noteworthy that at the time of the writing of the book, the aesthetic and philosophic problems of nineteenth-century realism were not conscious in Huysmans' mind. As he admitted in his Preface, "these reflections did not actually occur to me till much later."[137] This is why the first half of the novel can be regarded as an ironic exploration as well as a celebration of the inherent possibilities of hysteria as a cultural gesture. The notorious eccentricities of Des Esseintes were, in fact, stylized versions of typical performances that characterized bohemian culture of the period. Des Esseintes, like his bohemian contemporaries, was dedicated to the task of bringing about through artificial means as perfect a correspondence between life and art, external symbol and inner experience, as possible. A representative incident in a long list of amusing vignettes will illustrate the point. To commemorate his first episode of sexual impotence, Des Esseintes decided to stage a wake that would duplicate through formalized gestures and ceremonies an inner state of mourning and renunciation that he was feeling at the moment. He sent out black-framed invitations to friends, draped his house in black, devised a menu whose every item was black, and even provided black waitresses for the occasion, who were nude except for silver, teardrop embroidered stockings. The outrageous details of this banquet in black served only to exaggerate the aesthetic creed of all realistic writings, which was based on the assumption that the external details of physical life were capable of being treated as readable texts of the inner conditions of modern experience.

Des Esseintes's decision to break with his extravagant habits in Paris and to move to the relative isolation of Fontenay on the outskirts of the city did not represent the abandonment of his bohemian project. On the contrary, it simply meant its continuation in a controlled environment cleansed of the impurities and unforeseen disturbances of everyday life. Des Esseintes's theatrical and improvised gestures, characteristic of his life as a Parisian man about town, were to find more precise and disciplined expression in the laboratory setting of his artificial house, which was set up expressly for the purpose of recreating the perfect environment for the novelistic project. In a real sense, Des Esseintes's actions recapitulated the experiences of an earlier generation of bohemians, who had abandoned public performance for the rigors of scientific observation. Like them, Des Esseintes went through a process of reassessment and came to the conclusion that "the extraordinary clothes he had donned and the grotesque decorations he had lavished on his house" appeared as "puerile and out-of-date displays of eccentricity."[138]

The purified environment of Fontenay, however, yielded unexpected results that eventually undermined not only Des Esseintes' efforts to create a distinctly artistic way of life, but also the very premises of the realistic novel as an art form. The crucial issue that determined the outcome of the experiment was Des Esseintes's growing inability to reconcile and create a seamless identity between cultural and aesthetic images of hysteria, on the one hand; and the unmediated, physical experience of the disease, on the other.

Hysteria as art was spectacularly displayed by a painting of Gustave Moreau's, which was among Des Esseintes's prize possessions at Fontenay. The image represented Salome dancing in front of Herodotus and was the very embodiment of Des Esseintes's aesthetic ideal of the spiritual universe made visible through its physical incarnation. Contemplating the painting would plunge Des Esseintes into a passionate reverie in which he saw Salome no longer as "merely the dancing-girl who extorts a cry of lust and concupiscence from an old man by the lascivious contortions of her body . . . she was now revealed in a sense as the symbolic incarnation of world-old Vice, the goddess of immortal Hysteria, the Curse of Beauty supreme above all other beauties by the cataleptic spasm that stirs her flesh and steels her muscles."[139]

This brilliant vision of the aesthetic possibilities of hysteria was, however, radically undermined in the second half of the book, through a meticulous exploration of the physical and psychological implications of the disease. Des Esseintes developed a long list of excruciating ailments, which began with insomnia and culminated in the inability to swallow nourishment. Hysteria as aesthetic allegory retreated before hysteria as medical symptomology. As Des Esseintes's worsening condition made explicit, the experience of hysteria carried no inner significance; it held no clues about the meaning of the universe and about the mysterious unity of life and art. Given Charcot's centrality in creating the myth of hysteria, it was perhaps appropriate that the final pronouncement of this lesson was made by physicians grounded in a more up-to-date version of medical science. Both Des Esseintes's attending physician and the Parisian specialists he consulted commanded him to immediately abandon his experimental way of life and to return to the pursuits of ordinary society if he wished to avoid an untimely death.

The unraveling of Des Esseintes's carefully constructed laboratory experiment had wide-ranging cultural and aesthetic consequences that Huysmans spelled out toward the end of the book. Perhaps most strikingly, it implied disenchantment with the artistic café and cabaret as potentially redeeming public spaces, where the meaning of modern life could be acted out. Like Goudeau and Lévy, Huysmans, too, assumed initially that these institutions were a microcosm of modernity that gave access "to the state of mind and imagination of a whole generation." By the end, he grew disillusioned with this premise. They came to represent for Huysmans only "imbecile sentimentalism, combined with ferocity in practice [that] seemed to represent the dominant feeling of the age."[140]

Even Balzac's much-admired figure could not withstand the impact of Des Esseintes's psychological and physical collapse. "He had at one time adored the great Balzac," Des Esseintes confessed, "but in proportion as his organism had lost balance, as his nerves had gained the upper hand, his inclinations had been modified and his preferences changed. Soon even, and this although he was well aware of his injustice toward the marvelous author of the *La comédie humaine,* he had given up so much as even opening his books, the study of which irritated him; other aspirations stirred him now, that were in a sense incapable of precise definition."[141] The cutting of his ties with the literary heritage of urban realism seemed to be complete at this point. Hysteria had unraveled the final illusion that had linked fin-de-siècle modernity to its early nineteenth-century predecessor.

The closing lines of the novel simultaneously liberated Des Esseintes from his house of artifice and violently exposed him to the terrors of an unfathomable universe. "In two days more I shall be in Paris," he exclaimed. "[A]ll is over; like a flowing tide, the waves of human mediocrity rise to the heavens and they will engulf my last refuge; I am opening the sluice-gates myself, in spite of myself."[142] Des Esseintes was, of course, saying farewell to more than his personal illusions in this passage. The same meta-phor was used by Goudeau to end his own account of the dispersion and demise of bohemia. Its original members, he concluded, "have either dis-appeared or settled down. The quasi-oceanic life of Paris rumbles on as ever, like a turbulent, sometimes tempestuous flood tide."[143] The reference in both cases was to a well-known analogy of the time that had compared Montmartre to the biblical Mt. Ararat where Noah had anchored his ark after the flood.[144]

The apocalyptic vision of Noah's flood, with which both Huysmans and Goudeau closed their respective accounts of fin-de-siècle artistic life, had far-reaching implications for the history of bohemia. On one level, the figure simply gave recognition to the ephemeral nature of the bohemian experience, which, as Gautier had already foretold in 1849, needed to be reinvented by each generation. In the course of the nineteenth century, the bohemian effort to define a public art of modernity had suffered several shipwrecks. Gautier's abandoning of bohemia for the editorial offices of *La Presse* in 1836 and Baudelaire's retreat from empirical flânerie after 1848 can be considered comparable moments.

On a deeper level, however, the decline of bohemia in 1885 signaled a more radical disruption and dislocation than did these earlier events. As the metaphor of a biblical flood suggests, it implied the erasure not simply of the specific cultural spaces that had sustained creativity and identity for artists, but also of the more general urban culture that had provided the symbolic context for their activities. From the 1880s, the modern city itself had become problematic as a space capable of being rendered visible and legible for its inhabitants.[145] Goudeau acknowledged this subtle difference in *Dix ans de bohème* when he declared that future bohemias would emerge in the course of time, but that these would differ in fundamental ways from the one just ended.

How can we explain this deeper, more conclusive, sense of ending that characterized the bohemian generation of the 1880s? What was the source of the discontinuity between its experiences and those of its predecessors? Huysmans's final invocation at the conclusion of *À Rebours* provides a key to the problem. "Ah; but my courage fails me!" Huysmans's protagonist exclaims, "Lord, take pity on the Christian who doubts, on the skeptic who would fain believe, on the galley-slave of life who puts out to sea alone, in the darkness of night, beneath a firmament illumined no longer by the consoling beacon-fires of the ancient hope."[146] In light of Huysmans's much-publicized conversion to Catholicism in 1892, it is difficult not to read this passage as a religious crisis foreshadowing his return to the fold of the Church. Huysmans himself counsels against this conclusion, however. The novel's connection to Catholicism, he wrote in his preface of 1903, "remains, I confess, an insoluble problem to me." He further elaborated: "in the days when I wrote *Against the Grain,* I never set foot in a church, I did not know a single Catholic who regularly performed his religious duties, I had not a single priest among my acquaintances; I felt no Divine impulse drawing me toward the Church, I lived calmly and comfortably in my own style."[147]

Behind the spiritual distress articulated by Huysmans in *À Rebours* was a more general cultural-aesthetic crisis that Huysmans explicitly associated with the influence of Schopenhauer, whom he "admired beyond reason" at the time of the writing of *À Rebours.*[148] Schopenhauerian pessimism, as it was customarily called at the time, conjured up a universe that could no longer be grasped through the categories of reason, nor experienced as a totality of lived relations. It was a universe of flux and estrangement that brought into question the very status of art as a reflection of reality. Realism, broadly defined since the 1830s as the art of modernity, had always been a precarious enterprise. Its aspiration to hold up a mirror to modern society was predicated on what Christopher Prendergast has called "the desire for stable knowledge, while encountering the condition of its impossibility."[149]

For much of the nineteenth century, however, the contradictions of this enterprise were kept in creative tension and resolved through the parodic gestures of bohemia. Bohemia as a cultural space and an aesthetic project was, in fact, built on the paradoxes inherent in the project of realism defined in the broadest terms. More than a transitional phase of an artist's career or a laboratory for unconventional lifestyles, nineteenth-century bohemia aspired to be a popular stage where the collective meanings of modernity could be illuminated, performed, and made comprehensible for an urban public that no longer had direct access to its inner truths.[150] The bohemian artist, in his changing guises as melodramatic hero, as anonymous journalist, as cabaret performer and, finally, as charismatic physician, had a common mission: to make transparent the hidden, mysterious, and fragmented aspects of modern experience. Des Esseintes's return to Paris signaled the final disintegration of this hope and a radical transformation in the relationship between modernist art and urban culture.

The beginnings of this transformation were to be undertaken by a younger generation of avant-garde artists in the middle of the 1880s, who defiantly proclaimed themselves to be Decadents, reclaiming the figure of Huysmans's paradigmatic hero for their own aesthetic purposes. In their hands, the religious iconography permeating Huysmans's novel was to find a secular meaning, signaling the possibility of aesthetic regeneration in a modern world that had become overly materialistic and wedded to external realities.

Decadence as an aesthetic movement owed a great deal to the polemical and journalistic activities of Anatole Baju, who in 1885 created the first example of the avant-garde manifesto in *Le Décadent*. As the programmatic editorials of the journal stridently proclaimed, Decadence was not a sign of social or political decay, but on the contrary, of artistic rebirth. "A literary revolution was inevitable," wrote one representative article, "and the Decadents, with their inveterate habit of speaking about essentials, were the only ones able to accomplish it, or to bring it to practical realization. Decadence is everywhere; fortunately, it is not to be feared. As we have maintained, it is only a happy transformation, the direct opposite of what happened in antiquity, whose decadent empires ended up disappearing forever."[151]

The Decadents, who defiantly accepted and manipulated the controversial term that had originally been applied to bohemians, did not succeed in their proclaimed task of rejuvenating the conditions of modern aesthetic life. Their efforts to create a new art of modernity could not be accomplished without the sustaining energies of everyday life and popular culture. It remained for the avant-garde of the early twentieth century to reinvent the terms and conditions of this enterprise.

5

The Primitivist Artist and the Discourse of Exoticism

In 1891 Paul Gauguin left Paris for Tahiti in search of a more congenial environment for his art, beyond the physical setting of bohemia. Gauguin did not find in Tahiti the island paradise that exoticist novels and colonial expositions had led him to expect.[1] What he did discover, however, was a radically new artistic identity that came to define one of the central myths of early twentieth-century modernism: the Primitivist artist.[2] Anticipating the myth, Octave Mirbeau wrote shortly before Gauguin's departure that he was the kind of man who flees civilization in order to discover outside of Europe a place "where nature is more in keeping with his dreams."[3]

Gauguin had few emulators, but his idiosyncratic journey had enormous symbolic importance for avant-garde artists and intellectuals of the early twentieth century. In the decade before World War I, they published hundreds of aesthetic manifestoes, personal testimonials, and theoretical essays, proclaiming the European artist's aesthetic and psychological affinities with the Primitive cultures of Africa, Polynesia, Indochina, Egypt, Persia, and even ancient Greece.[4] The modern Primitives, these apologists pointed out, had turned away from the material world of external appearances and had discovered in the realm of inner subjectivity the means for both spiritual renewal and artistic regeneration. According to Wilhelm Worringer, the author of possibly the most influential Primitivist manifesto of the age, the moderns were related to the Primitives not so much in their material circumstances as in their artistic volition, which stemmed from a growing similarity in their relationship to nature. After centuries of identification with the external aspects of the natural world, Worringer pointed out, the moderns had emancipated themselves from their naturalistic and rationalist illusions and had returned to a more ancient, more mythic attitude to the outside world, whose appropriate expression was abstraction.[5]

These declarations of aesthetic renewal and cultural rebirth were not entirely new to the Primitivists. The Decadent manifestoes of the mid-1880s, published by Anatole Baju and his followers, had already celebrated the creative and regenerative potential of modern art.[6] Unlike the Decadents, however, the Primitivists did more than proclaim the utopian future of modern art. They also redefined contemporary aesthetic idioms by severing their final links with nineteenth-century realism and naturalism. It was the Primitivists who carried through the momentous breakthrough to abstraction or "pure art" that was to characterize much of twentieth-century modernism. Less frequently thematized, however, were the cultural aspects of this revolution. For Primitivism signaled a realignment not only in avant-garde practices, but also in artistic identities. Indeed, with Primitivism, the nature of bohemia itself was reconstituted under the changed conditions of twentieth-century modernity.

The complexities of this cultural transformation would lead avant-garde artists to form a romantic identification with the non-European and the antimodern, as well as the exoticized images that Europeans themselves created to represent their colonial "Other." Paradoxically, it was through engagement with the problematic discourses of exoticism, Orientalism, and evolutionary theory that the modernist artists were to distill their own unique visions of the Primitive. Their dialogue with, and eventual transformation of, these popular forms of exoticism allows us to retrace the steps by which avant-garde artists recreated the empirical and imaginary spaces for radical art in the twentieth century.

The modernists of the early twentieth century invariably presented themselves as Primitives alienated from modern civilization. Yet they remained quintessentially urban artists, closely identified with the landscape of the modern city and with the varied manifestations of popular culture. Henri Matisse expressed this paradox in his defense of the Fauves (wild beasts) in 1908: "Whether we want to or not, we belong to our time and we share in its opinions, its feelings, even its delusions. All artists bear the imprint of their time, but the great artists are those in whom this is most profoundly marked . . . Whether we like it or not, however insistently we call ourselves exiles, between our period and ourselves an indissoluble bond is established."[7] Matisse's defiant identification with his age gains added meaning from the context in which it was made. His was a rebuttal to a conservative critic who found the Fauves' conventional appearance incongruous in light of their supposed radicalism. Despite their ferocious name, he accused, the Fauves "dressed like everyone else," and were "no more noticeable than the floor walkers in a department store."[8] The association of the young artists with the anonymous spaces of the department store and commodified urban culture was more telling than the critic realized. It placed the Primitivists in direct line of succession to the flâneurs and decadents of the nineteenth century who had inhabited the spaces of popular bohemia before them.

Indeed, the image of the Primitive was a long-established icon of popular urban culture, used by novelists since the 1830s to represent the mystery, unpredictability, and potential savagery of life in the modern city. By the mid–nineteenth century, Baudelaire began to appropriate this image for avant-garde art by making a direct connection between the Primitive and the modern artist. The modernist's love of external finery and artifice, he pointed out, resembled the aesthetic gestures of "those races which our confused and perverted civilization is pleased to treat as savage."[9]

These basic continuities between nineteenth- and twentieth-century aesthetic visions of the Primitive cannot be pushed too far, however. They were also quite different from each other, and had radically different implications for the enterprise of avant-garde art. For the nineteenth century, the Primitive served merely as an ornamental mask, whose function was to render visible and legible the anonymous surfaces of modern life. As Baudelaire put it, the nobility of the Primitive was inseparable from the "many-colored feathers, iridescent fabrics, the incomparable majesty of artificial forms" through which he distinguished himself from the ignonimity of nature.[10] For the twentieth century, however, the Primitive became a subjective condition, rather than an external façade. It implied a psychic fusion between the modern artist and the Primitive "Other" that led to a purified and radicalized inner state. The Primitivism of the modern artist, according to Worringer, represented a complex metamorphosis, through which the physical spaces of urban life came to be redefined as the internal spaces of the artist's consciousness.

Worringer and his contemporaries were elusive about the nature or dynamics of this transformation, which was presented as both an aesthetic break-through and a psychological epiphany. What, in fact, were the preconditions for, and implications of, a creative fusion between the Primitive and the modern? More puzzling still, why was this phenomenon associated with spiritual and aesthetic regeneration? The answer to these questions is neither direct nor unequivocal. Indeed, it cannot be separated from the institutional contexts and symbolic horizons within which Parisian modernists acquired their understanding of the Primitive in the early twentieth century. As is well known, their actual encounters with the arts and artifacts of tribal cultures took place in Europe, rather than in empirically foreign settings. They tended to meet the Primitive in ethnographic museums, worlds' fairs and colonial exhibitions, or zoos, cabarets, and music halls; where exoticized and Orientalized images of colonial peoples were habitually displayed. The Primitive of the avant-garde artists was, in other words, always already mediated by official and unofficial venues of mass culture.[11]

Paradoxically, this generalization is true even for Gauguin, whose encounter with the exoticized Primitive of French colonialism predated, and in a sense predetermined, his empirical experience of Tahiti. Gauguin formed his original vision of Tahiti at the colonial exposition of 1889, which he visited shortly before his departure for the South Seas. Impressed with the exhibit, he immediately created a fantasy of his life in Tahiti. "With the money I'll have," he wrote to a friend, "I can buy a native hut, like the ones you saw at the Universal Exposition. Made of wood and clay, thatched over (near a town, yet in the country). That costs next to nothing . . . I'll go out there and live withdrawn from the so-called civilized world and frequent only so-called savages."[12] Gauguin's familiarization with Tahitian culture continued through his reading Pierre Loti's popular novel, *Le mariage de Loti, (Loti's Marriage)* which recounted a tale of romantic love and exotic adventure in the idealized landscape of the island paradise.[13] Loti, probably the most important writer of exoticist fiction at the fin de siècle, set the standards for the genre. His novels of romantic adventure in colonial settings, which ranged from Tahiti and Turkey to North Africa and Japan, reached both a popular and an avant-garde audience and seemed to play an important role in framing Gauguin's own expectations of Tahiti.[14] Indeed, as we shall see shortly, they were even to structure aspects of his own autobiography of spiritual rebirth and aesthetic regeneration, that was to be published in 1901 under the title of *Noa Noa*. (Figures 37–40)

Exoticist fiction and colonial exhibitions were by no means the only sources of the Primitive available to artists at the turn of the century. Perhaps more than any other venue, it was the ethnographic museum that was to play a decisive role in mediating between avant-garde artists and Prim-

Figure 37. *Vue général de l'Exposition de 1889* (General view of the Exposition of 1889). From *Exposition de 1889*. Courtesy of Brown University Library.

Figure 38. *Le Palais du Trocadero* (The Trocadero pavilion). From *Exposition de 1889*. Courtesy of Brown University Library.

Figure 39. *Le Palais des colonies* (The Colonial pavilion). From *Exposition de 1889*. Courtesy of Brown University Library.

Figure 40. *Rue du Caire* (A Cairo street). From *Exposition de 1889*. Courtesy of Brown University Library.

itivist images. Most of the painters who became pioneers of abstraction first encountered Primitivist art and artifacts in the Trocadero Museum, Paris' major ethnographic collection that was built in conjunction with the World's Fair of 1879. Picasso himself began to seriously study *l'art nègre* in the Trocadero around 1907. Even foreign visitors to Paris like Wilhelm Worringer were irresistibly drawn to the museum in their search for aesthetic and intellectual inspiration. It was in the deserted halls of the Trocadero, he recalled in his Preface to *Abstraction and Empathy,* that the original inspiration for his Primitivist theoretical masterpiece came to him.[15]

In order to unravel the complex relationship between the Primitivist artist and the exoticized image of the Primitive that he encountered in venues of popular culture, it will be useful to look a little more closely at the cultural and ideological function of these institutions. The Trocadero Museum in particular was a symbolically charged place for Primitivist artists, and is perhaps an appropriate place to start. The Trocadero of the fin de siècle was, as James Clifford tellingly put it, a "scandalous museum," with exotic objects, fetishes, and curiosities scattered about without any systematic organization or scholarly classification. "Its arrangements," Clifford illustrated, "emphasized 'local color' or the evocation of formal settings: costumed mannequins, panoplies, dioramas, massed specimens."[16]

The "scandal" of the Trocadero did not lie exclusively, however, in the disorder and exotic profusion of its exhibits. It was implicit within the political and ideological messages encoded in the collection itself. Like most ethnographic museums of the time, the Trocadero conceived of itself not so much as an art museum as a scientific exposition of evolutionary theory. Its collection of primitive tools, artifacts, and fetishes were supposed to be "living survivals of our European prehistory" and the "missing link that the archeologist needed in order to provide a complete history of European man."[17] The ethnographic collections were, thus, not simply scientific displays, but also visual and tactile demonstrations of the distance traveled between the primitives and the moderns. In these displays, the Primitive became part of an evolutionary narrative of self-affirmation through which European middle-class culture defined its place in the historical and natural worlds. The ethnographic collection, wrote Simon Bonner, was concerned with demonstrating "how 'mechanized' modern man genteelly triumphed over primitive man yet retained his sensory excitement."[18]

The museum, as self-appointed guardian of evolutionary ideology, could not, however, maintain monopoly over the interpretation of the Primitive.

It faced increasingly successful competition from world's fairs, universal and colonial expositions, and even zoos, which often transformed the Primitive into exotic spectcle. Displays of primitive artifacts and tools were supplemented in these venues by more spectacular exhibitions such as reconstructed native villages, where indigenous people, imported from Africa, India, Samoa, even Ireland, reenacted their daily activities—dancing for women and wrestling for men were the most popular pastimes—for the benefit of European visitors. These recreations of tribal life erased physical distance between "civilization" and "primitivism," transporting Europeans into the midst of primitive experiences for the price of an admission ticket. At the same time, however, they also resurrected barriers between European and natives, by turning them into objects of spectacle. World's fairs made possible the experience of "vicarious tourism" for Europeans, who were supposed to be both entertained and instructed by these displays. Using the rhetoric of "learning through pleasure," world's fairs combined the prestige of science with the drawing power of pure entertainment in order to appeal to the crowds.[19]

Other venues of urban mass culture, however, such as cabarets, music halls and, above all, popular fiction, abandoned even such transparent pretence at scientific respectability. They featured Primitivist themes and Orientalist motifs exclusively as entertainment.[20] In these cases, the meta-narratives of evolutionary science were supplemented by older forms of exoticist and primitivist discourses reaching back to the eighteenth century, if not before. As Tzvetan Todorov has pointed out, such discourses traditionally crystallized around the trope of the noble savage, who lived in a state of economic and political equality, conformity with nature, spontaneity, and sexual freedom.[21] These were clearly fantasies, through which Europeans attempted to create alternate identities and social possibilities that lay outside the frame of Western modernity. They were, however, no more innocent or free of hegemonic implications than evolutionary theory was. Ultimately, both were about Western self-definitions in which the Primitive was the passive reflection of Western desires and domination.[22]

The uncomfortably close association between these exoticized images of the Primitive "Other" and avant-garde Primitivism has raised important questions of interpretation that continue to engage critics and cannot easily be sidestepped. To what extent was the avant-garde of the early twentieth century complicit with the hegemonic discourses of colonialism and exoticism? In what form did these discourses permeate and shape avant-garde aesthetic practices and sensibilities? According to some views, there can be no neat separation between avant-garde Primitivists and the world of popular exoticism from which they drew their creative visions. Both were based on control and domination. "The flow of ideas from so-called Primitive artists to modern Western artists," so the argument has been presented, needs to be seen as parallel to "the flow of raw materials from the colonized peoples of the Third World to the industrialized West."[23] As James Clifford summarized this position, avant-garde Primitivism was nothing more than an expression of Western culture's disturbing "taste for appropriating otherness, for constituting non-Western arts in its own image, for discovering universal, ahistorical 'human' capacities."[24]

The problem with such arguments, however, is that they draw too direct a link between the avant-garde Primitive and popular exoticism. They fail to take into account the complex processes of mediation, internalization, and reinterpretation that actually occurred in avant-garde engagement with, and appropriation of, the popular exotic.[25] In order to begin to explore this process, it is useful to retrace our steps to the Trocadero Museum to the moment of inspiration that gave birth to modern Primitivism. As it turns out, Picasso has left an intriguing depiction of his experience in the museum, which suggests a considerably more complex encounter than had appeared at first sight. In a conversation with André Malraux in 1937, Picasso recounted that his Primitivism, which found its first incarnation in the *Demoiselles d'Avignon,* was only obliquely related to the actual ethnographic displays in the Trocadero. Indeed, it was only after a period of resistance and even repulsion that he was able to appropriate and internalize the message of the museum. "When I went to the Trocadero it was disgusting," Picasso remembered. "The flea market. The smell. I was all alone. I wanted to get away. But I didn't leave. I stayed. I understood something very important: something was happening to me, wasn't it?" What exactly happened to Picasso in "that awful museum," as he called it, is difficult to reconstruct, but the moment of epiphany that he struggled to communicate had little to do with the stylistic impact of the exoticist collection. It was, rather, a radical intuition of a new way of conceiving the function of art and the artist that seemed to take possession of the would-be Primitivist artist. "[A]ll these fetishes," he cryptically summarized his epiphany, "were used for the same thing. They were weapons. To help people stop being dominated by spirits, to become independent. Tools. If we give form to the spirits, we become independent of them. The spirits, the unconscious (which wasn't much spoken then), emotions, it's the same thing. I understood why I was a painter . . . *Les Demoiselles d'Avignon* must have come to me that day, but not at all because of the forms: but because it was my first canvas of exorcism—yes, absolutely!"[26]

The extraordinary interest of this originary tale is that it problematizes any simple linkages between the avant-garde Primitive and the ethnographic Primitive. Modernist conceptions of the Primitive came into being, not through an act of emulation or direct transmission of ideas or styles; but in a moment of intense contemplation that made possible a creative fusion between the modernist sensibility and the ethnographic image. It is the imagination of the modern artist that brought into proximity and made possible the connection between the antithetical poles of the primitive and the hyper-modern. The experimental arts of the early twentieth century would come into being on this paradoxical site that collapsed the linear logic of historical narration and created a new, mythic space for the modernist imagination.

Perhaps no text provides more acute insight into how this process of aesthetic fusion between the modern and the primitive took place than Gauguin's autobiographical narrative, *Noa Noa.* (Figure 41) The idea for the book came to Gauguin in 1893, during his stay in Paris between his first and final trips to Tahiti. The immediate purpose of the book, as he confided in a letter to his estranged wife, was to provide for Parisian audiences a better understanding of his recent Tahitian paintings, which were being exhibited at the Duran-Ruet gallery between November and December 1893.[27] *Noa Noa,* however, was more than a publicity event to generate interest in Primitivist painting. It was also a complicated story of artistic and spiritual rebirth, cast in the form of an allegorical journey from civilization to Primitivism. Significantly, Gauguin conceived this project in the form of a dialogue between two diametrically opposite versions of the fin-de-siècle artistic sensibility: the "Primitive self," represented by Gauguin himself; and the "civilized self," represented by his friend, the art critic Charles Morice. Gauguin clarified his fundamental motivations behind this work right after the publication of *Noa Noa* in 1901. "For me, the collaboration had two objectives," he explained to Daniel de Monfried. "It seemed an original idea for me to write with a primitive simplicity, side-by-side with the style of a cultured man—Morice. So I conceived and directed the collaboration with this intention. What is more, not being a professional writer myself, I thought it might tell us a little about the relative value of

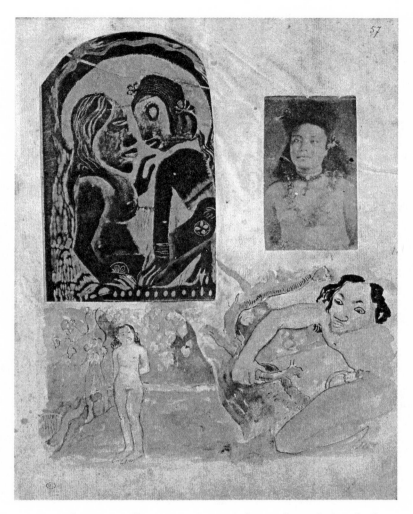

Figure 41. Paul Gauguin, *Album Noa Noa: Hina Tefaton and Hiro (with a photo)*.
Louvre, Paris. Copyright © Réunion des Musées Nationaux/Art Resource,
New York; photo of album page by Gérard Blot.

the two—the naïve clumsy savage or the corrupted [pourri] product of civilization."[28]

The projected coauthorship that was supposed to create the typology of the avant-garde artist out of the juxtaposition of opposites was full of technical complications and unavoidable delays. The final version of *Noa Noa* was published unilaterally by Morice in 1901, without Gauguin's knowledge or permission; a fact that has to some extent damaged the credibility and "authenticity" of the text itself. Yet, as Nicholas Wadley has persuasively argued, Morice's subsequent reputation as the "intrusive ghost-writing partner" who appropriated Gauguin's voice is not quite deserved.[29] The actual text of *Noa Noa* remained more or less faithful to the first draft that Gauguin had given Morice in 1893. More important still, it gave full expression to Gauguin's original intuition that the identity of the avant-garde Primitive should be understood in terms of a fusion of opposites; that it was only through the combined perspectives of the "civilized" European and the "primitive" native that the new kind of artistic sensibility could be legitimately presented.

The opening scene of *Noa Noa* has unmistakable parallels with Picasso's initial experience with the Trocadero Museum. Just as Picasso perceived the ethnographic museum as disappointing and even distasteful, so Gauguin found his first encounter with Papeeta, the capital city of Tahiti, profoundly disenchanting. It is far from coincidental that Gauguin's Tahitian narrative opens with the funeral of King Pomare, the last of the traditional Maori monarchs, an event that supposedly corresponded to his arrival to the island. The death symbolized for Gauguin the disappearance of Maori history and the impossibility of finding an authentic primitive culture in Tahiti. "A profound sadness took possession of me," he wrote. "The dream which has brought me to Tahiti was brutally disappointed by the actuality. It was the Tahiti of former times which I loved. The present filled me with horror."[30] Gauguin was repelled by the arrogance, pretension, and shabbiness of colonial Tahiti, whose leaders he despised and almost immediately antagonized. "Life in Papeeta soon became a burden," he confessed. "It was Europe—the Europe which I had thought to shake off—and under the aggravated circumstances of colonial snobbism, and the imitation, grotesque even to the point of caricature, of our customs, fashions, vices, and absurdities of civilization."[31]

Gauguin's quest for the Primitive began only at the point of realization that the exoticized Primitive of European imagination was either irretrievable or unalterably spoiled by colonial domination. It would lead to the transformation of the very idea of the Primitive from a concrete, ethnographic reality, into a dematerialized, psychological concept. The catalyst in this transmutation was, undoubtedly, a more intimate contact with Maori customs and the beauty of the Tahitian landscape. Gauguin moved away from Papeeta to a relatively uninhabited part of the island, where he assumed the outer life of the Maori. "My neighbors have become my friends," Gauguin wrote with undisguised satisfaction. "I dress like them, and partake of the same food as they. When I am not working, I share their life of indolence and joy, across which sometimes pass sudden moments of gravity."[32] Gauguin even acquired a Tahitian "wife" or *vahina,* who became a conduit to the long-lost tradition of Maori myths and customs that Gauguin had been seeking.[33]

The apparent similarities between Gauguin's and Pierre Loti's Tahitian stories—especially on the point of the "marriages"—cannot be ignored. The frame of exoticized popular fiction was never fully repudiated by the coauthors of *Noa Noa.* The familiar motifs of sexual adventure in a world of Edenic innocence were almost flaunted by them, as the inevitable admission prize for the more complicated story of inner transformation that was to be actually disclosed in the text. As Octave Mirbeau cautioned, *Noa Noa* may have superficially resembled tropical adventure stories, but it was "alive with strange beauties whose existence M. Pierre Loti never even suspected."[34] *Noa Noa,* in fact, both recapitulated and undermined inherited meta-narratives of Primitivist exoticism, and it is this double perspective that explains the complexity and ambiguity of the text itself.

The differences between Gauguin's Primitivist text and Pierre Loti's exoticist narrative become evident on closer view. Indeed, in many respects, they were the direct antithesis of each other. While Loti's exotic vision of Tahiti was essentially a psychological projection that elided all distinction between fantasy and reality, Gauguin's account depicted a process of psychological introjection that depended on the experience of difference and incommensurability. The final outcome of Gauguin's Tahitian sojourn was not nostalgia and escape, but self-purification and self-discovery. The encounter with true difference allowed Gauguin to shed acquired habits and identities that still inhibited inner creativity. Tahiti and the Primitive became an allegory of an inner transformation that was taking place within his psyche. "Civilization is falling from me little by little," Gauguin wrote toward the middle of this pilgrimage. "I am beginning to think simply, to feel only very little hatred for my neighbors—rather, to love him."[35] By the end of his stay, he had become "older by two years, but twenty years younger; more *barbarian* than when I arrived, much wiser."[36]

The final outcome of Gauguin's narrative of artistic rejuvenation was to dissolve all perceptible ties with established discourses of Primitivism based on evolutionary theory or exoticist fantasy. His particular vision of the Primitive could no longer be reduced to a geographic place, cultural condition, or scientific theory. It was characterized by semantic overload, a lack of stable references. Whether identified with "the art of living and happiness," or with the lesson "to know myself better," the Primitive was connected with the "deepest truth" of life, which ultimately could only be approached in the form of a question. "Was this thy secret, thou mysterious world? Oh mysterious world of all light, thou has made a light to shine within me, and I have grown in admiration of thy antique beauty, which is the immense youth of nature."[37]

The purified Primitive that emerged from the combined voices of Gauguin and Morice in *Noa Noa* was a new aesthetic state that, like Picasso's *Les Demoiselles d'Avignon,* had shed the outer casing of the ethnographic Primitive without, however, fully erasing its traces. It gave voice to a new conception of the avant-garde artist, who had been liberated from the invisible shackles of rationality and naturalism and empowered to create radical visions of the modern. Gauguin was remarkably self-conscious of the significance of this achievement. Indeed, he seems to have considered his exemplary act of self-creation in Tahiti to be of potentially greater value for contemporary art than even his painting. Writing to Daniel de Monfreid in 1903, shortly before his death, he summarized this intuition. "You know what I have wanted to establish for so long a time," he claimed. "The *right* to dare everything, my own ability (and the pecuniary difficulties that were too great for such a task) have not resulted in anything very great, but in spite of all that the machine is started. The public owes me nothing, for my work is only relatively good, but the painters of the day, who are now profiting by this enfranchisement, do owe me something."[38]

At least some of Gauguin's contemporaries were aware of the debt that Gauguin referred to in this letter and were capable of interpreting its meaning in terms of the artist's life. In 1907, the relatively unknown literary critic Georg Lukács reviewed *Noa Noa* in a Budapest journal and claimed to discover there "an answer to that very general question: what is the relationship between the modern artist and Life?" Far from considering

Noa Noa an exoticist tale of escape from European modernity, Lukács saw it as a heroic story of artistic reintegration and homecoming. "[A]bove all Tahiti restored Gauguin as a human being," Lukács wrote. "He had found his place in society, no longer an exotic luxury item in the hands of amateur collectors, nor a restless anarchist who threatened public safety. A primitive man pointed out to him—for the first time in his life—that he could produce what no one else could, that he was a useful human being. Gauguin felt he was useful, they loved him and he was happy. This intense sense of happiness and peace of mind permeates his last paintings." "Gauguin has reached his goal," Lukács concluded. "Every artist searches for his own Tahiti, and, other than Gauguin, none have found it, nor are they likely to find it, unless things change so radically that anyone can anywhere conjure up his imaginary Tahiti."[39] In a relatively brief space, Lukács was able to give concentrated expression to the essential feature of the modernist Primitive. Rather than being about exoticist escape or colonial adventure, he suggested, Gauguin's Tahitian sojourn was about the modern artist's search for relevance and usefulness in the modern world.

Lukács was not the only contemporary to become fascinated by Gauguin's self-creation as the modern Primitive. Probably the most theoretically sustained analysis of the implication of Gauguin's persona was to come from a young naval doctor with literary ambitions, Victor Segalen. Arriving to the Marquesas only three months after the painter's death, Segalen became Gauguin's "unofficial literary executor and posthumous apologist."[40] In a certain sense, however, he also constituted himself as Gauguin's alter ego, continuing to explore through his own experiences in Tahiti and later in China, the problem of exoticism and its relationship to modernism.

Segalen, a friend of Joris Huysmans, was well-situated to understand and explicate the broader implications of Gauguin's experimental life. In a Preface to the painter's letters published in 1916, Segalen claimed to discover in Gauguin's Tahitian exile "the eternal problem of the artist living in society." In contrast with Huysmans, who was able to create a relatively sheltered space for his art in Paris, Gauguin had to reinvent his ties to the modern world outside of France. His trip to Tahiti, Segalen concluded, may have been motivated by "the basest of domestic calculations—a cheaper way of life—but he received there the highest prize that any artist could have from a jury: the disclosure of his vocation."[41]

Segalen's enduring contribution to the problem of modern Primitivism was, however, his fragmentary *Essay on Exoticism,* which he began in 1908 and left unfinished at the time of his death in 1919. In this prolonged philosophic and aesthetic meditation on the nature of exoticism, Segalen explored and clarified some of the central issues that remained only implicit or partially acknowledged in the avant-garde practices of the prewar years. Segalen's reinterpretation revolved around the necessity of distinguishing between two different versions of exoticism: what he called a "future exoticism" and a "past exoticism."[42] This was to be, he wrote, a Herculean task of purification that required the destruction of all established associations with the word. "Throw overboard everything misused or rancid contained in the word exoticism," he demanded. "Strip it of all its cheap finery: palm tree and camel; tropical helmet; black skin and yellow sun; and, at the same time, get rid of all those who use it with an inane loquaciousness. My study will not be about the Bonnetains or Ajalberts of this world, nor about travel agents like Cook, nor about hurried and verbose travelers."[43]

Segalen intentionally avoided the word Primitive in references to the new ideal type he was trying to define and rescue from its hackneyed association with popular exoticism. He preferred the neologism *exot,* precisely because of the need to preserve the creative tensions and ambiguities inherent in the very concept of exoticism. The *exot,* stripped of his "cheap finery," and his "exclusively tropical, exclusively geographic meaning,"[44] was, as Segalen realized, only an abstraction. Juxtaposed, however, with its popular "Others" and reintegrated within contemporary discourses of exoticism, it became charged with negative energy that was itself a source of creative identity for the artist. Segalen's sensitivity to contexts and his uncanny ability to distill meaning from the popular linked him to his nineteenth-century bohemian prototypes, who had also insisted on reintegrating the avant-garde artist within the forms of popular culture.

It is thus not surprising that Segalen's method of conceptualizing the *exot* had striking parallels with the constructions of the flâneur in nineteenth-century physiologies and feuilletons. Just as the flâneur could only be defined in juxtaposition to the *badaud* (idler) and other problematic urban types who inhabited the nineteenth-century city; so the *exot* could only be imagined in opposition to the numerous false exoticists who emerged in a colonized and Europeanized global culture. There were, in fact, several versions of false *exots,* whom Segalen invoked as foils for the true *exots* of avant-garde culture: the tourist, the colonial administrator, and the bureaucrat.

The ordinary tourist, either in his guise as consumer of exoticist literature or as an actual traveler to foreign lands, was characterized by the inability to perceive the true meaning of the world he encountered. He was a "mediocre spectator," whose "kaleidoscopic vision" was unresponsive to the genuine strangeness and difference of others, and who inevitably projected his own emotions and attitudes onto others. Perfectly exemplified by the exoticized romanticism of Loti, such vicarious tourists "are mystically drunk with and unconscious of their object. They confuse it with themselves and passionately intermingle with it."[45]

The other doubles of the *exot* with whom he was likely to be confused were the colonial administrator and the bureaucrat. Like the ordinary tourist, these colonial types were also constitutionally incapable of perceiving the unique characteristics of others. The distinction between the tourist and the colonist lay in the nature of the self-created images that they projected onto the scenes they encountered. While the tourist saw the world through escapist fantasies, the colonist tended to create hegemonic constructs. "For the colonial," Segalen illustrated, "Diversity exists only in so far as it provides him with the means of duping others. As for the colonial bureaucrat, the very notion of a centralized administration and of laws for the good of everyone, which he *must* enforce, immediately distorts his judgment and renders him deaf to the *disharmonies* (or harmonies of Diversity). Neither of these figures can boast a sense of aesthetic contemplation."[46]

In contrast to these false observers of difference, the true *exots* were born travelers who were sensitive to the full wonder of the world they observed. "They are the ones," wrote Segalen, "who will recognize, beneath the cold and dry veneer of words and phrases, those unforgettable transports which arise from the kind of moments I have been speaking of: the moment of Exoticism."[47] The "moment of Exoticism," as Segalen entitled the transformative experience of "Otherness" that he was struggling to capture, meant literally reversing the perspective of the popular exoticist. "So, not Loti, nor Saint-Pol-Roux, nor Claudel," he meditated. "Something else! Something different from what they have done! . . . Why actually should I not *simply* take the *opposing view* from those views I am defending myself against? Why not strive to *counter-prove* their findings?"[48]

This "opposing view" that Segalen referred to was, in fact, a shift from the European to the native perspective. Curiously, the act of true identification with the Other resulted, not in homogenization and fusion; but, on the contrary, in greater differentiation and individuation. As was the case with Gauguin's experience in Tahiti and Picasso's epiphanic moment in the Trocadero Museum, Segalen's "moment of Exoticism" was a transformative experience that resulted in the creation of something new. The shift "from the traveler to the object of his gaze," he explained, "rebounds and makes what he sees vibrate."[49]

Redefined as the self capable of experiencing novelty, difference, excitement; the *exot* could be repatriated to Europe. Indeed, as Segalen admitted, the *exot* had never really left Europe and was indistinguishable from the creative artist. It was "from the depth of his own clump of patriarchal soil, [that the *exot*] calls to, desires, sniffs out those beyond. But in inhabiting them, savoring them, the clump of earth, the soil, suddenly and powerfully becomes *Diverse*. This double-edged balancing game results in an unflagging, inexhaustible diversity."[50] The inevitable consequence of Segalen's identification of "exoticism" with "diversity" was to bring back the exotic within the spaces of modernity. Divested of its "cheap finery," the exotic turned out to be "everything that until now was called foreign, strange, unexpected, surprising, mysterious, amorous, superhuman, heroic, and even divine, everything that is *Other*."[51]

With this realization, Segalen abolished the very subject of his investigation, collapsing back the phenomenon of the exotic within the phenomenon of avant-garde innovation and artistic renewal. Segalen himself had foreseen the possibility of this fusion. As he wrote to a friend in 1908, his projected work on exoticism was to be closely intertwined with the problems of modernist aesthetics. "As the *Soirées de Médan* did for naturalism," he explained, "this work will reveal the existence, not so much of a school or a group but of a sincere and fecund exotic moment."[52]

The "exotic moment" that Segalen had foreseen and attempted to theorize was to be a seemingly brief episode, whose traces were already fading by the years immediately preceding World War I. Apollinaire's aesthetic manifesto of 1913, *The Cubist Painters,* had only one passing reference to Primitivism, and even that was in connection with the technical discovery of a "fourth dimension" of space that allowed the new painters to transcend the limits of mimetic representation. It was, he declared, the contemplation of "Egyptian, negro, and oceanic sculptures," and the meditation on "various scientific works" that gave these artists a premonition of a new kind of "sublime art."[53] By 1920 Jean Cocteau considered Primitivism to be entirely of the past, declaring that "the Negro crisis has become as boring as Mallarméan *japonisme*."[54]

Primitivism as a flamboyant aesthetic gesture, self-consciously assumed by the avant-garde artist in relationship to a conformist public, was certainly a transient phenomenon that did not last beyond the war years. Indeed, it could be argued that the Primitivists were the last of the urban performers still associated with the public spaces of the modern city. They were, however, also the pioneers of a new conception of the modern that was to survive well into the 1920s and beyond. The sites of twentieth-century modernism they helped map out were to be abstract, shifting, and multiple, like the culture itself to which they gave expression. The new spaces of aesthetic modernity would be located in the unconscious of Freudian theory, in the automatism of Surrealist writing, in the improvisation of American jazz, and in the abstraction of nonrepresentational art. Though fragmented and seemingly unrelated to each other, these avant-garde practices did not lose all traces of their affinities with prewar Primitivism. Indeed, the image of the Primitive would repeatedly be invoked in connection with the twentieth-century avant-garde, whose characteristic products were often conceived in terms of a fusion between the ultra-modern and the Primitive. As Le Corbusier put it in connection with American jazz, the music combined scientific precision and primitivist emotion; it was "the melody of the soul joined with the rhythm of the machine."[55]

The continuities between the avant-gardes of the 1920s and their predecessors had deeper historical roots than this, however. Indeed, the conversation between avant-garde art and popular culture that constituted the core of popular bohemia was to continue in a more direct and explicit form in the twentieth century than in the nineteenth. A hundred years after the Jeunes France paraded through the streets of Paris in the exotic costumes of the melodrama, the surrealists were to discover in American popular cinema their own version of the marvelous in the midst of the modern. Philippe Soupault recounted this transformative experience in a fable of collective aesthetic renewal that began with the familiar tension between the "intense lives" of young artists and the banality of everyday existence. "We walked the cold and deserted streets," Soupault recalled, "seeking an accidental, a sudden, meeting with life." A chance encounter with an advertising poster for an American film was the epiphanic event that revealed to them the hidden mystery of modern life. The poster, depicting a masked man with a revolver pointing straight at the observer, liberated their slumbering imaginations and conveyed to them the sound of "galloping hoofs, the roar of motors, explosions, and cries of death."

We rushed into the cinema and realized immediately that everything had changed. On the screen appeared the smile of Pearl White—that almost ferocious smile which announced the revolution, the beginning of a new world. At last we knew that the cinema was not merely a perfected mechanical toy, but a terrible and magnificent reflection of life . . . The American cinema brought to light all the beauty of our epoch, and all the mystery of modern mechanics. But it was done so simply, so naturally, so unaffectedly, that one scarcely noticed. It was, however, one of the greatest and most important of artistic discoveries. It created at one blow a new world.[56]

The bohemian themes that Soupault gave voice to in this testimonial were not restricted to the surrealists of the 1920s. They would be echoed in various forms and combinations by the Beat generation of the 1950s, the counterculture of the 1960s, and even by elements of postmodernism in the 1980s. In spite of obvious continuities, however, the exact relationship between twentieth-century experimental culture and nineteenth-century bohemia remains deeply ambiguous. Historians and cultural critics have acknowledged the ongoing appeal of bohemia, yet they have also insisted on the impossibility of the bohemian project in the twentieth century. According to Jerrold Seigel, the "ground of Bohemian life seems to have slipped away" and the "free spaces—both real and metaphorical—once occupied by Bohemia have become narrower and harder to find."[57] In a less nostalgic mode, Elizabeth Wilson has compared the bohemian role to "an old fashioned frock" that has become too quaint to wear. "Although it still has a certain musty charm," she admitted, "it must be relegated . . . to the museum of ideas to which all good cultural phenomena go when they die."[58]

The decline of bohemia as a distinct cultural space and a radical identity has generally been attributed to its loss of autonomy in the twentieth century. Historical explanations about the causes of this development have varied greatly, depending on the political and ideological outlook of historians. Some have linked the crisis of bohemia with the rise of the consumer society that erased the boundaries between bohemian values and mainstream culture. Others have pointed to the politicization of everyday life after World War I that destroyed a leisured way of life. Still others have stressed the decline of revolutionary utopias with the rise of the Cold War after World War II. The underlying assumption in all these explanations, however, has been that the fate of bohemia was inextricably linked to traditional bourgeois culture and could not survive its demise. Bohemia, wrote Jerrold Seigel, corresponded "to the classic phase in the history of modern bourgeois society that extended between the French Revolution and the First World War."[59]

The dissolution of nineteenth-century bourgeois society, and with it, the boundaries of "classic Bohemia" have had unforeseen consequences, however. The process unquestionably rendered anachronistic the kind of bohemian subcultures whose prototype was depicted in Henry Murger' *Scènes de la vie de bohème* in the middle of the nineteenth century. But it also made visible the contours of a different kind of bohemia, more unstable, more paradoxical, more transgressive, that always existed in the shadow of "classic Bohemia" but was rarely thematized independently of it. Ironic or popular bohemia, as I have called this other bohemia, never subscribed to the myth of autonomy, whether applied to the self, to society, or to the work of art. It rejected all stable aesthetic truths or moral absolutes as incompatible with the unprecedented experiences of modernity. Yet, it also postulated the possibility of heroism in the modern world, based on acceptance rather than rejection of the flux and contingency of modern life. Far from declining in the twentieth century, this ironic bohemia, with its complex strategies of parody and aesthetic doubling, has become the dominant formula for personal freedom and artistic creativity in the modern world.

Notes

1. The Historical Bohemian

1. For a discussion of the historical differentiation of the concepts of the "modern" and the "contemporary" see Matei Calinescu, *Five Faces of Modernity: Modernism, Avant-Garde, Decadence, Kitsch, Postmodernism* (Durham: Duke University Press, 1987), 86–92.

2. See Albert Cassagne, *La Théorie de l'art pour l'art en France chez les derniers romantiques et les premiers réalistes* (1905; Paris: Lucien Dorbon, 1959); also Gene H. Bell-Villada, *Art for Art's Sake and Literary Life: How Politics and Markets Helped Shape the Ideology and Culture of Aestheticism, 1790–1990* (Lincoln: University of Nebraska Press, 1996).

3. This complex development that essentially transferred the power to define modernist aesthetics from the academy to popular culture was already remarked upon by Wilhelm Dilthey. In an essay of 1887, entitled "The Imagination of the Poet: Elements for a Poetics," he pronounced the death of formal aesthetic theory as a relevant factor in contemporary artistic life. "Our German aesthetics does indeed still survive in some universities," he admitted, "but no longer in the consciousness of the leading artists and critics where it should live above all . . . Since the French Revolution a new poetry current in London and Paris has attracted the interest of poets and public alike. As soon as Dickens and Balzac began to write the epic of modern life as found in these cities, the basic poetic principles once debated by Schiller, Goethe, and Humbolt in idyllic Weimar became irrelevant." Five years later, in "The Three Epochs of Modern Aesthetics and Its Present Task," Dilthey returned to the same problem, pointing to the central role that artists and critics had taken in the definition of the meaning of their own artistic practices. "We do not need to build up aesthetics anew," he wrote here. "For the artists themselves have already found it necessary to inquire into the true nature and means of the particular arts; they have had to create aesthetic principles for themselves. The aesthetics of our century must be sought elsewhere than in compendia and thick textbooks." Wilhelm Dilthey, *Poetry and*

Experience, ed. and intr. Rudolf A. Makkreel and Frithjof Rodi (Princeton, N.J.: Princeton University Press, 1985), 30–31, 179.

4. E. P. Thompson, *The Making of the English Working Classes* (New York: Vintage Books, 1966), 12.

5. In contrast to theorists of the "historic avant-garde," who have postulated a fundamental breach between modernism and the avant-garde, I will be using these terms as continuous phenomena associated with the ongoing aesthetic project of modernity. For definitions of the historic avant-garde, see Peter Bürger, *Theory of the Avant-Garde,* trans. Michael Shaw, forward Jochen Schulte-Sasse (Minneapolis: University of Minnesota Press, 1984); and Andreas Huyssen, *After the Great Divide: Modernism, Mass Culture, Postmodernism* (Bloomington: Indiana University Press, 1986). For arguments of continuity between modernism and the avant-garde, see Renato Poggioli, *The Theory of the Avant-Garde,* trans. Gerald Fitzgerald (Cambridge, Mass.: Harvard University Press, 1968); and Calinescu, *Five Faces of Modernity.*

6. Fredric Jameson, *A Singular Modernity: Essay on the Ontology of the Present* (London: Verso, 2002), 1.

7. Catherine Gallagher and Stephen Greenblatt, *Practicing New Historicism* (Chicago: University of Chicago Press, 2000), 8, 9.

8. Thomas Crow, "Modernism and Mass Culture in the Visual Arts," in *Modernism and Modernity: The Vancouver Conference Papers* (Halifax: Press of the Nova Scotia College of Art and Design, 1983), 215.

9. Kirk Varnedoe and Adam Gopnik, "Introduction," *High and Low: Modern Art and Popular Culture* (New York: Museum of Modern Art; Distributed by Harry N. Abrams, Inc., New York, 1990), 19.

10. Andreas Huyssen, *After the Great Divide,* vii.

11. Ibid., ix.

12. Calinescu, *Five Faces of Modernity,* 5.

13. Charles Taylor, *Sources of the Self: The Making of the Modern Identity* (Cambridge, Mass.: Harvard University Press, 1989), 422.

14. Pierre Bourdieu, *The Rules of Art: Genesis and Structure of the Literary Field,* trans. Susan Emanuel (Stanford, Calif.: Stanford University Press, 1995), 48.

15. Pierre Bourdieu, "Flaubert's Point of View," trans. Priscilla Parkhurst Ferguson, *Critical Inquiry,* 14, no. 3 (Spring 1988), 553 and 551.

16. See David S. Luft, *Robert Musil and the Crisis of European Culture, 1880–1942* (Berkeley: University of California Press, 1980); William J. McGrath, *Freud's Discovery of Psychoanalysis: The Politics of Hysteria* (Ithaca: Cornell University Press, 1986); Mary Gluck, *Georg Lukács and His Generation, 1900–1918* (Cambridge, Mass.: Harvard University Press, 1985); Debora L. Silverman, *Art Nouveau in Fin-de-Siècle France: Politics, Psychology, and Style* (Berkeley: University of California Press, 1989); Michael P. Steinberg, *The Meaning of the*

Salzburg Festival: Austria as Theater and Ideology, 1890–1938 (Ithaca: Cornell University Press, 1900).

17. Carl E. Schorske, *Thinking with History: Explorations in the Passage to Modernism* (Princeton, N.J.: Princeton University Press, 1998), 3.

18. Ibid., 4.

19. Ibid.

20. Silverman, *Art Nouveau in Fin-de-Siècle France,* 10.

21. Jürgen Habermas, *The Philosophic Discourse of Modernity: Twelve Lectures,* trans. Frederick Lawrence (Cambridge, Mass.: MIT Press, 1987).

22. David Frisby, *Fragments of Modernity: Theories of Modernity in the Work of Simmel, Kacauer and Benjamin* (Cambridge, Mass.: MIT Press, 1986), 1.

23. Scott Lash and Jonathan Friedman, "Introduction," in *Modernity and Identity,* ed. Scott Lash and Jonathan Friedman (Oxford: Blackwell, 1992), 2.

24. Calinescu, *Five Faces of Modernity,* 41.

25. Marshall Berman, "Why Modernism Still Matters," in *Modernity and Identity,* 33. See also Marshall Berman, *All That Is Solid Melts into Air: The Experience of Modernity* (New York: Simon and Schuster, 1982).

26. Walter Benjamin, *Charles Baudelaire: A Lyric Poet in the Era of High Capitalism* (London: Verso, 1983), 34.

27. Elizabeth Wilson, *Bohemians: The Glamorous Outcasts* (New Brunswick, N.J.: Rutgers University Press, 2000), 2.

28. Jerrold Seigel, *Bohemian Paris: Culture, Politics, and the Boundaries of Bourgeois Life, 1830–1930* (New York: Penguin Books, 1986), 12.

29. Ibid., 11.

30. Wilson, *Bohemians: The Glamorous Outcasts,* 24.

31. Seigel, *Bohemian Paris,* 295.

32. Wilson, *Bohemians: The Glamorous Outcasts,* 241.

33. *Le Charivari* (28 June 1848) in Loys Delteil, *Le Peintre-Graveur Illustre* (XIXe et XXe siècle), vol. 22: *Honoré Daumier, III* (Paris: Chez l'Auteur, 1926).

34. Wilson, *Bohemians: The Glamorous Outcasts,* 6.

35. Sainte-Beuve, *Nouveaux Lundis* (1866), quoted in Henry Murger, *Scènes de la vie de bohème,* intro. Loïc Chotard (Paris: Gallimard, 1988), 9.

36. Murger, *Scènes de la vie de bohème,* 26.

37. Ibid., 7.

38. Ibid., 9–10.

39. Murger, *Scènes de la vie de bohème,* 7–9.

40. Wilson, *Bohemians: The Glamorous Outcasts,* 240.

41. Murger, *Scènes de la vie de bohème,* 148–149.

42. Seigel, *Bohemian Paris,* 5.

43. Théophile Gautier, *Les Jeunes France: Romans goguenards,* intr. René Jainski (Paris: Flammarion, 1974), 25–26.

44. Ibid., 34.
45. Ibid., 35.
46. Richard Terdiman, *Discourse/Counter-Discourse: The Theory and Practice of Symbolic Resistance in Nineteenth-Century France* (Ithaca: Cornell University Press, 1985), 13.
47. See Linda Hutcheon, *A Theory of Parody: The Teachings of Twentieth-Century Art Forms* (Urbana: University of Illinois Press, 2000).

2. The Romantic Bohemian

1. See Jürgen Habermas, *The Structural Transformation of the Public Sphere: An Inquiry into a Category of Bourgeois Society* trans Thomas Burger with Frederick Lawrence (Cambridge, Mass.: MIT Press, 1989); and Richard Sennett, *The Fall of Public Man* (New York: W. W. Norton, 1974).
2. See Bruce Robbins, ed. *The Phantom Public Sphere* (Minneapolis, Minn.: University of Minnesota Press, 1993).
3. Sennett, *The Fall of Public Man,* 34–35.
4. There are many accounts of the "Battle of *Hernani*" that have served to reinforce the legendary quality of the event. See Orlo Williams, *Vie de Bohème: A Patch of Romantic Paris* (London: Martin Seckler, 1913); Malcolm Easton, *Artists and Writers in Paris: The Bohemian Idea, 1830–1867* (New York: St. Martin's Press, 1960); J. B. Priestly, *Literature and Western Man* (New York: Harper, 1960); René Jasinski, *Les années romantiques de Th. Gautier* (Paris: Librairie Vuibert, 1929).
5. For the reception of "Hernani," see Fernande Bassan, "La réception critique d'Hernani de Victor Hugo" in *Revue d'Histoire du Théâtre* 1984, vol. 36 (I).
6. The following account is based largely on Victor Hugo's own memoirs, "Victor Hugo raconté par un témoin de sa vie" in Victor Hugo, *Hernani, Ruy Blas: Suivi de la Bataille d'Hernani racontée par ses témoins* (Paris: Gallimard et Librairie Générale Française, 1969).
7. The excerpt from *La Quotidienne* is quoted in the text of "Victor Hugo raconté par un témoin de sa vie," Victor Hugo, *Hernani, Ruy Blas,* 459.
8. "Victor Hugo raconté par un témoin de sa vie," 456.
9. *La Gazette de France* 27 February 1830, in *Hernani, Ruy Blas* 518.
10. According to F. W. J. Hemmings, the scandal surrounding "Hernani" secured financial success not only for the author but also for the Comédie-Française. " 'Hernani' was, financially, a badly needed shot in the arm for the company, and its members did not mind contending with unruly audiences when the figures for receipts were so cheering: 12,000 francs netted from the first three performances had grown to 40,000 by the ninth and 76,000 by the nineteenth, which took place on 5 April." *Culture and Society in France, 1789–1848* (London: Peter Lang Publishing, Inc., 1987), 230.

11. Théophile Gautier, *La Presse* 22 January 1838, in *Hernani, Ruy Blas* 525.

12. Théophile Gautier, *Histoire du romantisme* (Paris: Les Introuvables, 1993), 79.

13. Ibid., 6.

14. See [Leo Gozlan] "Les Jeunes Frances," *Le Figaro* 30 (August 1831).

15. For a discussion of the symbolic role of costumes in culture see Elizabeth Wilson, *Adorned in Dreams: Fashion and Modernity* (London: Virago, 1985); and Amy de la Haye and Elizabeth Wilson, eds. *Defining Dress: Dress as Object, Meaning and Identity* (Manchester and New York: Manchester University Press, 1999).

16. "Victor Hugo raconté par un témoin de sa vie," *Hernani, Ruy Blas* 460.

17. Gautier, *Histoire du romantisme* 79.

18. Ibid., 77.

19. Although I use the concept of generations only implicitly in this study, it is noteworthy that the early nineteenth century saw the crystallization of cohorts of young people who were united by common cultural and ideological concerns. For the treatment of a slightly earlier phenomenon than I am concerned with, see Alan B. Spitzer, *The French Generation of 1820* (Princeton, N.J.: Princeton University Press, 1987).

20. Delecluze, "Les Barbus d'à présent et les barbus de MDCCC" in *Paris ou le livre des cent-et-un* (Paris: Chez Ladvocat, Libraire, 1832).

21. See Louis Maigron, *Le Romantisme et la mode, D'Après des documents inédits* (Paris: Librairie Ancienne Honoré Champion, 1911), 51–60.

22. Arsène Houssaye, *Man About Paris: The Confessions of Arsène Houssaye* trans. and ed. Henry Knepler (New York, 1970), 32.

23. Frances Trollope, *Paris and the Parisians in 1835* (2 vols.) (London: Richard Bentley, New Burlington St., 1836), I, 14.

24. Quoted in Louis Maigron, *Le Romantisme et la mode*, 65.

25. Elias Regnault, "L'Homme de lettre," in *Les Français peints par eux-mêmes* Vol. IV (Paris: L. Curmer, 1842), 226.

26. *Ibid.,* 226.

27. See in partiuclar Georg Lukács, *The Historical Novel* trans. Hannah and Stanley Mitchell, intr. Fredric Jameson (Lincoln: University of Nebraska Press, 1962), 19–27.

28. See Albert Joseph George, *Short Fiction in France, 1800–1850* (Syracuse, N.Y.: Syracuse University Press, 1964).

29. Houssaye, *Man About Paris,* 32.

30. Quoted in Louis Maigron, *Le Romantisme et la mode,* 54.

31. Gautier, *Histoire du romantisme,* 79.

32. For an account of these early bohemians, see George Levitine, *The Dawn of Bohemianism: The Barbu Rebellion and Primitivism in Neoclassical France* (University Park and London: Pennsylvania State University Press, 1978).

33. In 1832, both writers published journalistic accounts of the *Barbus.* See

Charles Nodier, "Les Barbus," *Le Temps* 5 October, 1832 and Etienne-Jean Delecluze, "Les Barbus d'à présent et les barbus de MDCCC."

34. Levitine, *The Dawn of Bohemianism*, 68.

35. Delecluze, "Les Barbus d'à présent et les barbus de MDCCC," 85.

36. Dick Hebdige, *Subculture: The Meaning of Style* (London and New York: Routledge, 1979) 80, 91, 92.

37. Jerrold Seigel, *Bohemian Paris: Culture, Politics, and the Boundaries of Bourgeois Life, 1830–1930* (New York: Penguin Books, 1986).

38. Gautier, *Histoire du romantisme* 83.

39. Sainte-Beuve, "De la littérature industrielle," *Revue des deux mondes* IV, no. 19, 1839, 676.

40. Ibid., 691.

41. Victor Hugo, *Préface de Cromwell,* intro. Michel Cambien (Paris: Librairie Larousse, 1971), 45–46.

42. See F. W. J. Hemmings, *Culture and Society in France 1789–1848* (New York: Peter Lang Publishing, Inc. 1987); Albert Joseph George, *The Development of French Romanticism: the Impact of the Industrial Literature on Literature* (Syracuse, N.Y.: Syracuse University Press, 1955); and James Smith Allen, *Popular French Romanticism: Authors, Readers, and Books in the Nineteenth Century* (Syracuse, N.Y.: Syracuse University Press, 1981).

43. Quoted in Hemmings, *Culture and Society in France 1789–1848,* 244.

44. For a description of the development of nineteenth-century newspaper culture in Paris, see Hemmings, *Culture and Society in France 1789–1848;* Richard Terdiman, *Discourse/Counter-Discourse: The Theory and Practice of Symbolic Resistance in Nineteenth-Century France* (Ithaca and London: Cornell University Press, 1985); Walter Benjamin, *Charles Baudelaire: A Lyric Poet in The Era of High Capitalism* (London and New York: Verso, 1997), and Dean de la Motte & Jeannene M. Przyblyski, *Making the News: Modernity and the Mass Press in Nineteenth-Century France* (Amherst: University of Massachusetts Press, 1999).

45. Désiré Nisard, "D'un commencement de réaction contre la littérature facile," *La Revue de Paris* (December 1833), in Richard Bolster ed., *Documents littéraires de l'époque romantique* (Paris: Lettres Modernes/Minard, 1983), 83.

46. Sainte-Beuve, "La littérature industrielle," 678.

47. Nisard, "D'un commencement de réaction contre la littérature facile," 91.

48. Sainte-Beuve, "La littérature industrielle," 680–81.

49. Ibid., 678.

50. See Albert Cassagne, *La théorie de l'art pour l'art en France chez les derniers romantiques et les premiers réalistes* (1905; Paris: Lucien Dorbon, 1959).

51. Jules Janin, "Manifeste de la jeune littérature, Réponse à M. Nisard," *La Revue de Paris* (January 1834), in Richard Bolster, ed., *Documents littéraire de l'époque romantique.*

52. Ibid., 121.
53. Ibid.
54. Ibid., 122.
55. The actual event that triggered the writing of the Preface was a controversy that Gautier found himself in during the spring and summer of 1834. The incident, trivial enough by itself, was symptomatic of the accelerated cultural power struggles of the time. In early 1834, Gautier had written an article about the medieval poet François Villon, as part of a series on France's less well-known poets, commissioned by the journal *La France littéraire*. Almost immediately after the publication of the Villon article, Gautier and *La France littéraire* found themselves under attack by a rival journalist from *Le Constitutionnel,* who accused them of helping to spread immorality by publicizing the work of a debauched and disreputable author. The journalistic polemic was followed in the summer of 1834 by a libel suit between the rival newspapers. The fact that *La France littéraire* lost the lawsuit galled Gautier, who used the Preface as a forum for rebutting and satirizing his opponents. See René Jasinski, *Les années romantiques de Th. Gautier.*
56. See Théophile Gautier, Préface, *Mademoiselle de Maupin* texte complet. 1835 [Texte établie avec introd. et notes par Adolphe Boschot] (Paris: Garnier Frères, 1966).
57. For English translation, see Théophile Gautier, *Mademoiselle de Maupin* trans. and intr. Joanna Richardson (New York: Penguin Books, 1981), 39.
58. For a traditional reading of the Preface to *Mademoiselle de Maupin,* see Matei Calinescu, *The Five Faces of Modernity* 45.
59. Sainte-Beuve, "La littérature industrielle," 691.
60. The melodrama has moved to the forefront of literary and critical debates during the past two decades since the publication of Peter Brooks' groundbreaking *The Melodramatic Imagination.* This recent body of research has essentially transformed the image of the melodrama from a vulgarized and unsophisticated popular genre into the essential prototype of all later forms of modern popular culture, including the novel. I am particularly indebted to these recent interpretations of the melodrama. See in particular, Peter Brooks, *The Melodramatic Imagination: Balzac, Henry James, Melodrama, and the Mode of Excess* (New Haven, Conn.: Yale University Press, 1976); John G. Cawelti, *Adventure, Mystery, and Romance: Formula Stories as Art and Popular Culture* (Chicago: University of Chicago Press, 1976); Julia Pryzbos, *L'Entreprise mélodramatique* (Paris: Librairie Jose Corti, 1987); Jean-Marie Thomasseau, *Le Mélodrame* (Paris: Presses Universitaire de France, 1984); Michael Hays and Anastasia Nikolopoulou, *Melodrama: the Cultural Emergence of a Genre* (New York: St. Martin's Press, 1996); Robert Bechtold Heilman, *Tragedy and Melodrama: Visions of Experience* (Seattle: University of

Washington Press, 1968); David Bradby, Louis James, Bernard Sharratt, eds. *Performance and Politics in Popular Drama: Aspects of Popular Entertainment in Theatre, Film and Television, 1800–1976* (New York: Cambridge University Press, 1980).

61. Théophile Gautier, "Porte-Saint-Martin, *La Juive de Constantine*," *Histoire de l'art dramatique en France depuis vingt-cinq ans* IV, 356.
62. Hugo, *Préface de Cromwell*, 29.
63. MM. A!A!A!, *Traité du mélodrame* (Paris, 1817), 4.
64. Ibid., 41.
65. Ibid., 7.
66. Peter Brooks, *The Melodramatic Imagination*, 13–14.
67. *Traité du mélodrame*, 9.
68. Ibid., 14.
69. Ibid., 10.
70. Ibid., 72.
71. Théophile Gautier, "Porte-Saint-Martin, *La Juive de Constantine*," *Histoire de l'art dramatique en France depuis vingt-cinq ans,* IV, 359–360.
72. *Figaro,* 8 February 1831.
73. Frances Trollope, *Paris and the Parisians (1835)* (New York: Alan Sutton, Gloucester, Hippocrane Books, Inc., 1985), 64.
74. Jules Janin, *The American in Paris* (London: Longman, Brown, Green, and Longman, 1843), 211.
75. Ibid., 211.
76. Ibid., 203.
77. *La Caricature* 14 July 1831, No. 37.
78. Lady Sydney Morgan, *France in 1829–30*, 2 vols. (London: Saunders and Otley, 1831), II, 97.
79. Janin, *The American in Paris*, 207.
80. Brander Matthews, *French Dramatists of the Nineteenth Century* (1881) (New York and London: Benjamin Blom, 1901), 84.
81. Janin, *The American in Paris,* 206.
82. Lady Morgan, *France in 1829–30*, II, 68.
83. Ibid., II, 70–71.
84. Janin, *The American in Paris,* 208.
85. See Louis Maigron, *Le Romantisme et la mode.*
86. Although the articles were published anonymously, it is almost certain that the author was the popular journalist Leo Gozlan, who had been associated with Gautier's circle and remained a friend of Balzac's.
87. "Les Jeunes Frances" *Le Figaro* 30 August 1831.
88. Ibid.
89. "Ameublement des Jeunes Frances" *Le Figaro* 12 September 1831.

90. "Le Festin des Jeunes Frances" *Le Figaro* 10 September 1831.

91. Théophile Gautier, *Les Jeunes France; roman goguenards* (Paris: Editions des Autres, 1979), 69.

92. Ibid.

93. Théophile Gautier, "Celle-ci et celle-là," *Les Jeunes France* 149.

94. Ibid., 161.

95. Beryl Schlossman, *The Orient of Style: Modernist Allegories of Conversion* (Durham and London: Duke University Press, 1991), 1.

96. For an account of Gautier's posthumous reputation as art critic, see James Kearns, "On his Knees to the Past? Gautier, Ingres and Forms of Modern Art," in *Impressions of French Modernity: Art and Literature in France, 1850–1900* ed. Richard Hobbs (Manchester, UK; New York: Manchester University Press, 1998).

97. Gautier's two identities were apparently so well insulated from each other, that even Mme. de Girardin, the wife of his editor, displayed astonishment on the occasion of the publication of Gautier's book of verses, *La comédie de la mort:* "What! Théophile Gautier a poet!" she supposedly exclaimed. "This prince of mockers, this master of irony, this great iconoclast, is also a dreamer of cascades, a melancholy inhabitant of the floating kingdom of clouds." In Joanna Richardson, *Théophile Gautier: His Life and Times* (London: M. Reinhardt, 1958), 38.

98. Between 1851, when the definitive edition of *Mademoiselle de Maupin* was published, and 1877, the novel was reprinted thirteen times. In 1877, a new edition appeared and by 1883 this had been reprinted nine times. For the fate of the novel in the late-nineteenth century, see Jean Pierrot, *The Decadent Imagination 1880–1900* trans. Derek Coltman (Chicago and London: University of Chicago Press, 1981), 43.

99. Théophile Gautier, "Port-Saint-Martin, *La Juive de Constantine,*" *Histoire de l'art dramatique en France depuis vingt-cinq ans,* IV, 356–357.

100. René Jasinski, *Les années romantiques de Th. Gautier,* 289.

101. See Jean-Marie Roulin, "Confusion des sexes, mélange des genres et quête du sens dans *Mademoiselle de Maupin*" in *Romantisme: Revue du dix-neuvième siècle* no. 103 (1999), 31–40.

102. Gautier, *Mademoiselle de Maupin,* 330.

103. The association between androgyny and modernism has frequently been made. See Walter Benjamin, *Charles Baudelaire: A Lyric Poet in the Era of High Capitalism;* Rita Felski, *The Gender of Modernity* (Cambridge, Mass.: Harvard University Press, 1995); Kari Weil, *Androgyny and the Denial of Difference* (Charlottesville and London: University Press of Virginia, 1992). See also Marjorie Garber, *Vested Interests: Cross-Dressing and Cultural Anxiety* (New York: Routledge, 1992); and Julia Epstein and Kristina Straub, eds. *Body*

Guards: The Cultural Politics of Gender Ambiguity (New York and London: Routledge, 1991).

104. For the first interpretation, see Matei Calinescu, *Five Faces of Modernity;* for the second, Pierre Bourdieu, *The Rules of Art: Genesis and Structure of the Literary Field.*

105. See Ralph Flores, *A Study of Allegory in Its Historical Context and Relationship to Contemporary Theory* (Lewiston, Queenston, Lamperer: Edwin Mellon Press, 1996).

106. Gautier, Preface to *Mademoiselle de Maupin,* 52.

107. Ibid., 53.

108. Ibid.

3. The Flâneur

1. Théophile Gautier, *Histoire de l'art dramatique en France depuis vingt-cinq ans* (6) (Paris: Librairie Magnin, Blanchard et Compagnie, 1859), 131.

2. Ibid., 130.

3. Théophile Gautier, *Baudelaire,* ed. Jean-Luc Steinmetz (Paris: Le Castor Astral, n.d.) 26, 31.

4. Un Flâneur, "Le Flâneur à Paris," *Paris, ou le livre des cent-et-un* (Paris: Librairie de Lavocat, 1831), VI, 96.

5. See Priscilla Parkhurst Ferguson, *Paris as Revolution: Writing the Nineteenth-Century City* (Berkeley, Los Angeles, London: University of California Press, 1994).

6. Elias Regnault, "L'Homme de lettres," *Les Français peints par eux-mêmes: Encyclopédie moral du dix-neuvième siècle* (Paris: L. Curmer, Editeur, 1841), III, 226.

7. Charles Baudelaire, "The Salon of 1846," *Art in Paris, 1845–1862: Salons and Other Exhibitions Reviewed by Charles Baudelaire* trans. and ed. Jonathan Mayne (London: Phaidon Press, 1965), 117.

8. Ibid., 119.

9. See Keith Tester, "Introduction," *The Flâneur* ed. Keith Tester (London and New York: Routledge, 1994).

10. Ibid., 1.

11. Janet Wolff, *Feminine Sentences: Essays on Women and Culture* (Berkeley and Los Angeles: University of California Press, 1990).

12. Elizabeth Wilson, "The Invisible Flâneur," *New Left Review* (Vol. 191, Jan.–Feb. 1992).

13. David Frisby, "The Flâneur in Social Theory," in *The Flâneur.*

14. Vanessa R. Schwartz, *Spectacular Realities: Early Mass Culture in Fin-de-Siècle*

Paris (Berkeley: University of California Press, 1998). See also Anne Friedberg, *Window Shopping: Cinema and the Postmodern* (Berkeley: University of California Press, 1993).

15. See Christopher Prendergast, *Paris and the Nineteenth Century* (Oxford, UK, and Cambridge, Mass.: Blackwell, 1992); John Rignall, *Realist Fiction and the Strolling Spectator* (London and New York: Routledge, 1992); Anke Gleber, *The Art of Taking a Walk: Flanerie, Literature, and Film in Weimar Culture* (Princeton, N.J.: Princeton University Press, 1999).

16. Walter Benjamin, *The Arcades Project* trans. Howard Eiland and Kevin McLaughlin (Cambridge, Mass.: Harvard University Press, 1999), 446.

17. For an interpretation of the complex relationship between journalism and art in this period, see Kevin McLaughlin, *Writing in Parts: Imitation and Exchange in Nineteenth-Century Literature* (Stanford, Calif.: Stanford University Press, 1995).

18. Regnault, "L'Homme de lettres," *Les Français peints par eux-mêmes,* 225.

19. Ibid., 226.

20. Ibid., 227.

21. Ibid., 252.

22. Ibid., 252.

23. Philippe Perrot, *Fashioning the Bourgeoisie: A History of Clothing in the Nineteenth Century* trans. Richard Bienvenu (Princeton, N.J.: Princeton University Press, 1994), 32.

24. John Harvey, *Men in Black* (Chicago: The University of Chicago Press, 1995), 19, 20.

25. Charles Baudelaire, "The Salon of 1846," *Art in Paris 1845–1862: Salons and Other Exhibitions* trans. and ed. Jonathan Mayne (London: Phaidon Press Ltd., 1965), 117, 120.

26. Théophile Gautier, *Baudelaire,* 29.

27. Baudelaire, "The Satan of 1846," *Art in Paris,* 119, 117.

28. Jules Janin, *The American in Paris* (London: Longman, Brown, Green, and Longmans, 1843), 169.

29. Un Flâneur, "Le Flâneur à Paris," 102.

30. Un Flâneur, "Le Flâneur à Paris," 100.

31. Janin, *The American in Paris,* 164.

32. "Le Flâneur parisien," *Figaro* 13 November 1831.

33. M. Louis Huart, Vignettes de MM. Adolphe, Daumier, et Maurisset, *Physiologie du flâneur* (Paris: Aubert et Lavigne, 1841), 10.

34. Auguste de Lacroix, "Le Flâneur," *Les Français peints par eux-mêmes* IV, 66.

35. Un Flâneur, "Le Flâneur à Paris," 98.

36. Huart, *Physiologie du flâneur,* 94–95.

37. Ibid., 51–52.
38. Ibid.
39. The association of urban modernity with the spectacle, spectatorship, and spectacularity is central to most contemporary interpretations of popular culture. For a recent presentation of this position, see Vanessa R. Schwartz, *Spectacular Realities* and Anne Friedberg, *Window Shopping*. Theoretically, this position was advocated in the 1960s by Guy Debord, *The Society of the Spectacle* (New York: Zone Books, 1994).
40. Benjamin, *The Arcades Project,* 430.
41. Un Flâneur, "Le Flâneur à Paris," 101.
42. Huart, *Physiologie du flâneur,* 96.
43. Charles Baudelaire, "The Salon of 1846," *Art in Paris,* 70, 103.
44. Charles Baudelaire, "The Painter of Modern Life," *The Painter of Modern Life and Other Essays* trans. and ed. Jonathan Mayne (New York: A Da Capo Paperback, 1964), 1.
45. Rebecca L. Spang, *The Invention of the Restaurant: Paris and Modern Gastronomic Culture* (Cambridge, Mass.: Harvard University Press, 2000).
46. de Lacroix, "Le Flâneur," 71–72.
47. Huart, *Physiologie du flâneur,* 124–125.
48. Janin, *The American in Paris,* 171–172.
49. de Lacroix, "Le Flâneur," 69.
50. *Les Français peints par eux-mêmes* Frontpiece to Volume III.
51. *Les Français peints par eux-mêmes* Endpiece of Volume IV.
52. *Les Français peints par eux-mêmes* Endpiece of Volume II.
53. *Les Français peints par eux-mêmes* Endpiece to Volume I.
54. See Margaret Cohen, "Panoramic Literature and the Invention of Everyday Genres" in *Cinema and the Invention of Modern Life,* eds. Leo Charney and Vanessa R. Schwartz (Berkeley: University of California Press); Richard Sieburth, "Same Difference: The French Physiologies, 1840–1842," *Notebooks in Cultural Analysis,* Norman Cantor, ed. Nathalia King, managing editor (Durham: Duke University Press, 1984); Judith Wechsler, *A Human Comedy: Physiognomy and Caricature in Nineteenth-Century Paris* foreword by Richard Sennett (Chicago: University of Chicago Press, 1982); Dean de la Motte and Jeannene M. Przyblyski eds., *Making the News: Modernity and the Mass Press in Nineteenth-Century Press* (Amherst: University of Massachusetts Press, 1999).
55. Representative examples of such panorama texts were: *Paris, ou le livre des cent-et-un,* 11 volumes, published in 1831; *Les Français peints par eux-mêmes* 8 vols., published in 1841; and *Le Diable à Paris, Paris et les Parisiens,* published in 1853.
56. Between 1840 and 1845, there were hundreds of physiologies published on

Parisian social types and professional groups. Most of these are now available on microfilm. See Andrée Lhéritié, ed. and intro., "Les Physiologies, 1840–1845" (Paris 1966), University of Michigan Microfilms.

57. The first physiology was Balzac's *Le physiologie du mariage* of 1828.

58. See the anonymous "Physiologie des physiologies" (Paris: Desloges, 1841), which paraphrased and parodied Balzac's Avant-Propos to *La comédie humaine*.

59. See Eugène Sue's depiction of the grisette, the artist, and the porter in *Les mystères de Paris*.

60. Janin, "Introduction," *Les Français peints par eux-mêmes* I, v.

61. Baudelaire, "The Salon of 1846," 116–119.

62. Honoré de Balzac, "Avant-Propos," *La comédie humaine* (Paris: Louis Conard, 1912), xxvii, xxix.

63. Janin, "Introduction," *Les Français peints par eux-mêmes* I, v.

64. Physiologie du fûmeur (Paris: Ernest Bourdin, 1841), 9–10.

65. Georg Lukács, *The Historical Novel* trans. Hannah and Stanley Mitchell (Lincoln: University of Nebraska, 1962), 23.

66. For an overview of the theoretical problems of the concept of "everydayness," see Ben Highmore, *Everyday Life and Cultural Theory: An Introduction* (London and New York: Routledge, 2002).

67. Anon. "Louis Lambert," *Bagatelle* (6 February, 1833) I, 184, reproduced in Bernard Weinberg, *French Realism: The Critical Reaction, 1830–1870* (Reprint of the Modern Language Association of America, General Series, 1937, Private Edition, Distributed by The University of Chicago Libraries, Chicago), 34–35.

68. Francis Girault, "Les Romanciers. Honoré de Balzac," *Bibliographe* (25 April, 2, 13 May, and 1 July 1841) in Weinberg, 61.

69. Quoted in Weinberg, 70–71.

70. For a discussion of Baudelaire's relationship to the world of caricatures, see Michele Hannoosh, *Baudelaire and Caricature: From the Comic to an Art of Modernity* (University Park: Pennsylvania State University Press, 1992).

71. Charles Baudelaire, *Les dessins de Daumier* (Paris: Aux Editions G. Cres et Cie, n.d.) 15–16.

72. For a contemporary exploration of the problem, see Sharon Marcus, *Apartment Stories: City and Home in Nineteenth-Century Paris and London* (Berkeley, Los Angeles, London: University of California Press, 1999).

73. Le Bibliophile Jacob, *Physiologie des rues de Paris* (Paris: Martinon, 1842), 1, 3.

74. Quoted in Peter Brooks, "The Text as the City," *Oppositions* Special Issue: Paris and the Academy: City and Ideology (Spring, 1977:78), 7.

75. Janin, "Introduction," *Les Français peints par eux-mêmes,* ix.

76. For one of the most important debates about realism and modernism, see *Aesthetics and Politics,* Ernst Bloch et al.; afterword by Fredric Jameson, trans. Ronald Taylor (London: NLB, 1977).

77. Christopher Prendergast, *The Triangle of Representation* (New York: Columbia University Press, 2000), 21, 119, 120.

78. Lukács, *The Historical Novel,* 36.

79. For an analysis of the relationship between social types and the physiognomies, see Judith Wechsler, *A Human Comedy* and Mary Cowling, *The Artist as Anthropologist: The Representation of Type and Character in Victorian Art* (Cambridge and New York: Cambridge University Press, 1989).

80. Janin, *The American in Paris,* 162.

81. Balzac, "Avant-Propos," *La comédie humaine,* xxvi.

82. Peter Brooks, "The Text of the City," 8.

83. Anonymous, *Physiologie des physiologies,* (Paris: Des Loges, 1841), 19.

84. Balzac, "Avant-Propos," *La comédie humaine,* xxix.

85. See in particular Christopher Prendergast, *The Triangle of Representation;* Margaret Cohen and Christopher Prendergast, eds., *Spectacles of Realism: Body, Gender, Genre* (Minneapolis, London: University of Minnesota Press, 1995).

86. Margaret Cohen, "Panoramic Literature and the Invention of Everyday Genres," in *Cinema and the Invention of Modern Life,* 234.

87. Balzac, "Avant-Propos," *La comédie humaine,* xxvii.

88. Ibid.

89. Albert Cassagne, *La Théorie de l'art pour l'art en France chez les derniers romantiques et les premiers réalistes* (1905; Paris: Lucien Dorbon, 1959), 28–29.

90. *Le Flâneur* (No. 1, 3 May 1848).

91. Susan Buck-Morss, "The Flâneur, the Sandwichman and the Whore: The Politics of Loitering," *New German Critique* (No. 39, Fall 1986), 105, 103.

92. Bernard Weinberg, *French Realism,* 1–5.

93. Fernand Desnoyers, "Du réalisme," *L'Artiste* (9 December 1855), No. 5, Vol. XVI, in Weinberg, *French Realism,* 122.

94. The series was published in *Le Charivari* between January 1848 and April 1850.

95. Champfleury, "Letter," *Le Figaro* 7 (August 1856), in Weinberg, *French Realism,* 122.

96. Sainte-Beuve, *"Madame Bovary"* in *Literary Criticism of Sainte-Beuve,* trans. and ed. Emerson R. Marks (Lincoln: University of Nebraska, 1971), 129.

97. Charles Baudelaire, *"Madame Bovary* by Gustave Flaubert," in *Baudelaire as Literary Critic: Selected Essays,* intr. and trans. Lois Boe Hyslop and Francis E. Hyslop, Jr. (University Park: The Pennsylvania State University Press, 1964), 143.

98. Ibid., 142.
99. Ibid., 143.
100. See Franco Moretti, *The Modern Epic: The World-System from Goethe to García Márquez,* trans. Quintin Hoare (London: Verso, 1996).
101. Priscilla Parkhurst Ferguson makes a similar distinction between the flâneur of the 1840s and the 1850s through a comparison between Balzac and Flaubert. See "The Flâneur and the Production of Culture," in *Cultural Participation: Trends since the Middle Ages,* ed. Ann Rigney and Douwe Fokkema (Amsterdam, Philadelphia: John Benjamin's Publishing Co., 1993).
102. Charles Baudelaire, "The Salon of 1859," *Art in Paris 1845–1862,* 154.
103. Jessica R. Feldman, *Gender on the Divide: The Dandy in Modernist Literature* (Ithaca and London: Cornell University Press, 1993), 140.
104. The art historian T.J. Clark implicitly questioned this choice of Baudelaire's by making Manet the center of his own study of nineteenth-century French modernism. See *The Painting of Modern Life: Paris in the Art of Manet and His Followers* (Princeton, N.J.: Princeton University Press, 1984).
105. Baudelaire, "The Painter of Modern Life," 13.
106. Ibid., 4–5.
107. Ibid., 9.
108. Ibid., 9.
109. Ibid., 28.
110. Quoted in Feldman, *Gender on the Divide,* 3.
111. Baudelaire, "The Painter of Modern Life," 9.
112. Feldman, *Gender on the Divide,* 140.
113. Baudelaire, "The Salon of 1859," 156.
114. Baudelaire, "The Painter of Modern Life," 11.
115. Ibid., 24.
116. Ibid., 18–24.
117. Ibid., 29.
118. Baudelaire, "The Painter of Modern Life," in *The Painter of Modern Life and Other Essays,* 4.
119. Baudelaire, "On the Essence of Laughter and, in General, on the Comic in the Plastic Arts," in *The Painter of Modern Life and Other Essays,* 152.
120. Ibid., 150.
121. Ibid., 153.

4. The Decadent

1. Anatole Baju's avant-garde journal, *Le Décadent,* published between April 1886 and April 1888 was important in creating publicity for the type.

2. Paul Bourget, "Études et portraits du moderne," *Le Parlemant* (31 May, 1883), in Daniel Grojnowski, *Le sujet d'à rebours* (Paris: Presses Universitaires du Septentrion, 1996), 109.

3. Théophile Gautier, *Baudelaire,* ed. Jean-Luc Steinmetz (Paris: Le Castor Astral, n.d.), 44.

4. See Asti Hustvedt, ed. *The Decadent Reader: Fiction, Fantasy, and Perversion from Fin-de-Siècle France* (New York: Zone Books, 1998); and André Billy, *L'Epoque 1900:1885–1905* (Paris: Editions Jules Tallandier, 1951).

5. J. K. Huysmans, *Against the Grain (À Rebours)* intr. Havelock Ellis (New York: Dover Publications, Inc., 1969), xxxvi.

6. Ibid., xlix.

7. Ibid., xlix.

8. Ibid., xlix.

9. Jerrold Seigel's *Bohemian Paris* does deal in detail with fin-de-siècle bohemia, but significantly, he focuses only on those bohemians who for various reasons have entered the canon of academic culture and leaves out of consideration those obscure actors, who failed to establish enduring artistic reputations, but who were, nevertheless, central to the bohemian enterprise of their time.

10. Billy, *L'Epoque 1900,* 188.

11. Probably the most ambitious plan to preserve the performances of fin-de-siècle bohemians was the publication of Jules Lévy, *Les Hydropathes: Prose et vers* (Paris: André Delpeuch, ed., 1928).

12. Daniel Grojnowski, "Hydropathes and Company," in *The Spirit of Montmartre: Cabarets, Humor, and the Avant-Garde, 1875–1905,* ed. Phillip Dennis Cate and Mary Shaw (Rutgers: Jane Voorhees Zimmerli Art Museum Rutgers, The State University of New Brunswick, New Jersey, 1996), 96.

13. Félicien Champsaur, *Dinah Samuel,* ed. Jean de Palacio (Paris: Segurier, 1999), 127, 132.

14. Emile Goudeau, *Dix ans de bohème* followed by *"Les hirsutes" de Leo Trézenik* intr. Michel Golfier and Jean-Didier Wagneur with the collaboration of Patrick Ramseyer (Paris: Champ Vallon, 2000), 119.

15. Coquelin Cadet, "Le Chat Noir," *Pirouettes* (Paris: Jules Levy, ed., 1888), 296.

16. Emile Goudeau, *L'Hydropathe* (19 February 1879), 3, quoted in Charles Rearick, *Pleasures of the Belle Epoque: Entertainment and Festivities in Turn-of-the-Century France* (New Haven and London: Yale University Press, 1985), 37.

17. The tune, called the "hydropathen-valsh," was by the Austrian composer Joseph Gungl and was performed at the concert Besseliève that Goudeau had attended with a few friends.

18. Goudeau, *Dix ans de bohème,* 185.

19. Ibid., 188.

20. Lévy, Introduction, *Les Hydropathes: Prose et vers,* 9.
21. Goudeau, *Dix ans de bohème,* 171.
22. Ibid., 192.
23. Ibid., 197.
24. Leo Trézenik, "Les Hirsutes," in Émile Goudeau, *Dix ans de bohème,* 390.
25. Champsaur, *Dinah Samuel,* 130.
26. Horace Valbel, *Les chansonniers et les cabarets artistiques* (Paris: E. Dentu, 1895), 75.
27. Coquelin Cadet, "Le Chat Noir," 278–88.
28. Jules Lévy, "L'Incohérence: son origine, son histoire, son avenir," *Le Courier Français* 12 March 1885, in Luce Abélès and Catherine Charpin, *Arts incohérents, académie du dérisoire* (Paris: Editions de la Réunion des Musées Nationaux, 1992), 14.
29. Catherine Charpin, *Les Arts incohérents, 1882–1893* (Paris: Editions Syros Alternatives, 1990), 22.
30. *Le Voltaire* 14 March 1885, in Abélès and Charpin, *Arts incohérents,* 26.
31. Seigel, *Bohemian Paris,* 216, 225.
32. Lionel Richard, *Cabaret, cabarets: Origines et décadence* (Paris: Plon, 1991), 61.
33. Rearick, *Pleasures of the Belle-Epoque,* 62.
34. Cate, "The Spirit of Montmartre," in *The Spirit of Montmartre,* 20, 32.
35. For a defense of impressionism, see Théodore Duret, *Critique d'avant-garde* (Paris: École nationale supérieure des Beaux-Arts, 1998).
36. Philip Nord, *Impressionists and Politics: Art and Democracy in the Nineteenth Century* (London and New York: Routledge, 2000), 38, 53.
37. For an account of the Goncourts' house, see Debora L. Silverman, *Art Nouveau in Fin-de-Siècle France: Politics, Psychology, and Style* (Berkeley, Los Angeles, Oxford: University of California Press, 1989).
38. For a theoretical discussion of the cultural significance of art collecting, see John Elsner and Roger Cardinal, eds. *The Cultures of Collecting* (Cambridge, Mass.: Harvard University Press, 1994).
39. Edmond de Goncourt, *La maison d'un artiste* (Paris: Ernest Flammerion, 1931), 1, 7–9.
40. Emile Goudeau, *La Revue Illustrée* (15 March 1887), quoted in Phillip Dennis Cate, "The Spirit of Montmartre," in *The Spirit of Montmartre,* 40.
41. Albert Millaud, *Physiologies parisiennes* (Paris: La Librairie illustrée, 1886), 139–14. Also quoted in Phillip Dennis Cate, *The Spirit of Montmartre,* 41. (Cate's translation used.)
42. For a theory of parody that discusses its creative function as the sources of artistic renewal, see Linda Hutcheon, *A Theory of Parody: The Teachings of Twentieth-Century Art Forms* (Urbana and Chicago: University of Illinois

Press, 1985). See also Simon Denith, *Parody* (London and New York: Routledge, 2000).

43. *Le Voltaire* (14 March 1885), in Abélès and Chapin, *Arts incohérents, académie du dérisoire,* 26.
44. Valbel, *Les chansonniers et les cabarets artistiques,* 62.
45. Ibid., 67–68.
46. For a recent study that makes this argument, see Richard Candida Smith, *Mallarmé's Children: Symbolism and the Renewal of Experience* (Berkeley, Los Angeles, London: University of California Press, 1999).
47. Grojnowski, "Hydropathes and Company," in *The Spirit of Montmartre,* 102.
48. Goudeau, *Dix ans de bohème,* 88.
49. Lévy, *Le courier Français* (12 March 1885), 4, in Catherine Chapin, *Les arts incohérents,* 110.
50. T. J. Clark, "The Bar at the Folies-Bergères," in *The Wolf and the Lamb: Popular Culture in France, From the Old Régime to the Twentieth Century* ed. Jacques Beauroy, Marc Bertrand, Edward T. Gargan (Saratoga, Calif.: Anma Libri, 1977), 247.
51. Ibid.
52. See Raymond Williams, *Culture and Society* (New York: Harper and Row, 1958),
53. Goudeau, *Dix ans de bohème,* 220–221.
54. Francisque Sarcey, *XIX. Siècle* (December 1878), in Goudeau, *Dix ans de bohème,* 222.
55. Daniel Grojnowski and Bernard Sarrazin, *L'Esprit fumiste et les rires fin de siècle* (Paris: Jose Corti, 1990), 17.
56. Goudeau, *Dix ans de bohème,* 192–196.
57. It seems that the monologue enjoyed unprecedented vogue during the early 1880s and was performed in salons, at soirées, and among friends. In 1881, the journal, *L'Illustration,* gave the following depiction of this newest artistic fashion: "There is in Paris a veritable monologue mania . . . Coquelin Cadet has invented the formula in contemporary entertainment. In place of the older, charming conversation, he has brought in this strange intellectual diversion, whose effect on the brain is like tickling on the sole of one's foot . . . The monologue is to the spirit what the somersault is to the clown in gymnastics. It is bewildering, rather than seductive. One asks oneself whether all this eccentricity does not lead the good people one day on the road to Charenton . . . The monologue is the distinctive sign of the age we live in. Political monologues, literary monologues, . . . monologues everywhere, a surfeit of monologues, an epidemic of monologues!" Quoted in Luce Abélès and Catherine Charpin, *Arts incohérents, académie du dérisoire,* 39.

58. According to Goudeau, the inventor of the monologue was the poet Charles Cros, who was one of the original members of the Hydropathes. See *Dix ans de bohème,* 166.

59. Coquelin Cadet, *Le monologue moderne* (Paris: Paul Ollendorff, 1881), 24–25.

60. Peter Brooks, *The Melodramatic Imagination: Balzac, Henry James, Melodrama, and the Mode of Excess* (New Haven and London: Yale University Press, 1976), 199.

61. A contemporary purgative, imported from Hungary.

62. Georges Fragerolle, "Le Fumisme," *L'Hydropathe* (12 May 1880), reprinted in Goudeau, *Dix ans de bohème,* 419.

63. bid., 420.

64. See Daniel Grojnowski and Bernard Sarrazin, *L'Esprit fumiste et les rires fin de siècle,* 470.

65. Coquelin Cadet, *Le monologue moderne,* 19–20.

66. Ibid., 10–11.

67. Ibid., 33–34.

68. Ibid., 12–13.

69. Quoted in Grojnowski and Sarrazin, *L'Esprit fumiste et les rires fin de siècle,* 20.

70. Goudeau, *La Revue Illustrée* (15 March 1887), quoted by Daniel Grojnowski, "Hydropathes and Company," *The Spirit of Montmartre,* 109.

71. Goudeau, editorial in *La Revue Illustrée* (15 March 1887), in Catherine Chapin, *Les arts incohérents,* 112.

72. See in particular, Jan Goldstein, *Console and Classify: The French Psychiatric Profession in the Nineteenth Century* (Cambridge, New York, New Rochelle, Melbourne, Sydney: Cambridge University Press, 1987); Robert A. Nye, *Crime, Madness, and Politics in Modern France: The Medical Concept of National Decline* (Princeton, N.J.: Princeton University Press, 1984); Janet Beiser, *Ventriloquized Bodies: Narratives of Hysteria in Nineteenth-Century France* (Ithaca and London: Cornell University Press, 1994), Jann Matlock, *Scenes of Seduction: Prostitution, Hysteria, and Reading Differences in Nineteenth-Century France* (New York: Columbia University Press, 1994), Ruth Harris, *Murders and Madness: Medicine, Law, and Society in the Fin de Siècle* (Oxford, UK: Clarendon Press, 1989); Martha Noel Evans, *Fits and Starts: A Genealogy of Hysteria in Modern France* (Ithaca and London: Cornell University Press, 1991); Mark S. Micale, *Approaching Hysteria: Disease and Its Interpretations* (Princeton, N.J.: Princeton University Press, 1995).

73. See Evans, *Fits and Starts.*

74. Micale, *Approaching Hysteri,* 218–219.

75. Beiser, *Ventriloquized Bodies*, 3.
76. Rae Beth Gordon, *Why the French Love Jerry Lewis: From Cabaret to Early Cinema* (Stanford, Calif.: Stanford University Press, 2000), vii.
77. Edmond and Jules de Goncourt, *Mémoirs de la vie littéraire,* 4 vols., cited in T. J. Clark, *The Painting of Modern Life: Paris in the Art of Manet and His Followers* (Princeton, N.J.: Princeton University Press, 1984), 207.
78. Evans, *Fits and Starts,* 13.
79. Jean Starobinski, Preface, Victor Segalen, *Les cliniciens ès lettres* (Saint-Clement-le-Rivière: Fata Morgana, 1980) 17.
80. J. L. Signoret, "Une leçon clinique à la Salpêtrière (1887) par André Brouillet," *Variété historique* 139, 12, 1983, 687–701.
81. Sigmund Freud displayed a copy of the painting in the waiting room of his office in Vienna and took it with him when he went into exile in London.
82. Axel Munthe, *The Story of San Michele* (London: John Murray, 1938), 239.
83. Gordon, *Why the French Love Jerry Lewis,* 1.
84. Micale, *Approaching Hysteria,* 200.
85. See in particular, G. Hahn, "Charcot et son influence sur l'opinion publique" *Revue des questions scientifiques* 6 (1899), in Micale, *Apporoaching Hysteria,* 199.
86. Coquelin Cadet, "Hydrothérapie," *Pirouettes,* 283.
87. Munthe, *The Story of San Michele,* 244.
88. Albert Millaud, "Les 'Carolines,' " *Physiologies parisiennes,* 219.
89. Georges Didi-Huberman, *Invention de l'hystérie: Charcot et l'iconographie photographique de la Salpêtrière* (Paris: Macula, 1982), 10.
90. Georges Guillain, ed. and trans. Pearce Bailey, *J.-M. Charcot, 1825–1893: His Life—His Work* (New York: Paul B. Hoeber, Inc., 1959), 135.
91. Micale, *Approaching Hysteria,* 180.
92. Jean-Martin Charcot, *Charcot, The Clinician: the Tuesday Lessons:—Excerpts from Nine Case Presentations on General Neurology Delivered at the Salpêtrière Hospital in 1887–88* trans. and commentary Christopher G. Goetz, MD (New York: Raven Press, 1987), xxiii.
93. Henry Meige, *Charcot, artiste* (Paris: Masson et Cie Editeurs, 1925), 12.
94. Quoted in Georges Didi-Huberman, *Invention de l'hystérie,* 30.
95. Meige, *Charcot, artiste,* 5.
96. Guillain, J. M., *Charcot,* 22.
97. Charcot, *Charcot, The Clinician,* 103–104.
98. Ibid., 104.
99. Pierre Janet, "J.-M. Charcot: Son oeuvre psychologique," *Revue philosophique* (June 1895), p. 576, quoted in Georges Did-Huberman, *Invention de l'hystérie,* 28.

100. Charcot, *Charcot, The Clinician,* 107.

101. The photographs, along with the case histories of particular hysterical patients, were published in Bourneville and P. Regnard, *Iconographies photographique de la Salpêtrière* (Paris: Aux Bureaux de Progrès Médical, 1876–77) and also Paul Richter and Gilles de la Tourette, eds., *Nouvelle iconographie de la Salpêtrière* 8 vols. (Paris, 1888–1895).

102. Evans, *Fits and Starts,* 24.

103. Quoted in Guillain, *J. M. Charcot,* 53–54.

104. Jacqueline Carroy-Thirard, "Hystérie, théâtre, littérature au dix-neuvième siècle," *Psychoanalyse à l'université* 7, no. 26 (March 1982), 312.

105. Ibid.

106. J. M. Charcot and Paul Richer, *Les démoniaques dans l'art* followed by *La foi qui guérit* by J. M. Charcot (Paris: Editions Macula, 1984), 91.

107. Ibid., 108.

108. *La révolution surréaliste* No. 11, IV (15 March 1928), 20, 22.

109. Charcot, *Charcot, The Clinician,* 111.

110. *Le courrier français* (25 Jan. 1891, quoted in Abélès and Charpin, *Arts incohérents,* 50.

111. For the earliest examples of such theories, see Benedict Augustin Morel, *Traité des dégénérescences physiques, intellectuelles et morales de l'espèce humaine* (1857) (New York: 1976) and Arthur de Gobineau, *Essai sur l'inégalité des races humaines* (Paris: P. Belfond, 1967).

112. Champsaur, *Dinah Samuel.*

113. Goudeau, *Dix ans de bohème,* 120–123.

114. Paul Bourget, Avant-Propos, *Essais de psychologie contemporaine* 2 vols. (Paris: Alphonse Lemerre, ed., 1895), vii–viii.

115. Bourget, *Essais de psychologie contemporaine,* 20.

116. Decadence as an aesthetic category came into common usage in the 1860s and was usually identified with the stylistic innovation of modern writers like Baudelaire and Flaubert. Perhaps the most important statement of this position was Théophile Gautier's Notice to Baudelaire's collected work in 1867, which was analyzed at the beginning of this chapter.

117. Ibid., 13.

118. Charles Bernheimer has recently referred to a similar ambiguity of surrounding contemporary understandings of "decadence." "In current parlance," he writes, "the notion of decadence is inhabited by a doubleness that puts fundamental moral and social values in question. There is an implicit appeal to a norm that sustains society's assumptions about what is natural, good, right, life-sustaining, progressive, and so forth. But there is also the suggestion that this appeal constricts human potential, denies opportunities for pleasure, and discredits the attraction of the perverse and destructive."

"Unknowing Decadence," in *Perennial Decay: On the Aesthetics and Politics of Decadence* eds. Liz Constable, Matthew Potolsky, and Dennis Denisoff (Philadelphia: University of Pennsylvania Press, 1999), 50–51.

119. Max Nordau, *Degeneration* (New York: D. Appleton and Company, 1895), 15.
120. Paul Bourget, "Etudes et portraits du moderne," in Grojnowski, *Le subject d'a rebours,* 109.
121. Ibid., 116.
122. Quoted in Robert Baldick, *The Life of J.-K. Huysmans* (London: Oxford at the Clarendon Press, 1955), 78.
123. Ibid.
124. Billy, *L'Époque 1900:1885–1905,* 72.
125. J. Barbey d'Aurevilly, "J.-K. Huysmans *À Rebours,*" (*Constitutionnel,* 28 July 1884), in *Le Roman contemporain* (Paris: Alphonse Lemerre, 1902), 273.
126. Quoted in Michael Issacharoff, *J.-K. Huysmans devant la critique en France, 1874–1960* (Paris: Editions Klincksieck, 1970), 65.
127. David Weir, *Decadence and the Making of Modernism* (Amherst: University of Massachusetts Press, 1995), 83.
128. *Gil Blas* (20 June 1884) quoted in Issacharoff, *J.-K. Huysmans devant la critique en France,* 72.
129. Huysmans's work has frequently been read as an example of the interiorization of the self that found expression in the "psychologie nouvelle" of the period. As Debora Silverman wrote, "This diachronic line extends from the Goncourts, via Huysmans and de Montesquiou, to Marcel Proust." *Art Nouveau in Fin-de-Siècle France,* 77.
130. Huysmans, *Against the Grain,* 17.
131. Segalen, *Les cliniciens ès lettres,* 113.
132. Huysmans was, in fact, a connoisseur of the café concert. For an admiring and knowledgeable depiction of its program and environment, see J.-K. Huysmans, "Les Folies-Bergères en 1879," in *Croquis Parisiens* (Lausanne: Mermod, 1955).
133. Grojnowski, *Le sujet d'a rebours,* 72.
134. Charpin, *Les arts incohérents,* 18.
135. J. K. Huysmans, *Against the Grain,* xxxv.
136. Ibid., xlv.
137. Ibid., xxxvi.
138. Ibid., 12.
139. Ibid., 53.
140. Ibid., 163.
141. Ibid., 167.
142. Ibid., 206.

143. Goudeau, *Dix ans de bohème,* 269.
144. The original article had been published by Jacques Lehardy in *Le Chat Noir.*
145. For more extended discussions of the same phenomenon, see T. J. Clarke, "The View from Notre-Dame," in *The Painting of Modern Life,* and Priscilla Parkhurst Ferguson, *Paris as Revolution: Writing the Nineteenth-Century City* (Berkeley: University of California Press, 1994).
146. Huysmans, *Against the Grain,* 206.
147. Ibid., xlvi.
148. Ibid., xxxvii.
149. Christopher Prendergast, "Introduction: Realism, God's Secret, and the Body," in *Spectacles of Realism: Body, Gender, Genre* eds. Margaret Cohen and Christopher Prendergast, (Minneapolis, London: University of Minnesota Press, 1995), 7.
150. This dilemma found poignant expression in Georg Lukács's *Theory of the Novel* in 1915, which was an exploration of the philosophic and existential consequences of the crisis of nineteenth-century realism. It is not at all co-incidental that his depiction of the tragic circumstances of the hero of the novel echoes almost word for word the final paragraph of Huysmans's novel.
151. Pierre Vareille, "Décadence," *Le Décadent* (24 April, 1886).

5. The Primitivist Artist

1. For an account of Gauguin's everyday life in Tahiti, see Bengt Danielsson, *Gauguin in the South Seas,* trans. Reginald Spink (London: George Allen and Unwin Ltd., 1965).
2. Gauguin was to become the victim of his own image as the Primitive artist. Wishing to return to Paris in 1903 for treatment of a medical condition that caused his death, he was dissuaded by his friend Daniel de Monfreid. "It is to be feared," de Monfreid wrote Gauguin, "that your return would only derange the growing and slowly conceived ideas with which public opinion has surrounded you. Now you are that legendary artist, who, from the depth of Polynesia, sends forth disconcertingly inimitable work—the definitive work of a man who has disappeared from the world." (*Gauguin's Letters from the South Seas,* trans. Ruth Pielkovo, foreward Frederick O'Brien (New York: Dover Publications, Inc., 1992), 98.
3. Quoted in Alfred Werner, Introduction, Paul Gauguin, *Noa Noa* (New York: Farrar, Straus and Giroux, 1957), vii.
4. For an example of such manifestoes, see Charles Harrison and Paul Wood, eds., *Art in Theory, 1900–1990: An Anthology of Changing Ideas* (Oxford, UK; Cambridge, Mass.: Blackwell, 1993).
5. For a reconsideration of the explicitly religious implications of Gauguin's

paintings, see Debora Silverman, *Van Gogh and Gauguin: The Search for Sacred Art* (New York: Farrar, Straus and Giroux, 2000) for Worringer's work, see Wilhelm Worringer, *Abstraction and Empathy: A Contribution to the Psychology of Style* trans. Michael Bullock (New York: International Universities Press, Inc.: 1967).

6. For a study of the manifesto as a cultural form, see Marjorie Perloff, *The Futurist Moment: Avant-Garde, Avant-Guerre, and the Language of Rupture* (Chicago and London: The University of Chicago Press, 1986) and Janet Lyon, *Manifestoes: Provocations of the Modern* (Ithaca: Cornell University Press, 1999).

7. Henri Matisse, "Notes d'un peintre," in *La Grande Revue* (Paris, 25 December, 1908), quoted in *Art in Theory, 1900–1990*, 78.

8. Ibid., 77.

9. Charles Baudelaire, "The Painter of Modern Life," in *The Painter of Modern Life and Other Essays* trans. and ed. Jonathan Mayne (New York: A Da Capo Paperback: 1964), 32.

10. Ibid.

11. For an older account of this process, see Robert Goldwater, *Primitivism in Modern Art* (Cambridge, Mass. and London, England: The Belknap Press of Harvard University Press, 1986). See also Jill Lloyd, *German Expressionism: Primitivism and Modernity* (New Haven and London: Yale University Press, 1991).

12. Quoted in Jehanne Teilhet-Fiske, *Paradise Reviewed: An Interpretation of Gauguin's Polynesian Symbolism* (Ann Arbor, Mich.: UMI Research Press, 1983), 9.

13. Pierre Loti, *Tahiti (The Marriage of Loti)* trans. Clara Bell (New York: Frederick A. Stokes Company, 1925).

14. For accounts of Loti, see Michael G. Lerner, *Pierre Loti* (New York: Twayne Publishers, Inc., 1974) and Tzvetan Todorov, *On Human Diversity: Nationalism, Racism, and Exoticism in French Thought* trans. Catherine Porter (Cambridge, Mass. and London: Harvard University Press, 1993).

15. See Wilhelm Worringer, "Foreward to the New Impression, 1948" in *Abstraction and Empathy*. For an analysis of the text, see Mary Gluck, "Interpreting Primitivism, Mass Culture and Modernism: The Making of Wilhelm Worringer's *Abstraction and Empathy*" in *New German Critique* 80 (Spring–Summer 2000).

16. James Clifford, *The Predicament of Culture: Twentieth-Century Ethnography, Literature, and Art* (Cambridge, Mass.: Harvard University Press, 1988), 135.

17. Annie E. Coombes, *Reinventing Africa: Museums, Material Culture and Popular Imagination in late Victorian and Edwardian England* (New Haven and London: Yale University Press, 1994), 120.

18. Simon Bonner, "Object Lessons: The Work of Ethnographic Museums and Collections," in *Consuming Visions: Accumulation and Display of Goods in America, 1880–1920,* Simon Bonner, ed. (New York, London: W. W. Norton & Co., 1989), 224–225.

19. See Annie E. Coombes, "Ethnography and the Formation of National and Cultural Identities," in *The Myth of Primitivism: Perspectives on Art,* Susan Hiller, ed. (London and New York: Routledge, 1991).

20. See Lloyd, *German Expressionism: Primitivism and Modernity.*

21. Tzvetan Todorov, *On Human Diversity: Nationalism, Racism, and Exoticism in French Thought,* 271–277.

22. See Marianna Torgovnick, *Gone Primitive: Savage Intellects, Modern Lives* (Chicago and London: The University of Chicago Press, 1990).

23. Introduction, *Primitivism and Twentieth-Century Art: A Documentary History,* Jack Flam and Miriam Deutch, eds. (Berkeley, Los Angeles, London: University of California Press, 2003), 19.

24. James Clifford, *The Predicament of Culture: Twentieth-Century Ethnography, Literature, and Art,* 192.

25. Scholars like Lisa Lowe have made a similar argument when she pointed out that it is impossible to isolate a "master narrative or a singular history" for exoticist and Primitivist discourses. *Critical Terrains: French and British Orientalisms* (Ithaca: Cornell University Press, 1991), 4. See also Roger Celestin, *From Cannibals to Radicals: Figures and Limits of Exoticism* (Minneapolis: University of Minnesota Press, 1996), Peter Mason, *Infelicities: Representations of the Exotic* (Baltimore: The Johns Hopkins University Press, 1998), Chris Bongie, *Exotic Memories: Literature, Colonialism, and the Fin de Siècle* (Stanford, Calif.: Stanford University Press, 1991).

26. Excerpt from André Malraux, *La tête d'obsidienne* (Paris: Gallimard, 1974), 17–19, in *Primitivism and Twentieth-Century Art: A Documentary History,* 33.

27. Nicholas Wadley, ed. and intr. *Noa Noa: Gauguin's Tahiti* trans. Jonathan Griffin (Salem, N.H.: Salem House, 1985), 85.

28. Quoted in Wadley, *Noa Noa: Gauguin's Tahiti,* 105. Also published in Paul Gauguin, *Gauguin's Letters from the South Seas,* trans. Ruth Pielkovo, foreword Frederick O'Brien (New York: Dover Publications, Inc., 1992), 96.

29. Wadley, *Noa Noa: Gauguin's Tahiti,* 121.

30. Paul Gauguin, *Noa Noa: The Tahitian Journal* trans. O. F. Theis (New York: Dover Publications, Inc., 1985), 7.

31. Ibid., 2.

32. Ibid., 15.

33. It seems that the source for these myths, which are presented at the end of *Noa Noa* as part of the recollection of Gauguin's Tahitian lover, Tehura, was actually a work of nineteenth-century ethnography that had been lent Gauguin by a French colonial in Papeete in the spring of 1892. J. A. Moerenhout's

two-volume *Voyages aux iles du grand océan* (1837) made a strong impression on Gauguin and even influenced his paintings. In Nicholas Wadley, *Noa Noa: Gauguin's Tahiti,* 109–112.

34. Octave Mirbeau, "Retour de Tahiti," *Echo de Paris* (Nov. 14, 1893), in Wadley, *Noa Noa: Gauguin's Tahiti,* 144.
35. Gauguin, *Noa Noa,* 17.
36. Ibid., 65.
37. Ibid.
38. Gauguin, *Gauguin's Letters from the South Seas,* 100.
39. Georg Lukács, "Paul Gauguin," in *The Lukács Reader,* Árpád Kadarkay, ed. (Oxford, UK and Cambridge, Mass.: Blackwell, 1995), 160, 163, 164. Lukács's original essay, "Gauguin," was first published in Hungarian in *Huszadik Század* (June, Vol. VIII, No. 6, 1907), 559–562.
40. Charles Forsdick, *Victor Segalen and the Aesthetics of Diversity: Journeys between Cultures* (Oxford and New York: Oxford University Press, 2000), 5.
41. Victor Segalen, "Homage à Gauguin," in Segalen, *Gauguin dans son dernier décor et autres textes de Tahiti* (Fontfroide: Bibliothèque Artistique et Littéraire, 1986), 87, 130.
42. Victor Segalen, *Essay on Exoticism: An Aesthetics of Diversity* trans. and ed. Yael Rachel Schlick, foreword Harry Harootunian (Durham and London: Duke University Press, 2002), 14.
43. Arman Bonnetain (1883–1973), sculptor and creator of ornamental medals. Jean Ajalbert (1863–1947), popular novelists; Segalen, *Essay on Exoticism,* 18.
44. Ibid.
45. Ibid., 34.
46. Ibid., 35.
47. Ibid., 20.
48. Ibid., 14.
49. Ibid.
50. Ibid., 41.
51. Ibid., 67.
52. Ibid., 18.
53. Guillaume Apollinaire, *The Cubist Painters: Aesthetic Meditations, 1913* trans. Lionel Abel (New York: George Wittenborn, 1970), 14.
54. Quoted in *Primitivism and Twentieth-Century Art,* 12.
55. Le Corbusier, "The Spirit of the Machine and Negroes in America," in *When the Cathedrals Were White: A Journey to the Country of Timid People* (New York: Reynal and Hitchcock, 1947), 158.
56. Philippe Soupault, *The American Influence in France* (Seattle: University of Washington Book Store, 1930), 12–17.

57. Jerrold Seigel, *Bohemian Paris: Culture, Politics, and the Boundaries of Bourgeois Life, 1830–1930* (New York: Penguin Books, 1986), 396.
58. Elizabeth Wilson, *Bohemians, the Glamorous Outcasts* (New Brunswick, N.J.: Rutgers University Press, 2000), 246.
59. Seigel, *Bohemian Paris,* 396.

Index